TURNER **CLASSIC** MOVIES

20TH CENTURY-FOX

DARRYL F. ZANUCK AND THE CREATION OF THE MODERN FILM STUDIO

TURNER **CLASSIC** MOVIES

20TH CENTURY-FOX

DARRYL F. ZANUCK AND THE CREATION
OF THE MODERN FILM STUDIO

SCOTT EYMAN

RUNNING PRESS
PHILADELPHIA

Running Press
Hachette Book Group
1290 Avenue of the Americas, New York, NY 10104
www.runningpress.com
@Running_Press

Printed in the United States
First Edition: September 2021

Published by Running Press, an imprint of Perseus Books, LLC, a subsidiary of Hachette Book
Group, Inc. The Running Press name and logo is a trademark of the Hachette Book Group.

The Hachette Speakers Bureau provides a wide range of authors for speaking events.
To find out more, go to www.hachettespeakersbureau.com or call (866) 376-6591.

The publisher is not responsible for websites (or their content) that are not owned
by the publisher.

All images courtesy of Turner Classic Movies and author's collection.
Print book cover and interior design by Susan Van Horn.

Library of Congress Cataloging-in-Publication Data

Names: Eyman, Scott, 1951– author.
Title: 20th Century-Fox: Darryl F. Zanuck and the creation of the modern
    film studio / Scott Eyman.
Other titles: Twentieth Century-Fox
Description: First edition. | Philadelphia: Running Press, 2021. |
    Includes bibliographical references and index.
Identifiers: LCCN 2021006340 | ISBN 9780762470938 (hardcover) | ISBN
    9780762470921 (ebook)
Subjects: LCSH: Twentieth Century-Fox Film Corporation—History. | Motion
    picture studios—California—Los Angeles—History.
Classification: LCC PN1999.T8 E96 2021 | DDC 384/.80979494—dc23 .
LC record available at https://lccn.loc.gov/2021006340

ISBNs: 978-0-7624-7093-8 (hardcover), 978-0-7624-7092-1 (ebook)

LSC-C

Printing 1, 2021

For Lynn, who has
watched movies with me
for 38 years.

Contents

≡ Introduction ≡

BEGIN WITH THE BEGINNING.

A vibrant drumroll announces what could be the arrival of an emperor come to inspect his subjects. The drumroll is more or less a lift from John Philip Sousa—many of his marches start with the same riff, a fact that would have been obvious to audiences in the thirties, when Alfred Newman first composed the music.

The screen lightens to reveal a deco monolith that reads "20th Century Fox" as searchlights sweep across the sky. As the drums finish, the brass kicks in with a stentorian conclusion to the fanfare, rising to a final crash of percussion as the logo darkens to transition to the main title. The theme for the brass is in F major, and the score specifies that it be played "Majestically." As the composer Neil Brand says, "It's a basic call to arms/roman fanfare that doesn't move off its root note."

It's a magnificent musical equivalent of the logo itself: big, arresting, and at the same time graceful, holding the promise of something wonderful.

Nearly twenty years after composing the original fanfare, Alfred Newman added another eight bars, taking the piece to a loftier, more resolved plane. The addition was to herald a separate panel after the Fox logo, announcing that the film was shot in "CinemaScope." Newman's addition meant that the fanfare resolved with a B flat minor 6th, concluding on a triumphant F major final note.

The original eight-bar fanfare and logo were created in 1933, for Darryl Zanuck's new company, called Twentieth Century Pictures. When Twentieth Century merged with Fox Pictures in 1935, creating 20th Century-Fox, that logo and fanfare introduced nearly every Fox film.[*]

Before Alfred Newman's fanfare, the introduction of the studio's films had been an unprepossessing polyglot. Sometimes it read "William Fox Presents," sometimes "Fox Film Presents."

But Newman's fanfare gave the studio an identity that lasted for more than three quarters of a century—a vibrant signature that was revitalized in 1977, when John Williams and a huge orchestra re-recorded the complete sixteen-bar fanfare for *Star Wars*, if only because Williams had written the opening of his landmark score in F major as well. It was a hand across time from one great composer of film music to another, and it made the Fox trademark sound thrillingly new and modern.

For more than fifty years of its existence, the Fox studio was dominated by two alpha males: First, William Fox, the founder of the feast, a feral, single-minded character who saw himself less as a movie mogul and more as a vaultingly ambitious American legend in the making—a Jewish Vanderbilt. Then there was Darryl Zanuck, who combined Fox's company with his own and ran the result, said one of his stars, "like a Swiss watch."

Fox was born Wilhelm Fuchs in Hungary in 1879 and came to America when he was nine months old. He grew up poor, in the American equivalent of a *shtetl*—the Lower East Side of New York. There were thirteen children in the Fuchs family, seven of whom died young.

---

[*] Among the exceptions without the fanfare: *The Razor's Edge*, in which Newman's thundering main title theme underscores the Fox logo.

Zanuck was born in Wahoo, Nebraska, in 1902, and many people thought that in some primary way he never quite grew up at all. Wahoo would prove far too limiting for a man of Zanuck's energies. He meant to put himself at the center of the whirlwind, and if he had to create the whirlwind himself, so much the better. As he told a gathering of his peers at the Screen Producer's Guild, "I decided to become a genius, and being a genius, I had to live that way."

William Fox single-mindedly built an empire of theaters and eventually began making movies in order to keep more of the money for himself. Money was Fox's armor, his status, the way he measured how far he had come on the path from poverty. He raised the level of his films incrementally from a production policy that schizophrenically flicked from a focus on mother-love to blatant exploitation and back again until a flowering in the 1920s with some of the enduring classics of silent film: *The Iron Horse, Sunrise, What Price Glory?, 7th Heaven.* It was only the unforeseen cataclysm of the 1929 stock market crash that destroyed Fox's plan to dominate the entire American movie industry.

Zanuck was more or less indifferent to theaters, not particularly obsessed by money, cared only about movies, all kinds of movies— their construction, their making, their editing, their presentation. He devoured movies the same way he devoured life—command was his prerogative. He would go on safaris, he would ride horses beyond the edge of danger, he would go to war, he would make love to beautiful actresses. Nothing else would do.

And he would make more than a thousand movies, some of them classics then and now: *The Grapes of Wrath, How Green Was My Valley, My Darling Clementine, All About Eve.*

Under both men, Fox was a studio with innovation in its DNA. Fox never had a great deal of what you could call elegance (that would be

Paramount) or the most money (that would be MGM) or the biggest stars (MGM again).

But you could make a serious case that, from the mid-twenties on, it was the Fox studio that led the way creatively. William Fox placed his bet on sound on film, whereas Warner Bros. placed the same bet on an inferior technology—a record running in theoretical synch with a 35mm projector. Because they were on the same driveshaft, if the film and record started out in synch they would presumably stay that way—unless the record skipped, or the film broke. The Fox system was obviously superior and became the industry standard within three years.

At the same time, Fox invited the man he regarded as the world's greatest director to create a great film without regard to budget. F. W. Murnau made *Sunrise*, a masterpiece of mood and photographic ingenuity that won a special Oscar at the first Academy Award ceremonies.

Fox placed another bet on 70mm widescreen. He produced several films as demonstration objects, including a western epic titled *The Big Trail*, the film that introduced a young man newly christened John Wayne to the world.

When the movie industry entered a postwar commercial trough caused largely by television landing with both feet, it was Zanuck and 20th Century-Fox that brought widescreen out of the attic. This iteration was called CinemaScope, and the dozen competing widescreen processes that came after nudged the box office upward so that the industry could once again compete.

When Darryl Zanuck took control of the Fox studio in 1935, many people thought he would attempt to replicate the success he had achieved as the production head at Warner Bros.—movies that were fast and tough, quick and dirty, and almost always urban. The stories that Zanuck put on the screen invariably involved people who had been places and done things. (Sometimes they had been things and done places.) Almost all of them were people in his own image, men and women who seized their piece of the world and dared anybody to take it away from them. Warners stocked their shelves with sleazy shysters (Warren William) and a profusion of streetwise mugs (James Cagney, Edward G. Robinson) who embodied male aggression as a prerequisite for survival, not to mention leading ladies (Barbara Stanwyck, Bette Davis) who matched up nicely with the men.

What Warners put on the screen was matched by what went on behind the scenes. Harry Warner had a visceral dislike of anybody who made as much money as he did, and his brother Jack had the soul of a racetrack tout. Warners had directors such as the brusque Michael Curtiz, who didn't like "actor-bums," and Raoul Walsh, who wore an eye patch, for God's sake. "We're talking major Tough Guys here," wrote Ethan Mordden, "charged with bringing every film off with the efficient fury of a pirate raid."

But Zanuck understood that times had changed; the Production Code had come into force midway through 1934, and movies exclusively centered on an intermingling of power, violence, and sex were no longer possible. Besides that, the stars Zanuck inherited from the Fox regime numbered precisely four: Shirley Temple, Will Rogers, Warner Baxter, and Janet Gaynor—not a roster that could populate a gangster picture.

Zanuck not only had to reinvent his new studio, he had to reinvent Darryl Zanuck. As one historian noted, "Zanuck was a first-rate mogul on a second-rate lot. Warners was cheap but it was loaded with talent. Fox had no major directors besides John Ford and no major writers besides Dudley Nichols and Nunnally Johnson." This is giving Fox in 1935 a great benefit of the doubt—in terms of its scattershot product and stars, Fox was closer to RKO than to Paramount or MGM.

Zanuck confounded expectations by devising a three-pronged system of colorful entertainment for the masses involving historical epics (*In Old Chicago*); bright, flouncy musicals starring what came to be known as Fox blondes (Betty Grable, Alice Faye, June Haver, Marilyn Monroe); and serious dramas about beleaguered families beset by changing times (*The Grapes of Wrath, How Green Was My Valley, A Tree Grows in Brooklyn*). Added to that was the occasional social problem film (*Gentleman's Agreement, No Way Out*). At the same time he more or less created the matrix for the Hollywood biography with films such as *Young Mr. Lincoln* and *Stanley and Livingston*. After World War II, he instituted a series of successful neorealist films shot entirely on location: *Call Northside 777, The House on 92nd Street*.

It was always like that for 20th Century-Fox. In due time, when the studio was being run by a second-generation Zanuck, movies like *M*A*S*H* and *The French Connection* led the way to the gritty, truth-telling 1970s. After Richard Zanuck went on his way, *Stars Wars* gradually but firmly reversed the equation. *Young Frankenstein* perfected genre parody, and *The Rocky Horror Picture Show* invented the phenomenon of the midnight movie. And when everybody said that yet another version of *Titanic* was pointless—Zanuck had made a good version of that story in 1953—20th Century-Fox stepped up to co-finance James Cameron's hugely expensive version that became the most successful movie of its time.

In short, for more than a century, Fox flourished by creating trends rather than following them. And then, in 2018, the studio was bought by Disney. William Fox and Darryl Zanuck would have been astonished, for they had known Disney only as a boutique studio, responsible for a few features a year for the family trade. Of those, only the animated pictures attracted much attention. But on reflection they would have understood perfectly. Both men understood that corporations age and decline just like human beings, to be replaced by more aggressive companies better equipped to invest and retool for the future.

With the specific character, history, and lineage of 20th Century-Fox now overtaken by a more narrowly focused company, an overview of what went right and what went wrong for more than a century is now possible.

Here is the story of 20th Century-Fox; here is the story of the movies.

CHAPTER ONE

SUNRISE

W ILLIAM FOX'S PROFESSIONAL AND PERSONAL APOGEE
arrived in March 1929, when he announced his purchase from
the estate of Marcus Loew of a controlling interest in Loew's Inc. He
paid $50 million (1929 dollars) for 400,000 shares whose market value
was about $33 million. Carrie, Arthur, and David Loew would receive
$40 million, and the remaining $10 million would go to Nicholas
Schenck, who had taken over Loew's Inc.—the parent company of Metro-
Goldwyn-Mayer—when Marcus Loew died in 1927, and managed the
deal for the estate. Fox also agreed to buy an additional 37,500 shares of
Loew's stock that was held by Schenck and the retired actor David Warf-
ield, who had been a good friend of Marcus Loew.

Fox was paying slightly less than double the market value for the
Loew's stock, but as far as he was concerned the deal was a bargain. The
worm in this particular apple was the fact that most of the money Fox
was using was borrowed. Specifically, of the $50 million, $27 million had
been borrowed: $15 million from AT&T and $12 million from the bank-
ing firm of Halsey Stuart. Both loans would fall due in April 1930. Fox
planned to pay off the loans by merging Fox with Loew's, slashing payroll,
and then selling stock in the new company.

What made it particularly maddening to Louis B. Mayer and his partners Irving Thalberg and J. Robert Rubin was that Schenck had sold the
company and its employees down the river without so much as a by-your-
leave. This was going to cost them a great deal of money. (Mayer's group
split 20 percent of MGM's yearly profits among themselves.) Mayer's private name for Schenck had always been "Nick Skunk," but he had finally
been given a specific reason for his distrust and dislike. As for Fox, he had
never had much use for friends so long as he had his family.

Money was cheap in the spring of 1929, so nobody seemed concerned
about the vast amount of debt Fox was taking on. Before completing the

original deal, Fox had checked with President Calvin Coolidge's attorney general, William Donovan, later to be known as "Wild Bill" Donovan, the creator of the Office of Strategic Services during World War II. Donovan told him that he didn't see the amalgamation of Loew's/MGM and Fox as an antitrust problem.

The purchase of Loew's would have made Fox the unquestioned czar of Hollywood. Besides the Loew's chain, generally regarded as the best theaters on the best corners in the country, Fox would own MGM—a Loew's subsidiary and the most successful studio in Hollywood, with an unparalleled roster of stars: Greta Garbo, John Gilbert, Joan Crawford, Lon Chaney, et cetera.

And that wasn't all. Beginning in 1927, Fox had begun investing in a process he would call Grandeur, a system for making and exhibiting 70mm movies. The 70mm film, twice as wide as 35mm, produced a screen image twice as wide as it was high—perfectly calculated for showcasing spectacle. The Mitchell Camera Company—another Fox subsidiary—was hired to build the 70mm Grandeur cameras and projectors.

Besides that, Fox had spent $60,000 to buy the patent on the German sound-on-film system known as Tri-Ergon, which had the distinct possibility of making Fox the owner of all workable sound-on-film systems throughout the world. It was the purchase of the Tri-Ergon patents that had led Fox to exclaim, "Now I've got the sons of bitches by the balls, and don't think I won't twist them!"

The purchase would theoretically entitle him to collect damages from every company who exhibited sound pictures that violated the Tri-Ergon patents, or nearly everybody besides the Fox studio. Not only that, it would make him the de facto part owner of the fourteen thousand theaters in America that had been equipped for sound.

In short, William Fox had cornered the American movie industry.

It wasn't Fox's fault that it all came crashing down. In March 1929, Herbert Hoover was about to be inaugurated president, and William Donovan's opinion was irrelevant. Louis B. Mayer had been friendly with Hoover through Mayer's executive secretary, Ida Koverman, who was a power in the California Republican Party. Between Mayer and Koverman, Hoover listened, and the word went out. The Justice Department began investigating Fox for antitrust activities.

"You must have known that I have moved heaven and earth to prevent this consolidation," Mayer told Fox. "Surely you felt that someone used his influence to have the government change its opinion with reference to these shares. I was responsible."

In July, Fox barely survived a car accident that killed his chauffeur. The accident laid him up for three months, but he maintained his buying spree; from August through early October, he bought more than a hundred additional theaters in America and was negotiating to buy the UFA circuit in Germany. In October 1929, he owned 54 percent of the Fox Film Corporation and 93 percent of Fox theaters, all one thousand of them.

William Fox was a very rich man, and a very satisfied one, so much so that he felt comfortable referring to himself in the third person. "When a man reaches fifty," he told a group of reporters on October 12, "three courses lie ahead. He may dream of his past accomplishments, he may rest on his oars, or may make ambitious plans for the future. The latter of these possibilities appeals to William Fox."

The general tone of self-approbation would shortly be banished, for Fox was blissfully unaware that the stock market crash that arrived at the end of October was not a correction, but a generational catastrophe that would devastate the world economy and destroy his empire. The studio and theaters he had bought with borrowed money were now worth much less than he had paid for them—the value of the Loew's shares alone dropped to about $24 million, less than half of what he had paid. Within a year, the indebtedness of the Fox empire was in the vicinity of $100,000,000, and its shares were worth less than half of their pre-crash levels and dropping.

William Fox had risen out of poverty because of a relentless appetite for work, for property, for money, for status, for *more*. He had been focused, he had been relentless, and he had been lucky. Suddenly, permanently, his luck had run out.

On November 27, 1929, a few weeks after the cataclysm on Wall Street, the United States Attorney General filed suit against the Fox Film Corporation as well as Warner Bros. for restraint of trade, the latter because Warners had recently purchased First National Pictures from Fox.

In a sense, the antitrust business was irrelevant. The stock market crash had ravaged the value of the shares Fox had bought for a premium price, and they would be worth even less over the next several years. He still owed about $70 million for his purchases, and the banks that had loaned him the money were attempting to stave off their own failure. And so the slow-motion collapse of the Fox empire began.

It wasn't until July 1931 that the courts ordered Fox Film Corporation to divest itself of the Loew's stock. But before that, the Fox Film Corporation had divested itself of the man who had founded it, brought it to international status, and made it one of the two or three leading studios in Hollywood.

William Fox was now that saddest of men: a movie mogul without a studio.

As for Fox's Tri-Ergon patents, in 1935, only twenty-two weeks after it decided that Fox's patents were indeed valid, the Supreme Court would revisit its initial decision and decide that the Tri-Ergon patents were no longer valid.

Game, set, match.

As an example of immigrant daring undone by hubris and malevolent fate, you can't do better than the story of William Fox.

Wilhelm Fuchs was born in Tolcsva, Hungary, in 1879, and came to America at the age of nine months. He was a child of the Lower East Side, with a dialect to match—he always pronounced "films" as "fill-ums." The defining characteristic of his life was early poverty—Fox's father, a machinist, never earned more than $1,000 a year. Fox despised his father, believed him to be fatally passive and ineffectual. "All I remember of those early years," he said, "is my father slurping up Mama's chicken soup at the dinner table. There was no talking allowed at meals unless my father said something, which he rarely did." The result of all this was a man determined to obliterate his father by exceeding his father's meager accomplishments. The most succinct way of doing that would be a relentless focus on money and property.

He began his schooling at the age of six and ended it when he was eleven, because he had to go to work to help support the family. He had dozens of jobs during his adolescence. For a time he sold candy in Central Park, or stove polish for five cents a can. Other times he would hire other children to work for him. In the summer he would earn as much as $11 or $12 a week. It was in this period that he fell off the back of a truck and broke his left arm in three places. The family could not afford a doctor, so a dentist removed the boy's elbow joint, leaving his arm permanently bent—a constant reminder of the burdens imposed on him by his father.

By the time he was thirteen he was pretending to be sixteen and was a foreman supervising a dozen men and boys sewing linings in coats for

S. Cohen & Son in the garment district. He was paid $17 a week and worked eleven hours a day, six days a week. On the seventh day, he only worked five hours.

Wilhelm adored his mother and came to regard his father as a parasite. It was a psychological tic shared by a number of the first-generation movie moguls: Louis B. Mayer and Jack Warner were also fervent mama's boys, if only because their fathers abdicated any kind of responsibility for their own or their children's lives. When his father died in 1936, Fox spat on the coffin and muttered, "You son of a bitch."

Practically speaking, Wilhelm was the family breadwinner by the time he hit puberty. In his successful middle years, he would say, "I do not remember anything about play, because I never remember playing." When the date of his bar mitzvah arrived, he took a sick day in order to become a man.

When he requested a raise, he was informed that at $17 a week, he was already overpaid. Years later, when he was worth many millions of dollars, Fox would pat his vest in satisfaction at the workings of fate and opine that Mr. S. Cohen just might have been right. "It would have been so easy to spend all that I saved in those days," he said. "Every penny was something that I denied myself, with the thought in mind that if I was going forward I had to have money. I saw that capital was what I needed. Either I had to be content to work for someone else all my life, or fight for independence. The latter course made it necessary to deny myself everything I could possibly contrive to do without until I had accomplished my aim and could afford to permit myself the things I missed."

Wilhelm Fuchs embodied the classic immigrant mindset: if he wasn't hustling, he was losing. By the time he was twenty, he had $580 in his bank account—a man of means, if not property. He married Eva Leo on December 31, 1899, one day before his twenty-first birthday. It was a big wedding—more than forty guests, and it reduced Fox's bank account to $325. They moved into a five-room flat on Myrtle Avenue in Brooklyn for a monthly rent of $11. Because of Wilhelm's experience in the garment district, he opened a cloth examining and shrinking business, mostly because it didn't require much capital. The mills would ship their cloth to Fox and he would examine it for imperfections and control any shrinkage before the fabric was sewn into suits. After two years in business, he was ahead by $10,000. He eventually sold the Knickerbocker Cloth Examining and Shrinking Company for $50,000.

The money came at considerable cost. His life and experience combined to produce a grinding personality with little time for sentiment, kindness, or empathy, if only because he had no experience of them. Environment and character had combined to create a loner, a man described by his niece as someone who "invited enemies." In time, he would boast that if he died, all the executives in his company put together would be helpless to run the business.

A brief, incongruous spell in vaudeville as part of a comedy team called The Schmaltz Brothers led to arcades, which led to theaters. In 1904, Fox invested in a Brooklyn nickelodeon with 146 seats. He bought one-third of the business for $1,666.67.

He opened his theater and . . . nobody came.

"All of it was in this one thing," he remembered in 1927. "I saw beautiful visions of going back and asking for my job, in which the maximum salary I had ever earned before I went into business for myself was $17 a week. I saw visions of that and leaving this thing that held out the world to me and I wondered what to do and why the thing was not doing business."

Fox knew an advance man for Barnum & Bailey's circus, who suggested publicity, ballyhoo, something that would make the public sit up and take notice. A sword swallower ran $2 a night, a fire-eater $3 a night;

a sleight-of-hand magician, however, could pocket as many coins as he could filch. Fox contracted for one of each, and it worked. The sword swallower was particularly potent; his act began in the street and concluded inside the theater, and the public dutifully anted up their nickels and followed him in.

The result, as Fox remembered, was that "this little bit of a theater into which I had put $1,600 brought in, in five years, approximately $250,000. . . . It was that little establishment that made it possible for me to build the organization we now have and it was that method that had to be employed to convince the people of this country ultimately that the motion picture was not just something that might run along but something that would prove worthwhile and something that the nation at large would accept."

Fox began what would be more than two decades of relentless expansion. "Every time we got $1,600 more we opened another just like it. Under the law, the maximum number of chairs at that time was two hundred and ninety nine. The minute you had more than two hundred and ninety nine seats, you were obliged to build under certain fire regulations and you had to have a modern, fireproof building. We kept investing our money in these two hundred and ninety nine seat theaters until one day they passed a law permitting us to seat six hundred people in a building that was semi-fireproof. The day after that law was passed these theaters were obsolete and we could not use them anymore. Later we built theaters seating a thousand or fifteen hundred people."

Fox was slightly shading his narrative, which was typical. The impetus to build larger theaters involved profit—the more seats, the more money Fox could make. With the exception of the occasional business downturn—the Spanish flu epidemic of 1918, for instance—the story of silent film would be one of constant aesthetic and business expansion.

Fox's chain of nickelodeons spread throughout Brooklyn, ending up with fifteen establishments. He would often configure the route through the building so that patrons would exit through a Kinetoscope parlor, which made it likely that they would spend more money before they hit the street. When he got enough money, he would buy out any partners. The first theater he purchased outright was the Gaiety, an old seven-hundred-seat vaudeville house at 194 Grand Street in Brooklyn. He paid $20,000 for the land and building.

Fox was not New York born, but he was New York bred. He knew how to go along to get along, and he seems to have ingested with his mother's milk a knowledge of power and how to use it. A lot of Fox's expansion over the years was because of a money stream that exceeded his profits from theaters. It largely derived from Tammany Hall, the Democratic political machine that ran the five boroughs. Tammany could easily launder money through Fox's expanding empire, and get a percentage in return—a win-win. His patron at Tammany was Big Tim Sullivan, who had already formed the Sullivan & Considine vaudeville circuit, which involved 140 theaters nationwide. The result of Fox's management and Tammany's money was that by 1914, Fox owned fourteen movie theaters in New York City and had spent more than $4 million on property and construction.

Fox's estimation of his patrons was blunt: "The motion picture did not appeal to the native born. He had other forms of recreation and entertainment. The motion picture appealed mainly to the foreign born, who could not speak or understand our tongue, who had no theater where he could hear his own tongue. He was a Pole, a Russian, a Slav or of some other foreign nationality. He wanted a diversion and found it in the motion picture."

All this illustrates the logical, businesslike progression of Fox's mind and career, which was duplicated in the early careers of most of the first generation of movie moguls, most of whom began as exhibitors. Louis B. Mayer and the Warner brothers all began with a single theater, then methodically expanded as theatrical entrepreneurs, then expanded further by moving into production, which made more sense than renting other people's hit-and-miss films. If they made their own movies, they could own both ends of the business, the production end feeding the exhibition end. Result: profits from both sides of the equation. The difference was that Fuchs was willing to walk on the shady side of the street in return for the capital he needed.

William Fox began producing movies toward the end of 1914; his first film was *Life's Shop Window*, based on a novel by one Victoria Cross, the rights to which cost Fox $100. The entire picture cost $6,000. It was a neo-Dickensian story about an impoverished orphan who marries and almost betrays her husband before returning to her loyal spouse. *Life's Shop Window* made money. And just like that, William Fox was a movie producer.

In these early years, Fox's wife, Eva, worked hand in hand with her husband. She was a compulsive reader and acted as his story editor, telling him what stories and novels to buy. Fox gave little thought to art; he was in a commercial medium and his ambition revolved around making money. When D. W. Griffith made *The Birth of a Nation* in 1915, Fox rushed out *The Nigger* within a week of the Griffith film's release. Based on a play by Edward Sheldon, a good friend of John Barrymore's, the Fox film told a relatively progressive story about a partly Black Southerner who passes for white and runs for governor. After business interests threaten him with exposure if he passes a bill hostile to their interests, he signs the bill, resigns his position, and moves up north.

Fox officially formed the Fox Film Corporation on February 1, 1915, with a capital investment of $400,000. That same year he hit the ground running with *A Fool There Was*, starring Theda Bara. By the end of the first year of Fox Film, the company had released twenty-six features at a cost of $767,000. Those twenty-six features brought back rentals of $3.2 million, which would have left Fox with a net profit in the vicinity of a million dollars.

While all this was going on, Fox was also engaged in another battle, with the Patents Company that had been created by Thomas Edison and allied companies to protect its patents on cameras and other equipment. The Patents Company demanded large license fees, which made it, in essence, a protection racket that strangled competition. The Supreme Court issued an antitrust ruling in 1917 that ended the stranglehold of the Patents Company and made it possible for anyone who wanted to make a movie to go ahead and do it without paying a bounty to anybody.

Fox took the victory personally, placing full-page ads in trade journals, proclaiming: "I fought in the United States courts and won." Fox, of course, had a bountiful supply of skeletons well hidden in the closet. As Vanda Krefft, his best biographer, wrote, "A founder who had made his name by allying himself with the most corrupt political machine in America . . . these were the people who launched the Fox Film Corporation. It wasn't the way Fox wanted to do business, but it was, he believed, the way he had to do business."

William Fox had chosen the perfect time to go into the movie business. Within fourteen years, the company would issue $10,000,000 in dividends.

For the first five years of its existence, Fox Film focused on a steady stream of programmers, five- and six-reel pictures produced at a reasonable cost that were almost guaranteed to bring in a profit from a world crazy for movies. Fox chose the stories, assigned directors, and watched the rushes closely while dictating notes to the editor. When the shoot was done, he helped write the titles and ginned up publicity instructions. A fair number of his films were adaptations of classics, such as *A Tale of Two Cities* and *Les Miserables*, partially because they were famous titles, partially because they were in the public domain and he didn't have to pay for the rights.

The film that turned Fox's head was called *Over the Hill to the Poorhouse*, a tear-jerker based on a poem that brought in rentals of more than $2 million, for a profit of $1.25 million.

Success didn't gentle Fox's character. Glendon Allvine worked for Fox for a number of years, and he characterized his boss bluntly: "Among the early pioneers, William Fox was not a loveable character, like Uncle Carl Laemmle or Joe Schenck."

That was putting it mildly. "He didn't want money for pleasure or for egotistical display," Fox's niece said. "He wanted money because he believed it gave him control." His press agents referred to him as "the lone eagle" of the movie business, but Angela Fox Dunn believed that "a notoriously savage lone wolf" was closer to the truth.

To a remarkable extent, it was a one-man organization—Fox delegated only what bored him, which was very little. There were very few conferences or meetings to decide policy or production plans. He didn't wear a watch because as far as he was concerned time was irrelevant; he only left his office when his desk was cleared of paper, and if that meant he had to stay till ten p.m. or later, so be it.

Every so often, he would explode in a burst of self-aggrandizement: "I knew the condition of every nation we traded with. No question could arise that by the push of a button could not be answered in the extensive files that I had adjoining my office. I had it completely systematized, so that I knew every move that was made throughout the organization . . .

"Again and again I didn't go to bed at all during the twenty four hours. There was work to do. I was working not only for myself, but to help others. I had an ambition to build this monumental institution."

Within his frankly commercial instincts, Fox wanted to make films for the family, assuming that the family in question was not averse to strong emotional components—filial devotion, sexual attraction, et cetera. He was sensitive about one thing: he was homely and knew it, so disliked being photographed. He was especially sensitive about his crooked arm. He hated to use the telephone, preferring to put everything in writing. Therefore he dealt mainly in telegrams and night letters. Like Michael Corleone, he settled all family—and company—business. He would send his sister a peremptory telegram one month in advance of every visit he made to the West Coast, and that was the only notice he gave.

In slightly more than twenty years, William Fox ran a $1,600 investment in a single nickelodeon into a film empire he estimated to be worth $300 million. It was an overstatement—we're dealing with the movie business here—but not an unreasonable one.

Fox's roster of stars was initially a majority of one: Theda Bara, real name Theodosia Goodman from Cincinnati. She was a pleasant woman who had been a jobbing actress of no renown whatever until Fox's publicists got hold of her. They proclaimed her to be the former leading lady of the Théâtre Antoine in Paris, said she had won acclaim in Vienna and Berlin. In reality she had never been to Europe, let alone acted there, and had never achieved any level of fame anywhere until Fox hired her for $75 a week to play the vamp in *A Fool There Was*.

The idea of a woman who drained men of both their money and their—ahem—vitality until the woebegone husk had little option but suicide hit a latently misogynist nerve in the population. *A Fool There Was* became a huge hit, and Bara ground out forty pictures for Fox in the next three years, the destructive yang to the wholesome yin of Mary Pickford and Lillian Gish.

Bara propelled Fox Film to revenues of $3.21 million in 1915, compared with $272,401 that Box Office Attraction Company, Fox's corporate predecessor, had earned the year before. Net profits amounted to $523,000.

Bara played a procession of fictional as well as historical vamps (Cleopatra, Salome, Madame Du Barry). Fox occasionally broke up the monotony with something different—Bara also played Juliet in an adaptation of *Romeo and Juliet*, and Esmerelda in a film called *The Darling of Paris*, a riff on *The Hunchback of Notre Dame*. Bara's publicity was every bit as exotic as her screen image. As one film historian noted, "She wore indigo makeup to emphasize her pallor; surrounded herself with symbols of death, such as human skulls, ravens, etc; rode in a white limousine; was served by 'Nubian slaves'; and received the press while stroking a snake in a room permeated with incense."

For a culture only recently emerged from the Victorian era, Bara's projection of evil carnality was a stunning, erotic corrective to Dickens's doomed ingénues. In 1919, Bara was making $4,000 a week, which seemed insufficient to counter her exhaustion and her boredom with a predominantly repetitive characterization. She quit the Fox studio, only to find that the public was every bit as exhausted as she was. Her last film was a two-reeler for Hal Roach in 1926 called *Madame Mystery*. After that, she lived out her years in apparently contented retirement in Beverly Hills as the wife of the director Charles Brabin. Only one complete Bara film has survived (*A Fool There Was*), and it does her no favors—it's flatly directed and she's small, squat, and lacks anything approaching subtlety.*

Fox's primary leading man of this period was William Farnum, a short, barrel-chested actor who proved exceedingly successful and exceedingly versatile. Farnum played the dual parts of Charles Darnay and Sydney Carton in *A Tale of Two Cities*, he played Jean Valjean in *Les Miserables*, he played François Villon in the movie of the same name, and when the tank of classic literature grew empty, he played western heroes in *Riders of the Purple Sage* and *Drag Harlan*.

An actor with that kind of versatility is prized by his employers, which helped William Fox overlook the fact that Farnum was a showy actor who did most of his acting with his flashing eyes and massive chest. Farnum held down the fort at Fox for close to ten years, and his career continued with smaller parts in the sound era. Although his chest slid inexorably into his stomach, Farnum's acting technique remained tied to the silent era. One of his last appearances was in Cecil B. DeMille's 1949 *Samson and Delilah*, where his flashing eyes got yet another workout. Since silent film acting was not merely valued by DeMille, but required, Farnum fit right in.

A different demographic was serviced by Tom Mix, the third great cowboy star of the movies, after Bronco Billy Anderson and William S. Hart. William Fox hired Mix away from the Selig company in 1916 for $350 a week to make a series of two-reelers, but he was quickly promoted to features. Said promotion came with a $50 raise.

---

* Archaeological excavations of the early years of the Fox studio have been limited by the fact that a 1937 vault fire at the studio's East Coast storage facility destroyed something like three-quarters of the Fox product before 1930. The original negative of Murnau's *Sunrise* burned, which has resulted in the darkish cast of surviving prints. Similarly, Tom Mix made eighty-five pictures for Fox, but only about a dozen survived in America, although more have turned up overseas.

As with Bara, William Fox emphasized quantity over quality—Mix averaged six pictures a year.

Mix set up his studio in Silver Lake, at a ranch that became known as Mixville. It had a false-front Western town, barns and corrals, plenty of open space to simulate the Wild West, all only minutes from downtown Los Angeles. Fox allowed Mix a good deal of autonomy, and many of the cowboys and actors who worked with him lived around Silver Lake. Mix's chuck wagon chef prepared the meals, and it could be said that they were living the West while simultaneously making movies about the West. William Fox would open a studio in Hollywood at the corner of Sunset and Western, but Mix continued to shoot at Mixville until the mid-twenties.

Tom Mix's rise can be gauged simply by charting his salary. He was making $600 a week in 1919, but by the end of the year was making $1,500 a week. By 1925, he was making $6,500 a week, and in the late 1920s he topped out at $7,500 a week, even though Fox publicity claimed that he was making $10,000 a week.

Mix had only a fifth-grade education but worked hard to broaden his horizons. When he would be scheduled to meet some dignitary, he would read up on them so he could discuss their work with some level of sophistication. "He had a photographic memory," said his daughter Thomasina, "and he would read up on all his guest's interests and accomplishments. He'd be able to talk with them about what they were interested in and put them immediately at ease."

Mix always put on a good show, playing the part of the glamorous cowboy star to the hilt and beyond. Even if he wore a tux to a social event, Mix made sure to wear cowboy boots and his Stetson. Similarly, he drove a Stutz but strove to give the impression that he'd rather be on a horse. While his press agent reported that Mix did all his own stunts, in truth he was frequently doubled, but "this fact was considered top secret," wrote

Lambert Hillyer, who directed him as well as William S. Hart. There was no question who ran a Mix set; if he didn't like the way a stunt looked, he'd occasionally do the stunt himself, danger be damned. "Mix was himself a good man with a rifle, rope or six-gun," wrote Hillyer.

"Tom was temperamental," remembered the director George Marshall, "but it ran in streaks. Every once in a while this would come to the surface, particularly if he was drinking. One picture would sail along with not a problem; the next would be full of them and he would be sullen and unapproachable. As a whole, though, his better nature prevailed, as he loved his work."

Mix's alcohol intake would be something of a continuing issue. In 1924, Victoria Forde, Mix's wife, shot him in the arm during a booze-fueled brawl. The bullet went through his arm and lodged near his spine, and surgery was required to get it out. It could have been worse. During a 1933 property settlement hearing, Mix testified that his wife had emptied the pistol at him, but only hit him once. Mrs. Mix countered by asserting that Mix was beating her at the time she brought out the hardware.

Mix's surviving films attest to his charm and charisma, although they're hampered somewhat by Fox's habit of giving Mix only ordinary directors to work with. Mix made only one film with John Ford, although they remained friendly. When Mix was killed in a car crash in 1940, Ford pulled strings and got permission to bury Mix in a military cemetery, despite the fact that Mix had deserted in 1902. For much of his career, Mix was stuck with Lynn Reynolds, who was mainly efficient. Mix was short, but the cameramen managed to hide that fact, and Mix cooperated by making sure to hire only actors and actresses who were shorter than he was.

Surviving Mix films such as *Sky High*, *Just Tony*, and *Riders of the Purple Sage* tend to be brisk programmers of about an hour each that reflect the casual, lighthearted fun of the early Douglas Fairbanks pictures. As with Fairbanks, Mix made sure to salt a few good stunts throughout each film. It's no accident that, as with Fairbanks, Mix was the hero of nearly every little boy who went to the movies.

Mix obviously worked hard, but Fox always acted as if he was doing the actor a favor by keeping him employed. Actually, Mix made Fox a lot of money. *Riders of the Purple Sage* cost $141,000, brought in world rentals of $375,000, and made a profit of $100,000. Mix's six pictures a year could drop more than a half million dollars into the Fox coffers all by themselves.

Every sentient movie mogul knew that when a star hit, it made sense to duplicate them. After Mix became popular, the studio tapped a man named Buck Gebhardt from the roster of cowboys who had been working with Mix and made him their second-string western star under the name Buck Jones. Jones proved popular, although he was never a genuine threat to Mix, who had a lighter, more boyish quality. The Jones pictures were purely commercial, but Fox refused to lower his standards: "Reviewed Buck Jones picture," he wired in December 1919. "Impossible to release. Worst amateurish direction I have ever reviewed Dismiss director immediately Hire someone else to complete present picture Will shelve picture we have here."

Buck Jones's Fox pictures cost between $50,000 and $75,000 and returned about $125,000 apiece. Jones's profits were less, but they still cumulatively returned around $150,000 in profits in an average year. Jones remained a popular star of B westerns until his tragic death in a Boston nightclub fire in 1942.

William Fox regarded himself as a confirmed New Yorker and went to Los Angeles only when absolutely necessary. This meant that the supervision of Mix and the rest of the California operation fell to Sol Wurtzel and, eventually, Winfield Sheehan, who worked in New York until Fox sent him west in the mid-twenties. Wurtzel had been Fox's secretary until he was promoted to studio manager for the West Coast studio at the bare-bones salary of $100 a week.

Sheehan's background was nearly as exotic as the movie business. He had been the secretary to New York Police Commissioner Rhinelander Waldo, where he earned a reputation for carefree corruption. In July 1912, Sheehan fell under suspicion as a suspect in the murder of one Herman Rosenthal. The late Mr. Rosenthal had collected graft payments for Big Tim Sullivan, William Fox's partner in the City Theater and much else, and had been providing information about corruption in the city to the district attorney. A New York police lieutenant named Charles Becker went to the electric chair in 1915 for the killing, but there was always a suspicion that Becker was the fall guy for Big Tim Sullivan and Sheehan, a suspicion fed by Fox himself in 1930. By that time Fox had been deposed from his studio and was lashing about in all directions when he told Upton Sinclair that he had "rescued" Sheehan from a murder charge by hiring him as his general manager, despite the fact that he had no experience whatever in the entertainment business.

Fox managed his growing operation by sending a steady stream of mostly abusive night letters to Sol Wurtzel. The dynamic that emerges from these letters is identical to that of Ebenezer Scrooge and his relentless brow-beating of Bob Cratchit.

Solomon Maximilian Wurtzel was born in 1890 on the Lower East Side of New York. His brother Harry became an agent with A-list clients such as John Ford, Henry King, and Gene Autry, but Sol Wurtzel took the brunt of Fox's predominantly charmless personality. Fox seemed to wake up every morning convinced that all and sundry were out to rob him blind through either bad character or lack of talent.

Fox's preferred method of management involved threats, either veiled or open. As Fox wrote to Wurtzel, "I have over-burdened you with work, and probably the job has gotten beyond you. . . . I [feel] you should be relieved of a portion of your work for at least two months . . ." Carla Winter noted, "He was the prototype of the tyrannical father who would keep his children obedient by berating and humiliating them."

Gladys Brockwell, one of the company's minor stars, wrote Fox in 1918 asking for a $500 loan to help her pay for an operation on her mother. As the correspondence between Wurtzel and Fox reveals, there were a lot of mothers needing surgery in these years, and Fox wasn't having it. Fox wrote Wurtzel, "I don't want to grant this loan of $500. You having this situation in hand should be able to judge just how long we will have to retain her services. I leave it to you to decide if you want to advance her this $500 and deduct it from her weekly salary. There might be a way of doing this, and take it out of her salary weekly, so that the entire amount will be paid before the expiration of her contract . . ."

Tom Mix was the studio workhorse, but when Wurtzel loaned him $2,500 in 1919 without clearing it with his boss first, Fox went through the roof. "By what authority [had] you to make this loan without first communicating with me . . . so that we could have had this loan approved by our executive committee, and then have it properly submitted to our Board of Directors. . . . I call your attention that when you first came to me, your salary per year was less than one thousand dollars. I have permitted you to grow to your heights. On what theory did you take it upon yourself to loan money belonging to the Company. . . . I would like your complete explanation of this action, and the necessity for it . . ."

Wurtzel explained that Mix had a chance to buy a house and needed $2,500 immediately. "He needed this money on short notice and I told him that I did not think the company would have any objection and arranged to loan him that sum."

Wurtzel realized he had made a serious mistake. "The only thing I can say is that it was a 'bonehead' piece of business and judgment on my part. I did not loan him the money without first securing your approval because I wanted to go beyond what I was privileged to do. I felt at the time I was doing it for the best interest of the company, and I realized soon after the transaction that I should have wired for your approval."

When Fox received a letter from the director Sidney Franklin saying that Fox's unhappiness with a recent Franklin picture was nothing more than a difference of opinion, Fox replied to Wurtzel, "I am not interested in the comment Franklin makes, nor am I interested in the comment you make. The final judgement with reference to any picture made by the Fox Film Corporation, you ought to know, is left with me and not with you or Mr. Franklin."

Fox carped, criticized, second-guessed, and demanded better pictures for less money while Wurtzel backtracked, placated, and cringed, sometimes throwing his hands up in utter bafflement at the impossibility of ever pleasing his boss. And just to keep Wurtzel even more off-balance, every once in a while Fox would give Wurtzel an unasked-for raise.

Communicating via letters was awkward, and Wurtzel would occasionally ask Fox to come to the West Coast so that they could talk face to face. Fox usually dodged. In time, Wurtzel developed chronic constipation and a facial tic that caused the side of his mouth to curve upward into a permanent smile. But Wurtzel never walked away, and he managed to find and sign directors such as John Ford and Frank Borzage to the Fox roster. And Fox always knew a good thing when he saw it. In mid-1918, he wrote Wurtzel, "I want you to make every effort to make the Tom Mix pictures splendid and vital, for I think he is on the road of a sure fire if we just pay attention to him."

It's impossible to read these letters without coming to the conclusion that Fox was carefully constructing a psychological veil of plausible deniability. The studio's successes were invariably ascribed by Fox to Fox and the impeccable management structure his genius had devised. Failure belonged strictly to Wurtzel.

In contrast to Fox, other moguls, such as Mayer, Thalberg, and Warner, only left Hollywood under duress. They hovered over the daily process of the making of their pictures, manipulating producers and directors alike in order to make sure their movies reflected *their* values, *their* needs.

Delegate authority? Not bloody likely. Authority delegated was authority dissipated.

Fox was making good money, but his movies were not impressing either the critics or his peers. *Variety* wrote that "there is behind all Fox productions a certain general scheme that is more important than any other consideration. This scheme is to put out melodramas that are heavy with sex appeal and blow air into the deadweight by swift action and unusual photography."

By 1920, the Fox Film Corporation had expanded to eighty-four exchanges and offices in America and the world. The list of stars at this point was evenly divided between brawny leading men and a few female leads: William Farnum, Pearl White, Tom Mix, George Walsh, William Russell, Buck Jones, and Shirley Mason.

Pearl White had made a huge splash in 1914 with *The Perils of Pauline*. She had a strange career—a great star in serials, less so in conventional features. She was only with Fox for a few years, after which she went back to Pathé and serials. White retired in 1924, although she occasionally played with the idea of a comeback. John Kenley, who worked for the Shubert brothers in the 1930s and '40s, remembered that White gave some thought to a comeback in the theater. "She was a drinking lady," Kenley noted, which may have accounted for her early death in 1938.

In truth, Fox's eye for actors was erratic. In 1921, he signed John Gilbert to a three-year contract and tried to force him into brawny, two-fisted parts of the sort that William Farnum was playing. Fox's version of *Monte Cristo* was particularly ludicrous, with Gilbert hidden behind some of the least convincing wigs and beards of the silent era. The problem was not Gilbert, but Fox's pictures. MGM picked up Gilbert after his Fox contract expired and quickly converted him into one of the legendary silent stars.

Fox knew he was underrepresented with women stars and was actively looking for a "Constance Talmadge type." The production plans for the post–World War I period mandated a whopping schedule of between fifty-five and sixty-five pictures with stars, plus a few pictures without stars.

Fox opened a splendidly appointed new corporate headquarters on W. 56th Street in New York while continuing to complain to Sol Wurtzel that Wurtzel's inability to control costs was going to drive the company off the cliff.

Fox somehow managed to sense whenever Wurtzel was forming a bond with one of his filmmakers and invariably ordered that filmmaker fired, the better to keep his loyal lieutenant off-balance. On more than one occasion, Wurtzel would keep the employee on the payroll under a different name. "Mr. Wurtzel is a special character entirely," noted *Fortune* magazine. "On the one hand, he wears the loudest golf clothes in Hollywood. On the other, he is extremely modest and unassuming, with a perpetual craving for work. . . . He it is who catches the studio hell, day in and day out, eight or ten or twelve hours a day."

Fox's modus operandi never changed. As Sol Wurtzel's daughter would note, "William Fox divided his employees into two categories and treated them in a diverse manner. With his important stars, directors and foreign managers, his behavior was impeccable, even to the point of generosity if required. He would save his spleen to vent unrestrainedly on his immediate working family of employees; those with whom he had continuing direct contact."

Another way of putting it was that Fox was polite to people he needed and nasty to people who could be replaced. To put it succinctly, there was Glendon Allvine, who worked in publicity for Fox from 1927 to 1932. "I never encountered him in an ugly mood, but Roxy and others shuddered at personal contacts with him. . . . His humor was primitive. Once, when he called me in to give Roxy hell . . . I was wearing a red necktie and he flicked it out, commenting, "What's the matter, boy? Got a nosebleed?"

Fox told Allvine that promoting the owner of the studio was useless. "This mug of mine will never sell any tickets, so just concentrate on getting the stars into magazines and newspapers and forget about me." His ego ran not to his face, but to his accomplishments and his need for the commercial equivalent of *lebensraum*: "I always bragged of the fact that no second of those contained in the twenty four hours ever passed but that the name of William Fox was on the screen, being exhibited in some theater in some part of the world."

For all his preference for managing through anger and intimidation, Fox was no fool. He knew good filmmaking when he saw it, as was proved by his enthusiasm for the work of a new director Wurtzel brought on board to direct Buck Jones. "I reviewed *The Big Punch*. It is a good Buck Jones picture. However there is as much difference in value between this picture and *Just Pals*, as there is between cream cheese and the full moon. *Just Pals* was one of the most artistically done pictures that I have reviewed in years. *The Big Punch* is just one more motion picture. . . . [John] Ford has proven that if Jones is properly directed he can play any part. He is daring and thrilling; has a charming personality and charming smile; strong face and therefore can play any part assigned to him providing he is properly directed."

Fox's enthusiasm for Ford's work would eventually lead him to slotting Ford to direct *The Iron Horse*, Fox's riposte to Paramount's *The Covered Wagon*, and the film that fired the starting gun for Ford's career as a major director. Shot in difficult conditions in Nevada, *The Iron Horse* cost a weighty $371,000 at a time when the average A picture cost from $150,000 to $200,000. But *The Iron Horse* had an authentic epic sweep and served as a marker for Ford's coming greatness. It had world rentals of $1.5 million with a profit of $650,000—Fox's biggest hit for 1924.

Before Fox gave Ford free rein to make his movie far from studio supervision, he was still focused on a steady supply of commercial programmers that would play a few days or a week and make way for the next one. Fox's average per-picture cost for 1924 was $78,000, which is one reason his profit for the year amounted to $2.2 million, compared with $2.7 million for Loew's Inc. and $9.4 million for Famous Players-Lasky, the latter attributable to their large investment in movie theaters.

The economics of westerns demonstrate why Fox made so many of them during the 1920s. By the mid-twenties, Fox was spending about $175,000 on each Tom Mix picture, which were generally allotted generous thirty-day production schedules, probably to accommodate attractive locations. Zion Canyon, Yellowstone, Lone Pine, and Royal Gorge all served as locations for Mix pictures.

By 1927, William Fox seems to have believed that he and Mix had outgrown each other. Mix was drinking more and enjoying it less, and the studio could no longer afford to adopt a laissez-faire attitude toward his films. A plethora of imitators also made it more difficult for the Mix films to stand out. Besides that, the studio was making a commitment to sound, and Mix had a strange way of talking that, along with age, would make his talkie career relatively unsuccessful—although his vocal timbre was fine, he spoke as if he had lockjaw, and tended to swallow his words.

In 1928, Fox let Mix's contract expire. William Fox had a belief that the most potent box office appeal of the average star was about five years, and it made sense to regularly shuffle the deck. Mix had spent eleven years at Fox, so in Fox's eyes he was overdue for a change of scenery. Mix's last picture for Fox eked out a profit of just $14,000.

Mix latched on at the FBO studio, a low-end producer of B pictures. It was a comedown; Mix was unhappy with the studio, and the studio was unhappy with him. He had been contracted for six pictures, but made only five. After that, there was trouble with the IRS that resulted in Mix paying $173,000 in tax and penalties, and a series of pictures for Universal with budgets that were about half of what Fox had spent. Then came a serial for Mascot. Mix toured with his own circus, which went belly-up in 1938. He died in a car wreck outside of Florence, Arizona, in 1940. It should be pointed out that even in the twenty-first century the best of his movies stand up nicely. Tom Mix was a true movie star.

CHAPTER TWO

WHAT PRICE GLORY?

IN MANY RESPECTS, THE STORY OF WILLIAM FOX IS ABOUT a business rather than a man, if only because he seems to have willfully obliterated anything resembling a personality in favor of the single-minded pursuit of achievement. You get a sense of grinding responsibility, a frightening level of aggression mixed with situational expedience, seasoned with a touch of megalomania. In short, a single-minded wolf at the door who could always justify himself by referencing the dozen family members he was carrying on his back.

For instance: Fox spent several years in the late 1920s manipulating his company's share price through secret trading that wasn't technically illegal until the Securities Exchange Act of 1934. Some of this involved short-selling his own companies. He did the same thing with Fox theaters, trading through as many as seven accounts at each of twenty-two brokerage houses, with all of the accounts carrying the names of relatives or employees.

In his private life, when the marriages of his daughters broke up, the surnames of his two grandsons were magically altered to Fox. Neither of them ever reclaimed their real names.

Because Fox was always determined to stay ahead of the pack, he was invariably a motivator of change. For instance: falling in line alongside the Warner Bros. when it came to sound.

Fox had sent an old friend named John Joy to look at the newfangled invention in March 1926 at the Case Research Lab in Auburn, New York. Theodore Case had been working on sound on film since 1911, initially with Lee De Forest, and had finally perfected his system. Joy was impressed by Case's demonstration films and persuaded Fox to watch Case's tests. The showing occurred at the Fox studio on 54th and Tenth Avenue in New York. It was nothing but a close-up of a canary singing, but Fox couldn't believe the evidence of his eyes and ears. Fox tended toward the suspicious—in later years he would lurch into outright para-noia—and he thought there was some sort of magician's trick. Ventrilo-quism? Nothing would do but that the projection room in his mansion be equipped.

After that, he went all in . . . sort of. On July 23, 1926, the two men formed the Fox-Case Corporation, with Case turning over all of his pat-ents to the new company. In return, he got a lot of stock in the new com-pany, a three-year contract, and $1 million to experiment with recording sound outdoors. Fox then began a modified stall, partially because of the same hesitance with which most of the founding generation of moguls regarded sound.

Earl Sponable, who had worked on the invention with Case, said that "Fox with his Movietone could have been ahead of [Warner's] Vitaphone if Fox had let us go ahead with theater demonstrations, but he kept me doing tests at the 54th Street studio." Fox thought sound was interesting, but he also thought it might be a fad, as did most of the moguls, if only because none of the previous attempts at synchronizing sound and film had caught on.

But all those other attempts had been made years earlier. In the interim, radio had achieved wide popularity and made the world safe for music and voices. Fox began screening Movietone shorts in February 1927 when he showed a random selection of sound shorts to fifty mem-bers of the New York City press, after which a selection of engineers answered questions from the reporters.

On April 30, the first advertised showing of Movietone newsreels was a four-minute segment featuring West Point cadets. These were coming attractions to the main event: at dawn on May 20, the Movietone news-reel cameras photographed and recorded Charles Lindbergh's takeoff from Long Island headed due east to Paris in his plane *The Spirit of St.*

Louis. The audience, filling all 6,200 seats at Fox's Roxy Theater for the premiere of the newsreel, responded with a ten-minute standing ovation—breaking news in a big way.

The New York Times reviewed the Lindbergh newsreel in laudatory terms: "Not only did one hear the whirring of the airplane's motor, but one also heard the cheers of the throng that saw the fearless young flyer take off on his dash to the French capital. This was Mr. Fox's second Movietone newsreel and there is no doubt but that he has started a valuable contribution to the screen. It is probably one that can be made more readily through the registering of the sound by light than when it is accomplished on a wax disk."

Thus encouraged, Fox began adding sound for the general release of some of his most prestigious silent films: *Sunrise* and *7th Heaven*, among others. Fox's use of sound for his newsreel operation made it easy for him to adapt sound recording for features, and his 1929 *In Old Arizona* won an Oscar for Warner Baxter in a flamboyantly atrocious performance as the Cisco Kid while also becoming one of the first all-talking films to make extensive use of outdoor locations.

The innovation of sound on film proved so successful that Fox began looking around for the next big thing in movie innovations. Fox's Grandeur Screen led the charge for 70mm film. Similar attempts were made by MGM and Warners, but the resulting films were all unsuccessful, and theater owners resisted outfitting their booths with new projectors just a year or two after buying expensive sound projectors.

These were years in which Fox was a whirlwind of action. In March 1927, he bought the Roxy Theater, which had cost $10 million. The Roxy had opened two weeks before, splendidly ornate but uneasily floating in an ocean of red ink. The theater was named after Samuel Rothafel, a famous theatrical impresario and newly christened radio star. Roxy was a brilliant showman, but he couldn't control either his costs or, as would soon become obvious, his new landlord.

1929 was the apogee of William Fox's power and prestige, not to mention his self-regard. A profile written by journalist Allene Talmey noted that "it is absurd to say that he is conceited. It is too puny a word. Megalomania afflicted with elephantiasis, that is the state of his self-esteem."

———

After more than a decade in movie production, it was clear that there was a central issue of identity and responsibility that Fox dodged. It's a mistake to lump Fox in with studio heads such as Jack Warner or Louis B. Mayer, when he was actually much closer to Adolph Zukor—an entertainment entrepreneur whose predominant passion was real estate, not movies. Like Zukor, Fox spent his time in New York with the financiers instead of in Hollywood with the moviemakers. "I only met him to say how do you do," said Janet Gaynor, Fox's biggest female star in the late 1920s and early 1930s. "He didn't seem to have anything to do with the running of the studio."

William Fox neither liked nor trusted most actors. Instead he bet on directors. His late 1920s roster of directorial talents included John Ford, F. W. Murnau, Frank Borzage, Raoul Walsh, and a young Howard Hawks—the directorial equivalent of the New York Yankees Murderer's Row (i.e., the best lineup in the business). Below them were the usual roster of camera mechanics that every studio needed in order to produce the necessary amount of product.

Fox signed F. W. Murnau to a contract in January 1925. This is itself a testament to Fox's nose for talent and determination to own as much of it as was available. *The Last Laugh* had premiered in Berlin only a week or so before Murnau agreed to come to America and work for Fox, long before anybody in Hollywood had heard of the film. (That would change soon enough.) Murnau had previously committed to making *Faust* for UFA, but would come to America to work for Fox when his last German film was finished.

The signing of Murnau kicked off a protean phase of the Fox studio. The same month he signed Murnau, William Fox announced that the studio would devote itself to "special features" that would eliminate "all hokum and unreality." Few people bought into the pronouncement. Joe Dannenberg, the columnist for *Film Daily*, wrote, "They never use hokum in the Fox studio. They never have. Of course, *Over the Hill*, well, that's different. And then too, Tom Mix with his hokum with [his horse] Tony—well, that's different. And of course, dear old Theda. With her big vamping eyes and tigerish movements—well, that's different."

Murnau finally arrived in America in July 1926, and Fox threw a banquet in his honor at the Ritz-Carlton. Fox's publicity announced that "Mr. Murnau will have his own technical staff and cameraman and all the vast facilities of the Fox company at his command. . . . He is a recognized genius, placed by many capable critics at the very top of the directorial field, and his innovations are certain to go far in bringing something distinctly new to the Fox program and in establishing new standards in the America studios."

In a 1927 address at Harvard arranged by Joseph P. Kennedy, Fox outlined his reasons for hiring Murnau. After calling him "the genius of his age," Fox said that Murnau's *The Last Laugh* was "the greatest motion picture of all time" because of Murnau's determination to "tell its story by picture and not by reading matter and he proceeded to make a motion picture that took two hours to unfold without a single word in titles. The only insert he had in his entire story was a copy of a letter one character had written to another. In other words, the story unfolded itself entirely with the camera. It was a huge success abroad, and, although the greatest motion picture of all time, was one of the greatest failures here."

All true. But there was something else at work besides his admiration for a director. In 1925, the *Film Daily Year Book* had done their annual canvassing of movie critics regarding the ten best films of the year. It had been a spectacular year for American movies: *The Gold Rush, The Merry Widow, Don Q, Son of Zorro, The Freshman, The Phantom of the Opera, The Big Parade*, and *Kiss Me Again* were all on the list. But not a single Fox picture made the roster. After ten years in the movie business, Fox was still in the business of appealing to the public rather than the critics. MGM, Paramount, and United Artists were manufacturing Cadillacs and Packards, while the Fox production line was grinding out Model Ts.

What flipped Fox's switch is impossible to ascertain, but his signing of Murnau marked the beginning of the greatest period of Fox films. From 1925 to 1929, there was no question that William Fox wanted it all and intended to have it all—money from the ever-expanding audience for quality silent films, as well as the plaudits of the critics.

The change began quietly. In October 1925, Fox closed down all production in New York and announced that his company would no longer use foreign locations. Winfield Sheehan had been sent out to California earlier in the year to be in charge of a new category of pictures that Fox called "super-specials," while Sol Wurtzel oversaw the "specials" (i.e., the program pictures) and George Marshall supervised the two-reel comedies. The planned "super-specials" included *7th Heaven, 3 Bad Men, What Price Glory?*, and *The Music Master*.

Not everybody thought this was a good idea. John Ford characterized Sheehan as "a smooth-talking Mick" and much preferred Sol Wurtzel, who he termed "very hard-boiled and tough, but very compassionate.

Very just." *Fortune* magazine described Sheehan as "pleasantly goblin-esque of form, with twinkling blue eyes and a genuine love for beautiful things." Glendon Allvine said that Sheehan treated him with "kindness, generosity, and consideration and we were friends as well as business associates." Allvine also said that Sheehan was "loved, feared and hated" because of his propensity for playing Dr. Jekyll or Mr. Hyde depending on his surroundings.

Put simply, Sheehan was a bluff Irishman with a well-earned reputation for genial corruption. He had been a reporter for the *New York World* before becoming enmeshed with the lords of Tammany and, later, the lords of Hollywood. Sheehan liked to play the nice guy while in LA and would hand out jobs to anybody who bought him a drink. After he left LA for his suite at the Savoy-Plaza in New York, he would stop in Santa Fe and wire Sol Wurtzel to fire all the new hires.

That said, Sheehan proved to be an effective executive, and he radically upgraded the Fox product. Among his other brainstorms was pairing Janet Gaynor with Charles Farrell in *7th Heaven*, which began a long series of costarring dramas and—after sound came in—musicals that carried the Fox studio for years.

Sheehan thought that the right name had to be attached to the right personality and once told Allvine that he thought the name Dixie Lee was a surefire box office name if they could only find the right actress. Sheehan told his publicity man that he wanted a red-headed blues singer to be cast as Dixie Lee. A young singer named Wilma Wyatt was cast and had a brief vogue in the early days of sound, until she married Bing Crosby and retired.

By 1926, Fox Film was estimated by the trade papers to be number seven in the roster of Hollywood studios. Fox himself was described as "a brilliant, noisy, excited energetic roughneck." By 1929, this "roughneck" had increased the number of his theaters by hundreds, including the Roxy. Fox had introduced sound on film, made the first all-talking short, the first sound film recorded outdoors, and the first sound newsreel.

What Price Glory? continued the unexpected interest in World War I films that had begun with MGM's *The Big Parade*, but the Fox film was in a lighter mode, with Victor McLaglen and Edmund Lowe playing a pair of brawling soldiers who fill the time between battles by chasing women. Although the film was directed by Raoul Walsh, it served as the matrix for many Howard Hawks pictures—a love story between two heterosexual men.

What Price Glory? was an expensive picture—the negative cost was $817,000—but the returns were lush: world rentals of $2.4 million, for a profit of $796,000. *What Price Glory?* had been ramrodded by Winfield Sheehan, and its success led to Fox giving Sheehan his head. *7th Heaven,* a profoundly beautiful romance directed by Frank Borzage, amassed world rentals of $1.7 million and a profit of nearly half a million dollars. The critics were every bit as impressed as the accountants. *Variety* crowed that "Borzage is entitled to the blue ribbon for this one. He has made a great picture . . . he brought to the fore a little girl who has been playing in pictures for two years and made a real star out of her overnight. . . . It took Borzage to take this young woman and let her smack the ball full on the nose by elevating herself into the Lillian Gish grade."

And then, after years of waiting, came Murnau's first American picture.

Sunrise was a special movie for Fox—he doted on it as if it was a beloved child, and so did most of the critics. When *Sunrise* premiered at the Times Square Theater on September 23, 1927, it was preceded by a Movietone newsreel that had Mussolini addressing the American audience, speaking in both Italian and English about the glories of international friendship.

The New York Times said that "Mr. Murnau proves by *Sunrise* that he can do just as fine work in Hollywood as he ever did in Germany." Trade papers also fell in line, although there were clearly some doubts as to the film's commercial potential. *Film Daily* devoted a front page editorial to the film: "The importance of *Sunrise* cannot be discounted. There will be arguments over its commercial value. That the picture falls into the division of big pictures will be admitted by all who see it. No one can foretell how its box-office valuation is to be rated, for it is a different type of motion picture. There is little precedent for which one may draw a conclusion."

When John Cohen, the movie critic for the New York *Sun*, was insufficiently enthusiastic about the picture, Fox was enraged and ordered that the *Sun* was not to have more than ten lines of advertising from any Fox picture. This was no small thing for the *Sun*, which was not that strong in the first place, and the editor of the paper appealed to Winfield Sheehan to come to his rescue. Unfortunately, Sheehan had no special argument that would convince Fox of anything, and lost the argument. It wasn't until Fox was deposed a few years later that the *Sun*'s ad quota from the Fox studio returned to what it had been.

The influence of *Sunrise* spread throughout the Fox studio. Directors as varied as John Ford and Frank Borzage integrated considerable amounts of Murnau's *stimmung* (moody atmosphere) into pictures as varied as *Four Sons, Street Angel, Lucky Star*, and *The River. Street Angel*, Borzage's follow-up to the huge hit *7th Heaven*, but in a more Expressionist mode, cost a modest $360,000, and made a profit of $757,000.

The general theory about Murnau's sojourn in Hollywood has always been that he was a noble experiment gone awry, a flop *d'estime*. But *Sunrise* was hardly a crushing financial failure. Fox figures show that it was the studio's third highest grossing picture of 1927, behind Borzage's

Street Angel and Ford's *Four Sons*. *Sunrise* earned $818,000 in rentals, that is to say, after the theaters deducted their share. Fox's accounting showed that the picture lost $80,000, which Fox probably considered a small price to pay for all the prestige that the picture brought him, not to mention a special Academy Award in the first year they were handed out.

Murnau made *Sunrise* on a one-picture contract that paid him $40,000 plus 4 percent of European distribution after 50 percent of the negative cost had been recouped from Europe. Both Murnau and Fox were sufficiently pleased by their working relationship to re-up. The new contract, which began in August 1927, was for four years, during which Murnau was to make one film a year for a fee that began at $125,000 for the first year and ascended to $200,000 in the final year of the contract.

Fox's upgrading of his product paid off commercially as well as critically. Fox films were now a regular presence on "ten best" lists, and in the first Academy Awards of 1927, eight Fox films placed. Janet Gaynor won Best Actress for *7th Heaven*, *Sunrise*, and *Street Angel*; Frank Borzage won Best Director for *7th Heaven*; and Charles Rosher and Karl Struss won Best Cinematography for *Sunrise*, which also won a special award for "Artistic Quality of Production."

MGM, eat your heart out.

In other areas, contention was the order of the day. Samuel "Roxy" Rothafel and Fox never got along. In particular, Rothafel resented sound pictures because they got in the way of the all-singing, all-dancing prologues that made him famous. "He resented the cans of film that came into his theater complete with music, and singing, dancing and talking actors," wrote Glendon Allvine.

The two men stopped speaking, and finally Fox had had enough. "Tell that bastard who calls himself a Major that it he isn't out of his office within 24 hours I will . . . throw him out of the theater," Fox told Allvine, who trooped over to the Roxy Theater to lower the boom on the theater's creator and namesake.

Murnau remained William Fox's proudest possession, which didn't stop him from requesting that the director shoot *4 Devils*, his follow-up to *Sunrise*, on a smaller budget. "I shall mail you a copy of the script and I certainly would like to hear from you and Mrs. Fox," wrote Murnau in December 1927. "Shortly after starting production, I shall forward to you a reel of tests of my principal cast, so that you will see the faces and contrasts of the types that I have selected for my story."

Murnau went on to inquire about the 70mm Grandeur camera that was currently in its testing phase, in the hope that "I could use it this summer." And he told Fox that "this summer I should like to make a picture named *Our Daily Bread*—a story that will tell a tale about WHEAT—about the 'sacredness of bread'—about the estrangement of the modern metropolitans from and their ignorance about Nature's sources of sustenance." *Our Daily Bread* would eventually be retitled *City Girl*.

Fox's reply: "After my talk with you in New York, I felt sure that you would make this picture at a reasonable cost, as expressed by you at that time. . . . I look forward to receiving a copy of your completed scenario [for *4 Devils*] which I will read promptly and will also have Mrs. Fox read it, after which I will send you our comment. . . . Some time between April and May we should have in our possession the Grandeur Film Color [camera] and projection machine. We are working on it day and night and just as soon as it is delivered to us it will be sent to Los Angeles and promptly shown to you so that you may use it in your next picture."

At Christmastime 1927, Murnau replied that "the estimated cost of the picture is reasonable, since exorbitant settings like in *Sunrise* are not required, and since I have also tried my utmost, in order not to be subjected to California weather-whims, to have all my settings on the

Hollywood stages, with only a very, very few exterior shots." Nor was Murnau ruling out the cautious use of sound: "I am glad that a Movietone recording truck has arrived here. I shall make use of it for some of my circus scenes." Murnau was probably planning a synchronized score for the film, which would also be his plan for *Our Daily Bread.*

With every director but Murnau, budgets were of paramount importance as far as William Fox was concerned. With Murnau, he spent what he spent. Despite Fox's expressed wishes, and the fact that *Sunrise* had basically been made without a budget, the circus story that was eventually titled *4 Devils* began shooting on January 3, 1928, and didn't finish shooting until the middle of May. It cost nearly as much as *Sunrise*—just over a million dollars.

Part of the problem seems to have been Murnau's particular—and peculiar—style of shooting. He would typically make dozens of takes of every shot, and instead of ordering a couple printed, he would have them all printed and make his final choice in the projection room. Film editor Harold Schuster remembered that he would have as many as 40 or 50 takes for a given shot. "We'd spend a whole evening just running one [shot]—picking maybe four takes out of the 40 or 50. They would have to be segregated by the assistants and maybe the next night we'd look at those four again. We'd run them over and over." Schuster's anecdote jibes with the memory of Charles Rosher, who shot *Sunrise* with Karl Struss. "I found it difficult to get Murnau to look through the camera," Rosher told Kevin Brownlow. "'I'll tell you if I like it in the projection room,' he used to say."

The Fox engineers devised a camera boom that facilitated Murnau's desire for shots that could follow the acrobats as they entered the arena on horses, and as they flew through the air. Fox publicity described the crane as "a gigantic apparatus in the center of the arena, devised by Murnau. . . . This consisted of a large steel upright, from which swung a big steel boom, on the end of which was a car carrying batteries of lights and cameras, capable of revolving at various heights and at dizzy speeds. This framework, which weighed twenty tons, was designed by the director to shoot the young players as they whirled through the air in their acrobatic feats."

Murnau took advantage of the camera boom's mobility and speed to terrify his extras. For a shot in which the acrobats fall to earth, Murnau had the boom high in the tent, then ordered it to descend rapidly toward the audience without warning in order to capture the subjective point of view of a falling aerialist. The extras on the ground believed they were about to be crushed, and naturally panicked. "People fell back, women fainted," remembered Janet Gaynor, "because they thought that the camera was loose and was coming down upon them. Of course this was the reaction he wanted. That's the way he directed it."

But for the first time in Murnau's Hollywood career, there was discord behind the scenes. *4 Devils* didn't do well in previews, which led to Murnau reshooting the ending to make it less tragic. The critics responded with a tone of bewildered respect: "From this sawdust story one gains the impression that Mr. Murnau exerts an amazing influence over his players, and when one might think he is digressing it soon turns out that he has something important to say. . . . Without any prismatic effects this picture seems to make an impression of varied colors as it surges along."

But *4 Devils* fell far short of *Sunrise*, with rentals of $581,000. The result was a loss of $212,000. Luckily, both 1928 and 1929 saw some great successes for Fox—*The Cockeyed World*, Raoul Walsh's sequel to *What Price Glory?*, and the musical *Sunnyside Up*, each earning profits of more than a million dollars.

Fox went ahead with *City Girl*, the third picture on Murnau's contract, which constituted a sort of narrative reversal of *Sunrise*. That film revolved around a naïve wife, a duplicitous husband, and a manipulative mistress whose plans are stymied by the magic of the big city. *City Girl* focuses on a naïve boy and the knowing woman he marries, who are brought together by the sensuality of nature.

But the studio made a crucial mistake. *City Girl* began production in Pendleton, Oregon, in the fateful summer of 1928. To be precise, shooting didn't begin until August 30 because Murnau had an appendectomy in July. By the time the picture got under way, it was already clear that the worst film with sound was out-grossing the best silent films. *Film Daily* of July 22, 1928, had reported that "overnight and like a tidal wave, sound pictures have stepped to the fore," which was why *4 Devils* actually had two premieres—the silent version opened in New York in October 1928, whereas the part-talking version (about 25 percent of the film) opened in June 1929.

In Oregon, Fox purchased a large field of standing wheat for the exterior sequences, which was sold for harvest after Murnau finished his location photography. L. W. O'Connell, one of the cameramen on the picture, said, "We took a whole apple orchard and planted it in wheat. You'd take stubs of wheat and put them in plaster of Paris all around the house. The old man was so wheat hungry that he planted the wheat right up to the door. . . . Such a perfectionist . . . everything had to be so real."

Murnau finished up the studio work by the end of the year, and after yet more discord over the edit, he left Fox in February 1929, by which time every studio was abandoning silent films as if they were distressed merchandise—which in fact they were. In March 1929, Winfield Sheehan announced that Fox would no longer make silent films, which left *City Girl* orphaned, not to mention endangered. In a farewell letter to Fox, Murnau wrote about some modifications he thought should be made to *City Girl*. "If talk should be added to the picture, I would suggest it start at the beginning of the final night sequence." He also recommended moving the incident when Tustine slaps Kate just after she arrives at the farm.

"I would take it out here, because there is no sufficient reason for this girl, after she has received the slap, to stay on with the family instead of returning to the city." Murnau suggested it be moved to near the end of the picture, after the father catches her with the brutish farmhand called Mac. He then proposed changes that would have mandated retakes by someone else: "In all scenes where [Mac] appears with the girl, build up the danger, so that in the climax the final night, it already has its danger-ous background. . . . On this final evening, the scene between Mac and the girl should be by far more sensuous, so that we, as an audience, really fear that the girl might surrender."

Murnau had little interest in injecting dialogue into a film that had been designed, shot, and edited as a silent, and he had nothing to do with the part-talkie versions of *4 Devils* and *City Girl*. By May of 1929, Murnau was in Tahiti preparing to shoot *Tabu*, which he financed with $150,000 he had saved from his Fox salary. While Fox diddled with *City Girl*, Mur-nau and his cameraman Floyd Crosby—the father of rock star David Crosby—made *Tabu* entirely on location.

The surviving silent version of *City Girl* was finalized in August 1929, six months after Murnau had left the studio. It fell under the purview of Katherine Hilliker and H. H. Caldwell, who were successful title writers and editors of the late 1920s, and are probably responsible for preserving as much of Murnau's intentions as was possible under the circumstances. Hilliker and Caldwell had written the titles for the American release of *Faust* as well as *Sunrise*, and were clearly friends with the director. Hilliker wrote Murnau that "*Sunrise* was the only picture we ever had handed to us that didn't have to be reconstructed in the editing and titles;

and in most cases we had to write in new sequences and have them shot in order to fill up the bad holes left by . . . writers."

The part-talkie version of *City Girl* didn't premiere until April 1930 at the down-market Globe Theater in New York, with 50 percent dialogue. "*City Girl* is mediocre material for the second runs," wrote *Variety*. "The grinds, of course, can use it." This sound version quickly failed, and has since disappeared. The near-magnificent silent version, which the film archivist David Shepard called "the final version before everybody walked away from it," was released mostly in Europe, where sound was slower to make inroads. It received very few bookings but survived mostly through blind luck.*

The surviving version of *City Girl* is a much sparser, more direct movie than *Sunrise* or, on the basis of the script, *4 Devils*. Most of the footage was probably shot by Murnau, but the picture only runs sixty-eight minutes and lacks his careful layering of visual and emotional coloring. Secondary characters in the script are nowhere to be seen in the movie itself. Also removed were entire scenes taking place in Chicago as well as at the farm. All that said, it's far from a negligible picture and contains some of Murnau's most ecstatic camerawork, as in a tracking shot that rushes through the wheat following Charles Farrell and Mary Duncan in the throes of exuberant passion until they collapse out of sight.

City Girl cost $730,000 and lost $517,000. William Fox had bankrolled three pictures by a man posterity has recognized as one of the great film artists and had lost a total of $800,000 for his trouble.

Murnau was in the South Seas from May 1929 to November 1930. He returned to a Hollywood that was, with the exception of Charlie Chaplin,

---

* In the early 1970s, the archivist Alex Gordon discovered a single print marked *City Girl* behind a radiator in a nitrate vault at Fox that was incorrectly labelled as starring Ricardo Cortez and Phyllis Brooks. It turned out to be Murnau's silent version with Charles Farrell and Mary Duncan, and was preserved by the Museum of Modern Art.

who was wrestling with *City Lights*, fully in thrall to sound. Murnau edited *Tabu* and supervised the musical score added to the otherwise silent movie. On March 11, 1931, Murnau was killed in a car accident near Santa Barbara. A week later, *Tabu* opened in New York City.

But Murnau's influence permeated not merely the Fox studio of that period, but an entire subspecies of film production that has survived through nearly a hundred years, from Ophuls to Kubrick to Malick—movies emphasizing the overpowering impact environment has on character, not to mention the audience.

In the short run, Murnau failed commercially; in the long run, he succeeded in every other way imaginable.

CHAPTER THREE

OVER THE HILL

By 1929, A CERTAIN AUDIENCE DISSATISFACTION WAS creeping in. The public indicated they could do without the cross-breeding of German Expressionism and American movie stars. Despite the presence of Janet Gaynor and Charles Farrell, Frank Borzage's exquisite *Lucky Star* lost $76,000, and *The River*, with Farrell and Mary Duncan, lost $250,000. Part of the problem—perhaps most of the problem—was that these films were silent, and sound was the rage.

In other areas, the studio was doing well. By 1929, Fox Film was releasing four newsreels a week to a hungry public. The incredible success of the newsreels undoubtedly played a part in Fox's decision to build a complete studio devoted to sound. On October 28, 1928, Movietone City had been inaugurated in what would become known as Westwood. It had been built in four months by 1,500 people working three shifts per day, seven days a week, at a cost of $10 million. The old studio at Sunset and Western gradually became the province of Sol Wurtzel's B picture unit.

While other studios were stalling under the assumption that sound was a fad that would burn itself out in six months or a year, Fox went all in. Let the other studios soundproof an existing stage or two, or even build a new stage—only William Fox understood sound would permanently change the technical equation of filmmaking.

———————

Compared with the penny-pinching of his early days, Fox was now spending real money on his pictures and was being rewarded with real money in return. This led him to a frankly baronial lifestyle, not to mention winters in Palm Beach, where he became an aficionado of the casino run by Major Edward Bradley. It was a high-end place for high rollers such as Joe Schenck. But Schenck and the other movie people who frequented Bradley's were mostly from the West Coast, while Fox stubbornly retained his East Coast identity, not to mention some of his less admirable qualities.

One night at Bradley's, Fox had a run of bad luck. The first thing that happened was that Fox lost an amount of money variously reported as $125,000 or $250,000. The second thing that happened was that he stopped payment on his check. That sort of thing simply didn't happen at Bradley's. The Major ran an honest casino, and he expected an equivalent response from his customers. Some stories say that Fox eventually paid off the debt, others say he didn't. What is certain is that he became permanently persona non grata at Bradley's, as well as most other places of chance.

Something similar happened a few years later when Fox was at a dinner for Jewish charities at the Waldorf-Astoria. Overcome by the emotion of the moment, he pledged $150,000. In the cold light of dawn, he reneged. Fox's lawyer, Saul Rogers, talked to him about it. "If your word is no good, how can you expect people to trust you?" asked Rogers. "Outside of your family and your golfing companions, you have very few real friends."

"The public be damned," replied Fox. "What do I need friends for when I am sitting on my money bags?"

Ladies and gentleman . . . William Fox.

After taking over Loew's Inc. Fox continued to expand, buying Gaumont British Pictures, which came with three hundred theaters in England. But 1929 was what *Fortune* magazine would call Fox's "Moscow year," referring to Napoleon's catastrophic invasion of Russia. "He did . . .

embark upon an expedition a bit too expensive for his resources, and he certainly retreated from it in extremely bad order."

When the stock market crashed in October 1929, Fox had leveraged his company into a leading position both critically and commercially—his purchase of the Loew's company as well as several other theater chains meant that he owned more than one thousand theaters world-wide. But the crash exposed the fact that Fox was massively over-extended financially and had little short-term capital. A month after the crash, the Justice Department filed an antitrust suit against Fox over his purchase of Loew's.

Over the next six months, Fox tried a series of increasingly desperate maneuvers to keep his company afloat, but he was eventually forced to sell a controlling interest with—Fox said—an understanding that he could buy back his stock whenever he was able to refinance his loans. When he attempted to do so, his partners refused to sell, said partners including Winfield Sheehan, who—Fox said—was a traitor.

William Fox lost control of his company on April 8, 1930. Fox in exile was no different than Fox on top of the world. He was up to his neck in lawsuits, but he could still speak out. He paid the journalist and novelist Upton Sinclair to sit and listen to him for weeks on end and self-publish a book titled *Upton Sinclair Presents William Fox*. It remains a primary text for people with a bent toward conspiracy theories involving Wall Street. In Fox's telling, AT&T, Winfield Sheehan, and Harley Clarke all conspired to shaft a man who embodied pristine innocence.

Journalists who had covered Fox for years thought the book was absurd. *Film Daily* wrote that "the dominating tenor of the book is Fox's persistent effort to prove he was framed and double-crossed all-around, that no act of his own was responsible for the difficulties into which his companies found themselves at the height of their expansion activities."

The paper didn't buy Fox's extensive prosecution of his perceived enemies. "Man's desire for more money than he can ever use, his ambition
for more power than he can wisely exercise—the urge to merge, amal-
gamate, control, without considering that the more surplus a few men
have, the greater is the privation among others—is at the bottom of all
catastrophes like the one recounted in this book."

Some journalists went even further. *Harrison's Reports* opined that
"The Fox Film Corporation had not occupied a high standing in the
industry until Winfield Sheehan took charge of production. . . . In his
early years, the name of 'Fox Film Corporation' was synonymous with
everything that was vile and low, because of the sex pictures William Fox
had made. . . . If it were not for Winfield Sheehan he would not have been
able to get for his company today eighteen cents let alone eighteen million dollars."

Pete Harrison went on to enumerate examples of Fox's mendacity
that he had strangely forgotten to include in his book: "He did not say
anything about his welching on that $250,000 gambling debt of his which
he contracted at Palm Beach. . . . Nor has he mentioned anything about
his exacting from D.W. Griffith $100,000 for the foreign rights of 'The
Two Orphans,' which had cost [Fox] only $13,000. Griffith overlooked
making a deal for these rights when he started 'Orphans of the Storm'
and . . . through an oversight, the Griffith New York office failed to pay
the $15,000 agreed upon . . . to the New York agent of the rights to the
book. . . . All the pleadings that his demand for $100,000 was excessive
were of no avail. And Griffith had to pay it."

Terry Ramsaye, who had already written *A Million and One Nights*,
a trenchant and still valuable history of the early days of the movie business, reviewed the book by saying, "Like all . . . Fox arguments, there are
only two sides, a right side which is theirs, a wrong side which is the other

fellow's. The rights are all right and the wrongs are all wrong, utterly, damnably, perniciously and eternally, with malice aforethought and conspiracy without end, until hell freezes over and three days past."

In June 1936, William Fox was forced into bankruptcy. He listed his assets as $100—a ridiculous underestimate—and his debts as $9.5 million. Splashing around in a toxic stew of rage and debt, Fox looked for an easy way out: bribery. He paid Judge J. Warren Davis, who would preside over his bankruptcy trial, $27,500 to go easy on him. The judge certainly did. Of five Fox bankruptcy cases that came before the judge between 1936 and 1938, all were decided in Fox's favor.

It all came tumbling down in 1940, when an FBI investigation of Davis's corruption ensnared Fox. In January 1941, William Fox was sentenced to a year and a day in a federal penitentiary for the crimes of conspiracy to obstruct justice and defraud the United States. After exhausting the appeals process, Fox finally entered the Lewisburg Federal Penitentiary on November 20, 1942. While Fox was in jail, his wife auctioned 126 paintings, including works by Van Dyke, Gainsborough, Rubens, Tintoretto, and Reynolds. The paintings brought a grand total of $39,025. Fox served five months and seventeen days before being released. Despite his manifest guilt, he was pardoned by President Harry Truman in 1947.

In April 1944, Fox opened an office on Fifth Avenue and vowed to return to the movie business. "I started with nothing and I'm not afraid to try again," he told a reporter for *The New York Times*. "Imagination and courage are still the essential elements for success in this business."

After his incarceration, William Fox occupied himself with the Mitchell Camera Company, the sole remnant of the show business empire he had spent thirty years building. He spent the years until his death in 1952 issuing bromidic plans for resuming film production interspersed with jeremiads against the men he insisted had euchred him out of the company that bore his name. Fox went to his grave believing that the only thing he was guilty of was being a bad judge of other people's character.

William Fox never made another movie. When he died in May 1952, the studio he had founded placed an ad in the trade papers: "His daring and initiative and courage enabled him to make a signal contribution to the growth and development of the motion picture industry.

"From the beginnings of his career he engaged in the production of films of magnitude and scope and blazed a trail for the industry in providing boxoffice attractions of wide popular appeal. He was truly a pioneer in foreseeing the present status of the screen as a medium of popular entertainment.

"Those who knew him best will long mourn his passing."

The *Hollywood Reporter* grudgingly agreed: "In the pages of any history written on the motion picture business, he will go down as probably the greatest of all in the building of this great business. Even the mighty Zukors and Loews of those early days must run second in the telling of the story of the movies."

Amidst a welter of counterclaims, only one thing is certain: after William Fox was separated from the company he had founded, Fox films began a slow, perilous drift into chaos.

———

From 1929 to 1932, the Fox studio managed to release at least one big commercial hit per year. There was also a distinct interest in creative experimentation, often by one of the journeymen directors on the lot, possibly because they were being encouraged so the premier directors could sail into sound with the kinks having been ironed out. *Sunnyside Up*, a 1929 Charles Farrell–Janet Gaynor musical directed by David Butler, has an opening reel full of camera moves that would have stressed Murnau. The camera glides down a long tenement street, swooping up and down from the street to higher stories in an extremely complicated shot.

Similarly, John Blystone directed a movie called *Through Different Eyes*, in which different versions of a murder are presented to a jury. The same event being shown from different points of view would seem revelatory in *Citizen Kane* and, later, *Rashomon*, simply because few people saw or remembered *Through Different Eyes*.

Sound wasn't a sufficient breakthrough for William Fox—he also wanted to revolutionize screen size. Shortly before he lost control of the company, Fox gave the OK for Raoul Walsh to make an epic of the pioneer trek west, to be shot almost entirely on location in 70mm. Not only that, there were to be multiple versions of *The Big Trail* shot at the same time for foreign markets: German, French, Italian.

Because the movie was going to be extremely expensive, economies were enforced regarding the cast, which is how a young, handsome twenty-three-year-old prop man/camera assistant/general dogsbody known around the Fox lot as Duke Morrison was hired to star. After Morrison agreed to change his name to John Wayne, the studio agreed to pay him $75 a week to star in a million-dollar movie, a considerable increase over the prop man's salary he had been earning. Wayne was dramatically inexperienced—he hadn't really acted since the senior play at Glendale High—but he was radiantly photogenic. His line readings were gauche but forceful, and the boy had charisma to burn—a born movie star. Raoul Walsh shot the film mostly on location around Jackson Hole, Wyoming, with a remarkable degree of documentary authenticity.

The Big Trail played in its 70mm version in precisely two theaters in America—one in New York, one in Los Angeles. The rest of the country saw it in the flat 35mm version, which considerably diminished the splendor of Walsh's accomplishments. With the various foreign-language versions driving up the cost, *The Big Trail* cost a whopping $1.7 million and lost $1 million.

Wayne had been tabbed by the studio as their replacement for Tom Mix, but he took the fall for the failure of *The Big Trail*. Fox dumped him and Wayne spent the next eight years on Poverty Row, grinding out five-day westerns for Monogram and ten-day westerns for Republic. By so doing, he learned how to act. John Ford eventually came to his rescue with *Stagecoach*. As for Raoul Walsh, he pulled in his horns and went back to directing programmers, including yet another sequel to *What Price Glory?*

The failure of *The Big Trail* was unfortunately typical for the studio in the early years of the Depression. In July 1931, more than a year after Fox had left the studio, the use of the main title text "William Fox Presents" was discontinued, and his name was banished from all advertising copy. Dividends were cut from $4 per share to $2.50, but the fact that the company was paying dividends at all was suspect. In 1930, Fox theaters ended with a $3.2 million loss, while the film company showed a profit, even though a more accurate accounting would indicate that in 1930 the studio showed a net loss of $4.2 million.

1931 did nothing to lessen the concern; Fox Film lost $2.8 million, while the theaters lost $3.4 million. The theaters were a particular drain; *Film Daily* carried a notice regarding the Latonia Theater in Oil City, Pennsylvania. William Fox had spent $400,000 to build the theater three years earlier, and it was sold at auction for $36,000.

The only consolation was that most of the other studios were in the same boat; Warner Bros. and its subsidiaries reported a net loss of $7.9

million for the year, and even MGM, the gold standard, had a 33 percent decline in profits, although they still managed to make some money—in March 1932, MGM reported profits of $5.2 million for the previous twenty-eight weeks.

Variety summed up the sad state of affairs: "Grosses for individual pictures have dropped to the point where a $750,000 total current rental income is deemed terrific. Outside of Chaplin's last picture [*City Lights*] it's doubtful if any distributor ran up $1 million on any one feature throughout 1931. That includes domestic and foreign sales. . . . Hence, what have $400,000 and $500,000 gross rentals meant to hit pictures which have cost from $300,000 to $800,000 to make?"

If 1931 was bad, 1932 was catastrophic—the low point of the Depression. RKO went into receivership when it defaulted on a loan of $3.5 million. Paramount, which would lose a stunning $21 million before the year was over, also went into receivership, while Warner Bros. and Fox were both teetering over the cliff. Between the theaters and the film operation, Fox lost $14.1 million in 1932. Between the theaters and the studio, Fox losses for 1931 and 1932 totaled $21 million. By May of that year, Fox stock had fallen to $1.25.

Two statistics paint the picture:

1) In 1929, there had been about 19,000 movie theaters in the country. Roughly 8,000 of them closed during the Depression, and most of those that remained open were struggling.

2) In 1929, there had been 110,000,000 admissions to American movies every week; in 1932, that figure was down to 60,000,000. The loss of nearly half of the audience plus a plethora of theaters worth far less than their mortgages were dragging the movie industry into the abyss.

Desperately scanning the horizon for something, anything, to stop the bleeding, Fox announced that they would reissue some successful films from the past—the very recent past. To be specific, from three years earlier. But reissues of *The Cockeyed World* and *Sunnyside Up* didn't draw audiences, and the plan was canceled.

The only bright spot in 1933 was *Cavalcade*, a $1.1. million Winfield Sheehan production of a Noel Coward play that told the story of England through the vicissitudes of one family. Seen today, it's stupefyingly dull, but the ever-present latent strain of Anglophilia in the American public propelled it to a profit of $664,000 and the honor of being Best Picture at the Academy Awards. Another hit was *State Fair*, which teamed Janet Gaynor with Will Rogers and made nearly as much money as *Cavalcade*. But these two pictures weren't enough to offset the accumulating losses from the rest of the program.

Near the end of February 1933, Fox shut down all production because the Chase Bank refused to provide any further financing. At this point, Chase was on the hook for somewhere between $100 million and $150 million in Fox loans. The bank eventually wrote off $55 million in losses.

Replacing that kind of money was not an easy task in the pit of the Depression. Basically, Fox had three choices: reorganize, merge, or declare bankruptcy. It was at this point that the trade papers published stories about a possible merger between Fox and Warners. Billy Wilkerson led off with one of his breathless page-one editorials in the *Hollywood Reporter*: "Understood here that the whole motivation of the deal is the opportunity of Fox to get the advantage of Warner-First National production organization. . . . The feeling around town is that the deal, if and when made, will provide for a substantial cash payment to the Warners, plus a participating interest, places on the board, etc., with [Sidney]

Kent heading both groups and [Darryl] Zanuck in charge of production for the joint companies."

It didn't happen, but there was no mistaking the message: Fox was in play.

Ultimately, Fox opted for reorganization. The studio issued new stock with six shares of the old stock equaling one share of new stock valued at $18.90, which would more or less enable them to get out from under their mountainous debt. Creditors had little choice; they could let the company go broke and lose their entire investment or agree to take a close shave with no guarantee of eventual success.

Despite the corporate heart palpitations, Fox Film managed a profit for the thirty-nine weeks ending December 1, 1933, of $1.4 million, largely because of British receipts for *Cavalcade*. It was a minor figure compared with MGM's profit of $4 million, but beggars couldn't be choosers.

1934 continued the marginally upward trend—Fox profits for the first quarter were $805,376. The problem was that the profits were the proverbial drop in the bucket compared with the company's overall indebtedness. The story department was still weak, and the studio's roster of directors, once the best in Hollywood, was sadly depleted. John Ford and Henry King were now the only undisputed A-list directors, with William K. Howard beneath them, and a roster of uninspired directors for hire beneath Howard: David Butler, John Blystone, George Marshall, James Tinling, et cetera. When *Harrison's Reports* ranked the studios for their money-making films, Fox ranked seventh out of eight.

The weakness of the story department was matched by weakness in the roster of actors. Fox's biggest leading man was Warner Baxter, followed by Will Rogers, and Janet Gaynor was still reasonably commercial. Beneath them was . . . nothing much. Winfield Sheehan again tried to place bets on directors. John Ford made *Pilgrimage*, a story that seemed more suited to Frank Borzage but beautifully managed. But it was a sad, emotionally ravaging film without stars and not the kind of movie that was ever going to attract a large audience.

Winfield Sheehan even gave Erich von Stroheim one last chance on a movie called *Walking Down Broadway*. Throughout the silent era, Stroheim had never seen a bridge he wouldn't torch via overspending and overshooting. The debacle of *Queen Kelly* in 1928 was the final black mark—the film was aborted before completion because of the tidal wave of sound and Gloria Swanson's fury at Stroheim's perceived licentiousness. After that, Stroheim was persona non grata for producers in both America and Europe, but his contract with Fox spelled out the limitations of length, so there could be no chance of him going off the reservation. Stroheim began shooting in August and completed the picture by mid-October, allowing for a two-week hiatus so Stroheim could make some extra money by acting in an RKO film called *The Lost Squadron*. *Walking Down Broadway* had been scheduled for a November release, and a double-page ad appeared in the trade papers: "Life Itself wrote this story—Genius brings living to your screen."

But the film seems to have been caught in internecine studio warfare—months earlier, when Stroheim was working on the script, he had been dismissed when Winfield Sheehan went on sick leave. When Sheehan returned to the studio, so did Stroheim. When the picture was finished, Sheehan ordered retakes done by other hands, and *Walking Down Broadway* finally made a brief appearance in 1933. *Film Daily*'s review said that the film "was for adults only. Its story is hackneyed and considerably off-color, with dialogue which at times cannot be described as wholesome." William K. Everson estimated that about 65 percent of the film is Stroheim's. It was another commercial disaster, and even if the disaster wasn't Stroheim's fault, it signaled the definitive end of his directorial career.

Between the Depression, a succession of bad pictures, production snafus like the Stroheim picture, and an inability to develop any new stars, Fox was in a very bad way. Sheehan tried a Hail Mary when he signed a contract with Lita Grey Chaplin and her two sons, Sydney and Charlie Jr., to appear in five films over three years. At this point, Lita Grey Chaplin had been divorced from her husband for years, and her acting career had consisted of a bit in *The Kid* and the leading female part in *The Gold Rush* until pregnancy intervened and the part was recast with Georgia Hale. Lita Grey Chaplin had no claim to acting credibility, but Sheehan was clearly desperate and trying to capitalize on a sensational divorce, which at that point was years in the past. It was all for naught; Charlie Chaplin quickly enjoined his ex-wife from exploiting their children, and Lita Grey Chaplin never appeared in a Fox film.

Fox's only real bright spots remained Charles Farrell, and, supremely, Janet Gaynor, whose audience remained loyal. Even long-standing favorites like Will Rogers were no longer sure things; several of his 1932 films lost money, and one, *Business and Pleasure*, amassed the biggest loss of the year, finishing $219,000 in the red.

What the filmmakers were up against was an unprecedented economic headwind. The industry tried to compete by making double features a common practice, which forced them to make more B pictures to fill the bottom half of the bill. Promotional giveaways such as Dish Night were other compensatory tactics. Fox could manufacture B films well enough—Sol Wurtzel was expert—but the problem remained the A pictures. For that, they looked to an outsider. Desperate to change the narrative, Fox hired Jesse Lasky to produce for the studio.

In 1913, Lasky had formed the Jesse L. Lasky Feature Play Corporation, with Cecil B. DeMille as the chief director. DeMille's genius for commercial drama drove the company to great success, and in 1916 the

Lasky company had merged with Adolph Zukor's Famous Players to form Famous Players-Lasky, the combine that would eventually become Paramount Pictures. Zukor's primary asset was Mary Pickford, while Lasky's primary asset was DeMille, the "Director-General" of the company—perhaps the most appropriate job title in movie history. Although Zukor's company got top billing in the merger, the fact was that Lasky's company was the more financially successful.

Through the teens and early 1920s, Famous Players-Lasky was by far the most successful company in the movies, but in the latter part of the 1920s they were overtaken by MGM. The Depression hit Jesse Lasky hard—his mother told friends that he lost more than $7 million in the stock market crash.

Somebody was going to take the fall, and it wasn't going to be Adolph Zukor, a far chillier character than the optimistic, likeable Lasky. In 1932, Lasky was shown the door. Adolph Zukor's explanation was remarkably vague: "Early in 1932 the company believed the production department was spending too much money—pictures didn't measure up to their cost. We wanted to investigate the studio situation . . . but were afraid it might embarrass Lasky, so we asked him to take a three months vacation and then went ahead with the investigation. As a result of that we made some changes and Lasky subsequently stepped out."

Fox was nobody's idea of the ideal place to land, but Lasky couldn't afford to be choosy. In August 1933, he filed for personal bankruptcy, listing $2,020,024 in liabilities and $134,718 in assets. Besides, Fox offered Lasky a good deal. His contract mandated he produce eight films per year for "a term of years." Fox would finance the films as well as Lasky's overhead, including an executive manager, an associate producer, and a story editor. After the studio approved a project, Lasky could make the picture without interference. After the studio deducted their production costs and a 30 percent distribution fee from the rentals, Lasky and the studio split the profits 50–50. All in all, it was a rich deal. What could possibly go wrong?

Basically, everything.

Lasky produced more than ten pictures for Fox, including *The Power and the Glory*, an original script by Preston Sturges that predates some of the storytelling style of *Citizen Kane*, and the idyllic *Zoo in Budapest*. Both of these pictures received good reviews, but both lost money—*The Power and the Glory* lost $52,000, while *Zoo in Budapest* lost $129,000. Lasky also produced *I Am Suzanne, The Worst Husband in Paris, Berkeley Square, As Husbands Go, Coming Out Party, Springtime for Henry, Grand Canary, The White Parade,* and *Helldorado*. Of this roster of obscurities, the only profitable picture was *The White Parade*, which made a profit of $237,000, against a cumulative loss of $1.3 million on the rest of the Lasky productions.

Besides the creative and financial issues represented by Lasky, his presence also caused political problems. There was serious jostling between Winfield Sheehan and Lasky because there was a faction of the studio that wanted Lasky to replace Sheehan. The primary argument against that was the string of flops that Lasky was currently producing. "Battlefront reports yesterday were that the Jesse Lasky-Winnie Sheehan situation was reaching the point of open warfare," noted the *Hollywood Reporter*. "Argument has grown up over new stories being considered, suggestions for casting, etc.

"The understanding is that the arrival of Sidney Kent before the end of this month is the only thing holding off the shooting . . ."

It was precisely at this point that there were glimmers of sun peeking through the rain clouds. Sure, there was the profusion of Lasky flops, and there was *Music in the Air*, a comeback attempt by Gloria Swanson that lost more money than any other 1934 Fox release: $389,000. But movie attendance was returning to a sustainable level of 70 million weekly, and Paramount began emerging from bankruptcy with a $6.3 million profit for 1934.

Lasky lost his battle with Sheehan and his contract was terminated. His next stop was at United Artists, where he formed a brief alliance with Mary Pickford and made two pictures, both unsuccessful. After a hiatus of several years, he found something of a home at Warner Bros., where he finally recaptured some success by producing *Sergeant York*, *The Adventures of Mark Twain*, and *Rhapsody in Blue*. But he fell into deep debt to the IRS, which was only ended by his death in 1958.

Part of the problem Lasky had at Fox was the hard fact that the studio had been remarkably inept when it came to developing stars, and during the Depression stars were the added value that often spelled the difference between profit and loss. In sound, Fox had supported a failed comeback attempt by Clara Bow and had signed young actors such as Humphrey Bogart, Jeanette MacDonald, Maureen O'Sullivan, Charles Boyer, Joel McCrea, Myrna Loy, John Wayne, and Spencer Tracy, only to see them all rise to fame at studios other than Fox. At the same time, Fox placed bets on Victor Jory, Elissa Landi, Marguerite Churchill, Alexander Kirkland, and Lilian Harvey.

In short, Fox was unsuccessful in creating new stars and relied on mediocre material foisted on a thin roster of preexisting stars. The creative problems were made obvious when scanning what other studios were doing. For instance, MGM had Greta Garbo, an entirely new kind of actress with an unusual combination of sensuality and diffidence. Paramount countered with Marlene Dietrich, who added irony to the mix.

Fox's answer was Elissa Landi, who had a roughly equivalent blonde affect, but who was a comparatively uninteresting actress. Fox publicity touted the story that she was a granddaughter of Emperor Franz Joseph of

Austria. Maybe, maybe not. Landi's high point was undoubtedly DeMille's *The Sign of the Cross*, but that was made on loan-out to Paramount, and its success failed to do anything to increase the commercial allure of Landi's projects at her home studio.

The contrast between the Fox studio of 1928 and the Fox studio of seven years later was and is startling. The studio was adrift.

Something had to be done.

CHAPTER FOUR

THE MARK OF ZANUCK

I N 1933, DARRYL FRANCIS ZANUCK HAD STALKED OUT OF his job as production chief at Warner Bros. after one final, nasty argument with Harry Warner. Zanuck had been at Warners since 1924 as a publicist, still later as a screenwriter so indefatigable that he had to adopt pseudonyms to camouflage the fact that he was writing a great number of Warner pictures.

He had been made production chief in 1930 and ramrodded the studio into an efficient machine for the manufacture of torn-from-the-headlines stories: *Public Enemy, Little Caesar, I Was a Fugitive from a Chain Gang, Wild Boys of the Road, Five Star Final.* Zanuck's films were populated by characters driven by ambition and rage, catapulting audiences into drama. Even a Zanuck musical such as *42nd Street* bore the marks of his view of life as a narrative in which people embody the traits of dogs quarreling over scraps. Warner Baxter's Julian Marsh has a heart condition and is desperate for a hit, although it's a toss-up as to whether he'll live long enough to see his show premiere. He tells Ruby Keeler, "You're going out there an unknown, but you've *got* to come back a star!"

Zanuck doesn't get much credit for the cycle of Warners musicals, but they were his creation. So many musicals were made in 1929 and 1930 that the genre burned itself out. An Irving Berlin musical called *Reaching for the Moon* was shot with numerous numbers, but by the time it was released in 1931, every number but one was excised because of public burnout.

But by 1932, Zanuck sensed that there was a way to bring the genre back from the dead. What he did was crossbreed the urban desperation of the Warner street films with the musical. *42nd Street* led to *Footlight Parade, Gold Diggers of 1933*, and *Gold Diggers of 1935*, with Busby Berkeley's masterpiece, the "Lullaby of Broadway" number. It has some sensational dancing—the sound of one hundred people tap-dancing in unison is terrifying—and tells a complete story that could be a particularly depressing Zanuck movie of the period: a girl comes to the Big City, falls in with café society, including a handsome boyfriend who isn't above romancing other women. The girl accidentally falls to her death. Back in her apartment building, her cat waits for someone to give it milk. Heartbreak all around.

"Come on along and listen to the lullaby of Broadway . . ."

Zanuck's stars were street kids grown large: James Cagney, Edward G. Robinson, Barbara Stanwyck. His movies bore the traces of a roughneck, and he liked directors with a similar temperament: William Wellman, Michael Curtiz. And he understood something about the movies, something profound: if the story moved fast enough, the actual quality of that story could be negligible.

Zanuck lived his life the same way his characters did: with the gas pedal jammed to the floor. A young man named Milton Sperling told a story about the first time they met. As he walked into Zanuck's office, "I saw an extraordinary scene. There were six men sitting around the walls of this enormous office, as in a ballroom, and the desk was at the far end. My eye went to the desk, and there was no one there. All these men were looking at the desk, and then turning and looking at me, then turning back to the desk, and then looking at me.

"As I stood there, Zanuck suddenly popped up from behind the desk and he had a [polo mallet] which he aimed at me and, simulating a Tommy gun, went 'tt-tt-tt.' And then, as I still stood there, Zanuck shouted, 'Fall down, you son of a bitch!' So I did. And then I heard him say to the others, 'That's the way Cagney played the scene. The guy walks in, Cagney's behind the desk, and he shoots the shit out of the guy as he comes through the door.' Then I saw a natty pair of custom-made shoes standing near my face, and a voice said, 'All right, kid, you can get up now.'"

Working for Zanuck was never dull. Sperling became Zanuck's secretary, in charge of writing down everything said at story conferences, then distributing the result to the attendees so there could be no doubt about what Zanuck had decided. During the planning of *Public Enemy*, Zanuck kept repeating, "Everyone in this movie is tough, tough, tough. People are going to say the characters are immoral, but they're not because they don't have any morals. They steal, they kill, they lie, they hump each other because that's the way they're made, and if you allow a decent human feeling or a pang of conscience to come into their makeup, you've lost 'em and changed the kind of movie we're making."

Zanuck assigned *Public Enemy* to William Wellman, a two-fisted man who had flown with the Lafayette Flying Corps in World War I and made *Wings*, the winner of the first Academy Award for Best Picture. Wellman gave Zanuck exactly what he wanted from *Public Enemy*, a film that made a lot of money and launched a huge star in James Cagney, who had originally been cast as the second lead behind Edward Woods. After a few days of shooting, Wellman went to Zanuck and told him they had to switch the actors—that Cagney was authentically tough and Woods was just acting tough and would kill the picture.

Cagney was the archetypal proletarian actor of the period, and his films ranged from the anarchic (*Public Enemy*) to the pro-union (*Taxi*). After *Taxi* was released in 1932, that film's screenwriter, John Bright, was walking on the Warner lot when he came across Zanuck reading a copy of *The Nation*. "I want to talk to you," said Zanuck. "Here's a review in a magazine I never heard of. Did you ever hear of it?"

"Yes," said Bright.

"This review says *Taxi* has great social significance."

"Yes?"

"Did you intend that?"

"Yes."

"I'll be a son of a bitch. I thought it was all cops and robbers."

In his years at Warner Bros., Zanuck created a studio style and made movies that remain among the most pleasurable experiences in American mass culture. His films were the antithesis of the sleek, stultifying melodramas Irving Thalberg and Louis B. Mayer were making at MGM. When Robert Montgomery left a woman, he made a wounded exit through one of Cedric Gibbons's Deco doorways; when James Cagney was done with a woman, he slammed a grapefruit into her face. One is more interesting than the other. Zanuck, his actors, and directors took the argot and behavior of the hoodlum and made an art form out of them.

Not everybody was in thrall to Zanuck's movies. As a reporter for the *Saturday Evening Post* noted, "Hollywood is divided into two camps: those who think [Zanuck] is a genius, and those who think he is a menace. There are no neutrals."

What everybody agreed on was that Zanuck worked very hard. He was brilliant in story conferences, where he would pace back and forth swinging a polo mallet while barking out his points. The story goes that once, while in a creative frenzy over a script, he declaimed, "And then, his love turned to hate." Screenwriter Katherine Scola was sitting there and asked, "But why does his love turn to hate?" Zanuck looked at her, then disappeared into the bathroom. After a decent interval followed by the flushing of the toilet, he reappeared and said, "All right. So his love doesn't turn to hate."

He was equally sure of himself when it came to watching different takes in the rushes. "That was better in the number two shot," would be often met with a director disagreeing, but when the takes were run back to back, the difference was usually clear.

When Zanuck was in his expounding mode, he would occasionally invent words, as in a conversation with the journalist Alva Johnson, when he said that the trend in motion pictures gave every opportunity for "betterment and correctment." Similarly, he pronounced "admirable" by tacking *able* onto *admire*. He could be touchy about his tendency toward language abuse; Johnson wrote that Zanuck had fired a man who had corrected him when he described a man as a "milestone around my neck."

The breach between Zanuck and the Warners came about after all Hollywood studio workers agreed to a temporary 50 percent salary reduction after President Roosevelt declared a nationwide bank holiday soon after he was inaugurated in 1933. The 50 percent pay cut was to avoid shutting down the studios.

The Academy of Motion Picture Arts and Sciences and Price and Waterhouse gave the all-clear to resume full salaries, but Harry and Jack Warner decided to stall for a few weeks before reinstating full salaries. Zanuck and Jack Warner generally got along, if only because they were both transparent—what you saw was what you got. But Harry Warner held himself above his younger brother, with whom he had little in common. Jack liked the movie business because it gave him a chance to be a big *macher* and to meet girls; Harry liked the movie business because he saw it as a force for social good. But Zanuck thought there was something intrinsically fraudulent about Harry that was revealed by his congenital cheapness.

Harry's reneging on his promise to restore salaries was the last straw. Zanuck had promised his people that their salaries would be restored when the Academy gave the green light, and here was Harry Warner making him a liar. Besides that, there was the matter of the company he was working for. Warner Bros. was a family business and, push come to shove, Darryl Zanuck was not a member of the family. It was time to move on.

The day after Zanuck confronted Harry about his chicanery, he released a statement to the press: "On April 10, as Head of Production of Warner Bros. I announced that the salary cut decided on March 15 last be restored immediately. This promise has now been repudiated, and since a matter of principle is involved and I obviously no longer enjoy the confidence of my immediate superiors, I have sent my resignation to the Chairman of the Company, Mr. Jack Warner."

Zanuck had no shortage of offers, but he was most intrigued by one from Joseph Schenck, the chairman of United Artists. Schenck had produced a series of pictures for UA in order to bulk up production, but by the time Zanuck became available, Schenck was in the process of shutting down his Art Cinema Corporation because of massive losses on such stillborn pictures as *Hallelujah I'm a Bum*, *Kiki*, *Reaching for the Moon*, *Secrets*, and *Puttin' On the Ritz*.

"I didn't know you were still interested in production," said Zanuck in a breakfast meeting that took place at the Brown Derby three days after he resigned from Warner Bros.

"I wasn't," replied Schenck, "but with you, I would be. Have you got a lot of confidence in yourself?"

"Yeah," replied Zanuck.

"All right," said Schenck. "You and I will start a producing company."

By the time they were finished with breakfast, they had come to an agreement, drawn up on a single sheet of paper without any legal advice whatever. Schenck produced a check for $100,000 as a binder. What was strange was that the check was signed by Louis B. Mayer. Zanuck looked at Schenck questioningly.

Schenck, the brother of Nick Schenck, the chairman of Loew's Incorporated, the parent company of MGM, explained that Mayer had a son-in-law problem. David Selznick was married to Mayer's daughter Irene and was already a force to be reckoned with in Hollywood, specifically, at MGM, where Selznick was about to start work. Mayer believed that he could get away with one son-in-law at his studio, but two would be a bridge too far. Yet, it was important that William Goetz have equivalent status to Selznick, because Goetz was married to Mayer's other daughter, Edie. With his $100,000, Mayer was buying Goetz that equivalence. Goetz had similar ambitions as Selznick but less traction and, frankly, less talent. Mayer's investment was to ensure a suitable position for William Goetz in the new company, and, equally as important, for Edie Mayer Goetz in Hollywood.

Schenck wanted to know if Zanuck had any qualms about what amounted to an MGM Trojan horse inside the new company. "Goetz wouldn't recognize a good script from a roll of toilet paper," snorted Zanuck. "So long as he keeps his father-in-law's money in our company, he can work for me as long as he likes."

And so Twentieth Century Pictures was formed in April 1933. Schenck was president; Zanuck, vice president in charge of production; William Goetz, second vice president.

Schenck and Goetz put up $1.2 million, while the Bank of America added $3 million and Consolidated Film Industries advanced $750,000 in exchange for the contract to process Twentieth Century's film. Zanuck's salary was set at $250,000 a year plus 10 percent of the profits, and he agreed to produce eight pictures in the company's first year. United Artists' distribution fee was set at 26 percent, the same rate Sam Goldwyn paid.

Zanuck decided to take a vacation before descending into the maelstrom. He set off for British Columbia via packhorse to the Columbia River. Accompanying him were Samuel Engel and Raymond Griffith, who would be associate producers on his new venture, and a crew of directors he had worked with at Warners: Lloyd Bacon, John Adolfi, Ray Enright, and Michael Curtiz.

Unfortunately, the forty-five-year-old Adolfi, who directed George Arliss pictures, suffered a stroke after the group got to the Columbia River territory and died. His body had to be strapped to a packhorse before it could be shipped to Los Angeles for burial. It was not an auspicious beginning for a new venture, but Zanuck seemed undeterred.

Schenck wanted the Twentieth Century output to bulk up the release schedule of United Artists, which was currently languishing because of the inactivity of its founders. Both Douglas Fairbanks and Mary Pickford were edging toward involuntary retirement, spurred by the public's disinterest in their recent pictures, while Charlie Chaplin took years between movies. The bulwark of the company at this point was Sam Goldwyn, who released two to three pictures annually.

The problem was that the United Artists lot on Santa Monica Boulevard—which had been known as the Pickford-Fairbanks lot during the 1920s—was small. There were two large stages and two small ones, and if two pictures were shooting, there was barely room for a third—a problem that would not go away.

Zanuck set to work building up an infrastructure from a standing start. He bought properties, hired staff, angled for actors. L. B. Mayer's method of protecting his investment was to loan out MGM stars to the new company, which is why Wallace Beery appeared in *The Bowery* in Twentieth Century's first year, and Clark Gable made *The Call of the Wild* the following year.

In the first year of Twentieth Century Pictures, Zanuck made twelve pictures, nine of them profitable, including the aforementioned Wallace Beery picture, which made a $304,000 profit. *Variety* said that *The Bowery* "gets the new company away to a grand start! A money magnet at any theater." Also highly successful were *House of Rothschild* with George Arliss and *Bulldog Drummond Strikes Back* with Ronald Colman. The latter picture had been ordered up from writer Nunnally Johnson, who was instructed to produce "a modest-budget blockbuster." Since Colman's first talkie success had been *Bulldog Drummond* in 1929, a sequel was just what the box office doctor ordered.

It was during *Bulldog Drummond Strikes Back* that Johnson realized Zanuck's rough genius. "Zanuck had a Geiger counter in his head," said Johnson. "When he read a script or watched the rushes, he knew the moment a movie got dull or a scene didn't move along. His Geiger counter would go tick-tick-tick and he would say at once, 'This is where it goes wrong. This is where the action stops.' And he would get out the script, leaf through the pages, and then point triumphantly and say, 'There!' And then he would begin to cut."

There were only a few flops. Twentieth Century produced *Born to Be Bad* with Cary Grant and Loretta Young, but the Production Code forced Zanuck to recut the picture. When he was through mollifying the Code, the movie ran sixty-one minutes and was what one critic called "an incoherent mess." It was also a flop at the box office. Both Grant and Young considered it a professional embarrassment.

In his first year at Twentieth Century, Zanuck spent $4.5 million on twelve films, an average of $375,000 apiece, more than the average at Warners, not quite as much as MGM. Both Schenck and Zanuck expected to be granted stock options for their second year of releasing through United Artists, but Goldwyn torpedoed the negotiations by requesting changes in the contract at the last minute.

Since Twentieth Century had accounted for more than half of United Artists' $23 million gross for the year, Zanuck and Schenck were properly outraged at the lack of reciprocity. Nevertheless, the second year's pictures maintained the company's standards and, in fact, upped Twentieth Century's game: *Clive of India* with Ronald Colman, *Les Miserables* with Charles Laughton and Fredric March, *Cardinal Richelieu* with George Arliss, and *The Call of the Wild* with Gable.

United Artists owned only a few theaters, which meant Zanuck was depending on the quality of his pictures for both American and foreign returns. He told the screenwriters of *Les Miserables* not to be daunted by the massive roster of characters in Victor Hugo's behemoth. "We must forget entirely the line of the book and just take the essence and dramatize it to fit our own needs." Stars help—Zanuck hired Fredric March, still in his matinee idol phase, to play Jean Valjean.

In April 1935, Zanuck came to New York for the dual premieres of *Les Miserables* and *Cardinal Richelieu*. It was the second anniversary of Twentieth Century Pictures. He was thirty-three years old, and his legend was already spreading. Frank Nugent of *The New York Times*—later to be a fine screenwriter for John Ford (*The Searchers*, *Fort Apache*)—showed up to interview him. "If an eight-footer with a long black beard, a bull whip, and the mannerisms of the Red Queen had come through the door, [I] would have arisen promptly and said, 'Hello, Mr. Zanuck.'"

But the man who presented himself to Nugent was "slim, dapper, youngish." He wore a gray flannel suit with pinstripes, his hair was sandy, he sported a trim mustache, spoke in a somewhat nasal, flat voice, and he loved his cigars. He spent most of the interview complaining about money—the high taxes in California, the possibility of the movie industry relocating to Florida or South Carolina.

The films Zanuck was making at Twentieth Century were a sort of halfway house between the films he had been making at Warners and the films he would make in a few years. But they pointed the way to his particular strengths. Zanuck understood movies, but that was not all that unusual within his peer group. What was unusual about Zanuck was the way he could see them in his head, live in them. David Selznick had many of the same characteristics, but Selznick lusted after class, and his films were top-heavy with dignity, at least until he had his affair with Jennifer Jones. Selznick never gave any director a long lead, whereas if Zanuck believed in you, he threw away the leash.

In fact, Zanuck was in the process of reinventing himself. He saw no percentage in extending the franchise he had invented at Warner Bros. Rather, he chose to express the ambition of a creative producer whose parameters were changing with age and responsibility.

"The most significant development . . . to my mind, is the impending change from mass production to individual production," wrote Zanuck. "In my opinion mass production is due for the discard because the day of 'cycles' is over. Practically every new type of picture has been made and there has been no background or type of story left untouched. . . . Each picture, henceforth, must be made as big and as good as possible. This can only be accomplished by full concentration on one picture at a time."

Zanuck was asserting that producers such as Goldwyn, Selznick, and, uh, Zanuck were the future of the business. Zanuck would do his best to implement this idea even as he would be engaged in mass production. The company he would control would make its share of programmers and B pictures, but Zanuck always sought to differentiate those pictures from his personal productions, when his name would appear in the credits, unlike those of the ordinary product.

But Twentieth Century's association with United Artists was due to come to a shuddering halt. Zanuck and Schenck had agreed to renew their deal with UA, but were cutting back production to ten pictures. Not only that, but there was a clause in the new contract that gave them what amounted to an out, ending the relationship with UA at any point. The crux of the disagreement was simple: Zanuck had been under the impression that his percentage of the profits was 10 percent of the gross. United Artists told him it was 10 percent of the net.

According to Zanuck, Douglas Fairbanks was on his side of the argument, but Charlie Chaplin was "violently opposed," despite the fact that, as Zanuck put it, "the pictures I was working on . . . had to carry the whole goddamn load." Nevertheless, the founding partners of UA saw no reason to take money out of their pockets and give it to Twentieth Century Pictures. Zanuck seems to have believed that Chaplin's animus was personal and derived from an exchange in the steam room at United Artists. "We were talking about comedians. I assumed that Chaplin realized I was excepting him when I said, 'The greatest comedian that ever lived was Lloyd Hamilton.' He didn't say anything. He went absolutely blue."

The prospective lineup for Twentieth Century's third year included *Ivanhoe*, *The Man Who Broke the Bank at Monte Carlo* with Ronald Colman, a musical with Lawrence Tibbett, *Shark Island* with Fredric March, and *Professional Soldier* starring Wallace Beery.

Zanuck would follow through on most of those pictures, but they wouldn't be released by United Artists. On May 28, 1935, *Film Daily* ran a headline regarding Hollywood's least surprising story. The Fox studio was merging with Twentieth Century: "FRAMING DETAILS OF FOX-20TH CENTURY MERGER."

"The merger will include the personal services of Schenck as chairman of the Fox board, while Darryl Zanuck, 20th Century production chief, will become a Fox vice-president. Schenck resigns his United Artists post, but remains as head of the UA theater circuit. . . .

85

"A minimum of 55 to 60 pictures a year will be made under the new affiliation, and there will not be any shakeup in the Fox organization, but merely a rearrangement of the executive and producing work."

Joe Schenck sold his stock back to UA for $550,000. He and his protégé were moving on . . . and up.

Those in the know were not surprised by what happened at UA. Fairbanks and Pickford's marriage was ending, and both Goldwyn and Chaplin were legendarily difficult in business. Between two partners who didn't want to be together anymore, and another two who didn't want to be in business with anybody but themselves, UA was in danger of seizing up.

The first overture seems to have been made by Fox in December or January. Would Zanuck and Schenck be interested in a merger? They were. The merger solved two problems. In 1935, Fox was listed as having assets of $35 million—two studios, and a lot of land—with profits of $1.8 million. Twentieth Century's assets were listed as $4 million—they didn't have a studio, but rented space at the United Artists studio on Formosa Avenue—but its profits had been $1.7 million. In other words, little Twentieth Century had no infrastructure, made far fewer pictures than Fox, but had nearly equivalent profits.

Imagine what Zanuck could accomplish with his own studio, production facilities, and contract list.

Zanuck immediately quickened to the possibility of a deal. As he succinctly put it, "Fox had the best distributing organization in the world and the worst films." MGM might have taken umbrage at the first part of that statement, but nobody in the movie business would have disagreed with the latter portion. The merger solved several problems for Zanuck—he would immediately acquire an impeccably modern studio instead of renting space from United Artists. More important, he would be master of his own fate.

Joe Schenck agreed to a salary of $2,500 a week as chairman of the board, while Zanuck took a salary of $260,000 a year, plus 10 percent of the company's gross profits, as well as stock options. Winfield Sheehan, who had been running production at Fox since 1926, would continue as vice president.

And then came the first sign of Zanuck's will to power and dominance. Sidney Kent wanted to call the new company Fox-20th Century, but Zanuck refused point-blank. It was 20th Century-Fox or nothing. Kent swallowed and agreed. Zanuck and his crew moved onto the Fox Westwood lot in June 1935.

In a sense, the merger was absurd. Twentieth Century Pictures had a library of about twenty films, no studio, no theaters, and no film exchanges. Fox Film had a worldwide production and distribution empire, not to mention a film library. But Twentieth Century had Darryl Zanuck, and that evened the equation.

With Zanuck, Fox would have something they had never had: leadership from a brilliant, aggressive young man on the cutting creative edge of the movie business. And just in case there was any doubt as to which component of the merger was most important, Zanuck made the pecking order obvious with the name of the post-merger company.

Within a week of moving onto the Fox lot, Zanuck plowed through all the current Fox scripts. He quickly threw out twelve of Sheehan's projects and pulled the plug on six more that were in preproduction on the grounds that they were "overpriced crap." Then he went through the roster of contract actors and crew, drawing lines through names of those that displeased or bored him. He called in the studio manager and told him to pay the people off at "the best price you can get." He brought in his core group of associates from Twentieth Century: screenwriters

Nunnally Johnson and Bess Meredyth, producers Raymond Griffith and Kenneth McGowan. And William Goetz.

The cuts went all the way to the top of the organization: a few weeks after Zanuck moved onto the Fox lot, Winfield Sheehan moved out, with a check for $360,000 in his pocket to gentle the hurt of being discarded. For Zanuck, it was a fait accompli: "Sheehan had started as a whirlwind, as a good discoverer of talent. . . . But when new films came along, the kind I had made at Twentieth Century, he was still making *The Farmer Takes a Wife*." Sheehan would make only two films as an independent producer—one of them was released by 20th Century-Fox—but neither was successful.

Darryl Zanuck was now in full charge of both his own movie studio and his destiny. They amounted to the same thing.

CHAPTER FIVE

HOW GREEN WAS MY VALLEY

THERE WAS ALWAYS UNANIMITY ABOUT THE PRIMARY gifts of Darryl Zanuck. He created an atmosphere of headlong enthusiasm—by the time Zanuck finished outlining a routine programmer, it sounded as if it was *Ben-Hur*. Philip Dunne termed him "a great creative executive: intelligent, decisive, totally in support of his subordinates as he was totally in charge of their work. No great screenwriter himself, he was an excellent editor. He recognized the strengths and weaknesses of his staff writers.

"To work with, he was exacting, demanding, stimulating, often irritating, and always rewarding. He was the boss but he always treated you as an equal in discussion.

"His greatest strength was his decisiveness. Right or wrong, he made his decisions quickly and firmly. He never vacillated. Next to this I would put his innate ability to handle people. . . . He knew which writer or director best responded to iron discipline, which to sweet persuasion. He stood behind his own work and the efforts of those who worked under his orders."

Zanuck sent one script back to Dunne with "Come to the point" written on the cover; another time a script came back with "Dig In!" scrawled on it. When Zanuck assigned Dunne to do a rewrite on a picture that inspired only apathy in Dunne, he asked Zanuck what exactly he was supposed to do with it.

"Put it in English!" Zanuck snapped.

Zanuck rarely accepted a first draft for production. Even high-end writers such as Ben Hecht and Charles Lederer were rewritten. The only (rare) exceptions were a few scripts by Philip Dunne and Lamar Trotti—Zanuck's favorites, both of whom would be promoted to the lofty realm of producer-writers. When Zanuck finally signed off on a script, that was it—the director was to shoot it as written.

Zanuck did not treat all writers with the respect he granted Dunne or Trotti. He had a script titled *Lucky Baldwin* that he would give to all new writers on the lot. *Lucky Baldwin* was Zanuck's version of a fraternity hazing—a legendarily bad script that the unsuspecting newbie was instructed to make shootable. The writer would sweat and strain for weeks, and triumphantly return with an improved version, only to be told that *Lucky Baldwin* was a running joke and would never be made.

Some of Zanuck's jokes could lurch over into outright cruelty—he enjoyed slipping cheese into the lunches of a subordinate who had an allergy to dairy products. When the man began to wheeze and break out in red blotches, Zanuck would chortle.

Directors who had been at Fox for years quickly learned that they could trust Zanuck. John Ford said that Zanuck "was head and shoulders above all other producers. . . . He was a great cutter, a great film editor." Henry King termed him "a model producer."

Directors are like actors in that they have to be correctly cast. Zanuck had a strong sense of the right material for the right director. John Ford had been a jobbing director at Fox for more than a decade by the time Zanuck arrived, turning his hand to all sorts of movies. Ford had made *The Iron Horse* in 1924, and, as Ethan Mordden observed, "the great scene in which the rails meet to join the continent has the ecstatic wonder of an epic poem and the honesty of an old photograph."

But after that, Fox and Winfield Sheehan had put Ford to work on whatever script came to hand. For every *3 Bad Men* and *Hangman's House*, Ford had to labor through dismal, hapless projects like *Lightnin'*, *Born Reckless*, or *The Brat*. But Zanuck understood that Ford's great gift was for the American landscape and human hearts. Soon after the merger, Zanuck tossed *The Prisoner of Shark Island* at Ford, and the director converted it into a picture so good even Warner Baxter was compelling.

After that, with few exceptions (*Four Men and a Prayer*), Zanuck carefully selected material for Ford, and the director responded with an astonishing run of great films carefully constructed for his wheelhouse: foundational examinations of America (*Drums Along the Mohawk, Young Mr. Lincoln*); families and cultures on the cusp of obliteration (*How Green Was My Valley, The Grapes of Wrath*); and solitary men wrangling the law in the barren, beautiful American West, specifically Monument Valley, which was far more Ford's native soil than his beloved Ireland (*My Darling Clementine*).

With the exception of Ford, Zanuck could be rough on directors. "I saw him treat Mike Curtiz like a slave," said Philip Dunne. Zanuck's core belief was that the movie belonged to him until the director began shooting, and it went right back to him as soon as the director finished shooting. Nunnally Johnson remembered a director named Steven Roberts who was in a conference with Zanuck in the early days after the merger. Roberts said, "I'll read the script over the weekend, and I'll kick it around." Zanuck flushed. "What do you mean, you'll kick it around? If you have any suggestions, I'll be glad to listen to them. But remember this—I'm the one who kicks things around here."

Milton Sperling said that Zanuck "had absolutely no respect for directors until they got on the set . . . they must have dreaded the script conferences to which he subjected them. He sat them all around the wall of his office, and there was one chair in the middle of the room right in front of his desk, and that of course was known around the studio as the Hot Seat. It was usually where the . . . writer . . . or the director . . . sat and it was a lonely spot, because all the criticisms and awkward questions were flung like bullets, in that direction.

"Everyone else had to sit absolutely still and listen while Zanuck walked up and down the office, tearing ideas out of his head, suggesting scenes and special shots, and then swinging on the Hot Seat and rasping, 'Waddya think of that? Does it grab ya?' Whether the poor guy agreed or not, he still had to say why he liked or disliked it."

By taking over Fox, Zanuck was returning to the days at Warners, but on a larger scale; he wasn't running a boutique operation like Twentieth Century anymore, but a combine that had to engage in mass production.

Zanuck was well aware of the fact that there weren't forty or fifty good scripts to be made at any movie studio in any given year, but his make-up meant that he had to convince himself that every script he worked on was, at worst, worth making, and, at best, a potential masterpiece.

If a director resisted taking on an assignment, Zanuck would tell them that his decision had been made and the director was going to make the movie, or else. Most of the time, they made the movie. "If you made a great picture, he was grateful, and happy for you," said Jean Negulesco. "But if you didn't make a good picture and you tried to apologize for it, he'd say, 'What are you trying to do, be a hero? I made all the decisions. Believe me, if a picture's great, I'll take the credit. But if it's not, then let's try not to make the same mistakes next time.'"

What particularly impressed Negulesco was Zanuck's obsessive devotion, not just to his own studio, but to the idea of movies in general. "After a day's work, after dinner, he'd look at the pictures of the small studios, like Republic, to compare them to what we were making. He'd ask one of us, one of his boys, to see it with him. Why? He'd say, 'It's making money. Let's find out what people like.' He wanted to make pictures that would keep his studio on top.

"There was no greater studio head than Darryl."

The founding generation of movie moguls were predominantly Eastern European Jews who came from Minsk, from Warsaw, from the Lower East Side of New York. They saw that the movie industry was there for the taking, largely because the predominantly WASP establishment that made up the American theater was utterly uninterested in the new invention.

Technically speaking, Darryl Zanuck was a second-generation mogul, which accounts for the fact that he was also the odd man out: an Episcopalian from the American plains. But in other respects, he was very much in the mold of Mayer, of Warner, of Goldwyn, in that he was an instinctive autocrat and had a very personal vision of what he wanted his movies to be.

Darryl Francis Zanuck was born in Wahoo, Nebraska, in 1902, the second child of Frank and Louise Zanuck. Wahoo is a farm town thirty miles west of Omaha. When Zanuck was born, it had a population of 2,500; today it's 4,500. Not much changes in Wahoo, which is why Zanuck got out early.

Zanuck's father was the manager of Wahoo's Grand Hotel, which was owned by Louise's father, and where he was born in a corner room on the second floor. The center of Darryl's emotional life became his grandfather, Henry Torpin, an engineer and surveyor who owned most of what Wahoo had to offer. Darryl had a brother named Donald who died four months after Darryl was born when he was kicked by a horse, so Darryl was effectively an only child.

The boy's childhood was, to put it gently, unsettled. His father gambled and drank, and his parents divorced in 1909, a time when few people got divorced. Zanuck summed up his father by saying, "Anyone who puts down his occupation as 'hotel night clerk' is admitting that he has no ambition for a start." It was, he said, "like admitting you're a mouse."

Zanuck's memories of Wahoo were fragmentary—sliding down the banister of the hotel where he was born. Once he fell in a cesspool, even though his mother had instructed him to stay away from it, which stimulated him to play right on its edge—a portent of life in Hollywood.

After his parents divorced, his mother moved to Glendale, California. Beginning in 1909, Darryl spent the fall, winter, and spring in Glendale with his mother and Joseph Norton, his stepfather. In the summer he was back in Nebraska, in a town called Oakdale, where his grandfather lived.

It was Henry Torpin who told him stories of the West that reeked of Manifest Destiny. Torpin had been a construction engineer for the Canadian Pacific Railroad, had scars on his back that he said came from Indian attacks, and generally seemed to be a mythical figure to the boy. Torpin's rough-hewn pioneer splendor threw a particularly harsh light on the feckless men who married his daughter.

Zanuck particularly loathed his stepfather, a Bible-thumper who drank as much as Frank Zanuck had, and enforced a reign of terror whenever he staggered home. "If I had a gun, I would have killed him a couple of times," Zanuck would remember. He spent time in a military school until his mother gave up and shipped him back to Nebraska. In later years, he kept his distance from his mother, probably blaming her for his unsettled childhood. Richard Zanuck, Darryl's son, said that he only met his grandmother a few times.

Darryl initially set out to be a writer. His grandfather had a few of the boy's pieces published in the local newspaper, and they are ambitious for a twelve-year-old. "We have two engines and are making forty miles an hour," he wrote in one story. "It is so hot the [writer] is compelled to stop writing. It is now three o'clock and I can write again. All we see now is desert with sagebrush every few inches. The porters says it will be like this the rest of the day so there is no more to write today."

Darryl was never much to look at—he stood no more than five feet six, was skinny, and had buck teeth. But none of that really mattered, because he aimed to do great things. Irven Wagner, who went to junior high with him, said that "Darryl was the type of a boy that had a very vivid imagination. He would talk whether it pertained to the subject the teachers asked the question on or not. . . . I remember Mrs. Leith saying, 'Darryl sit down. That doesn't pertain to the question at all.'"

In September 1917, Darryl told a prodigious lie about his age and enlisted in the Omaha National Guard one day before his fifteenth birthday. Henry Torpin was proud of his grandson and told him to go. "I'll take care of your mother," he told the boy, and evidently he was as good as his word. Zanuck managed to be sent to France as a private first class in World War I. He was not a model soldier—in March 1918, he was sentenced to "one month in quarters" for "disrespect to a non-commissioned officer."

He was in France for eight months, and was honorably discharged in August 1919, after which he returned to Nebraska and his grandfather. He was there less than a month. In September 1919, he arrived in Los Angeles, a move that coincided with the flowering of his ambitions. He bought an Underwood typewriter with which he intended to conquer the literary world. One of his first jobs while awaiting his destiny was as a riveter in the shipyards near Long Beach. The job paid $45 a week—suspiciously well for an entry-level job. The reason it paid well was that it was a horrible job. The stench of the burning metal was horrendous, and catching molten slugs of metal was dangerous.

"It was like being a catcher in a kind of lethal baseball game," Zanuck remembered. "Miss one of those rivets and it could burn a hole right through you. . . . Even when I bought the heavy reinforced apron and gauntlets that the job called for, I was in a constant muck sweat thinking I was going to fumble a red-hot rivet and get my balls burned off." Zanuck lasted a couple of months. That was followed by other dead-end jobs, but at least he wasn't risking life, limb, and balls.

In 1920, Zanuck broke into national print with sales to *Argosy* and *Physical Culture*, which began a frenetic period in which the young writer submitted a deluge of stories and proposals to anyone who might conceivably respond with a check. Pulp magazines, monthlies, movie studios—all were on the receiving end of Zanuck stories.

He was not, it must be said, a particularly skilled writer, purple prose being the specialty of the house. Reading Zanuck indicates that his own reading was probably limited to tabloid journalism and pulp novels. But he had a way of keeping the pot boiling.

To supplement his writing income, which was spotty, he took on part-time jobs—he thought he racked up eighteen of them in one year. He sold shirts, he worked for a drug company, sold magazine subscriptions while wearing his army uniform in order to stimulate patriotic solidarity. He took a correspondence course in commercial art and worked for a time tinting posters at the Orpheum Theater in downtown Los Angeles.

He was a member of the Los Angeles Athletic Club, and was complaining about his lack of success to Raymond Griffith, a gifted comedian whose star was beginning to ascend. Griffith was only half-listening and succinctly told Zanuck to "write a book." Zanuck never forgot this pithy piece of advice and years later employed Griffith as an associate producer at 20th Century-Fox.

Writing a book wasn't a bad idea, especially when he realized that he could take some of his unsold short stories and undertake a mild polish that would convert the stories into a novel. He asked a man named A. F. Foster, who had hired Zanuck to work on the advertising campaign for a hair oil called Yuccatone, to finance the publication of the book he called *Habit: A Thrilling Yarn That Starts Where Fiction Ends and Life Begins.*

Hardcover publication did not improve Zanuck's level of skill. Line by line, he consistently overwrites. The beginning of *Habit*, a variation on Griffith's *Broken Blossoms*, captures Zanuck's prose style: "Ling Foo Gow riveted his jet orbs on the burly figure that advanced on the narrow sidewalk of cracked asphalt, and with an excessive display of facial contortion, brought the aged lines of his poppy-hued countenance to an intensified scowl. His lean bony fingers with their three inch ceremonial nails, clenched fiercely about the handle of the bamboo basket they held, and tiny beads of perspiration glistened beneath the coiled wad of oily black hair that was his queue."

Zanuck's writing might be preposterous, but something is always happening, either to the characters or to the sentences. There's something charming and ingenuous in his ardor for his own work, and the transparent way he owns up to his inspiration: Darryl Francis Zanuck.

In "Say It With Dreams," one of the stories that makes up *Habit*, he writes, "And when I say that Harold was swayed by a peculiar passion for the emotionally exotic, the sensation, the grotesque, that he loved annoying people; that he had more blood and thunder and romance in his little toe than a dozen average mortals . . . I am again versed in my character. This time I am certain. I confess those failings are my personal detriments."

Surprisingly, *The New York Times* reviewed *Habit* and gave it a decent notice: "The four short stories that compose this volume, are all marked by ingenuity of plot and great fertility and variety in the invention of incident. Apparently when Mr. Zanuck sits down to write, he takes all the harness off his imagination and gets off at a gallup [*sic*] with bridle, halter or bit. . . . Even though they lack some of the essential qualities of good writing, his stories afford much entertainment."

Zanuck was nothing if not a hustler. Each of the four stories that made up *Habit* was sold to the movies, with the author pocketing a total of $11,000.

In 1922, he sold his first script, an adaptation of a play called *Storm*, to Universal, and a year after that he spent time as a gag writer at Mack Sennett studios, which led to short stints with Carter de Haven, Harold Lloyd, and Charlie Chaplin.

Zanuck didn't care for Chaplin, being put off by the comedian's habit of looking up words in a dictionary and then devising conversations in which he could show off his newly expanded vocabulary. He found he enjoyed writing comedy for Sennett, although not necessarily Sennett himself. "Working for Sennett was murder, because he was a real slave driver and he could be a son of a bitch if he thought you were wasting a minute of the time he was paying you for."

But Zanuck enjoyed the job because you weren't in it alone—writing comedy was a communal activity. "Five of us would sit around in a room and somebody would start off, 'A guy wakes up in the morning and can't find his paper . . .' and then someone else would take it up." As the story moved around the room, with each writer contributing the next story beat, a rough script gradually emerged. "The humor was all physical, completely physical. We would never show anything written to Sennett. He'd come and hear it.

"Sennett taught me two things about movie-making that I never forgot. One was that no matter how serious your picture is, no matter what momentous things you're trying to say or show, the moment you forget to keep the action going, you've lost them. Put in anything, any old gag, a girl's leg, a big explosion, a sudden scream, rather than let the audience's mind wander, and that goes for any kind of film, whether you are making *Heartbreak House* or *Charley's Aunt*. . . . Sennett knew that comedy is not words but action, and action is what movies are all about."

The time at Sennett was particularly valuable because Zanuck became friends with Mal St. Clair, a young writer who would become a successful director of comedy in the 1920s, and who finished up his career directing for Zanuck at 20th Century-Fox.

In January 1924, Zanuck married Virginia Fox, a former leading lady for Buster Keaton. (Fox was no relation to William Fox.) Virginia Oglesby Fox was born in Wheeling, West Virginia, in 1902. Her family was wealthy and sent her to boarding schools in St. Petersburg, Florida, and on regular vacations in California.

During one such vacation in 1919, Virginia became friends with Marie Prevost, who was working in Mack Sennett's comedies. Prevost took Fox to the studio and got her a screen test, which resulted in Sennett signing her as one of his Bathing Beauties. In August 1920, when Buster Keaton went looking for a new leading lady for his two-reel comedies, he chose Virginia, possibly because of her size—she was no more than five feet tall and 110 pounds, which made Keaton look much larger, although he was only five six. Keaton must have liked working with her—she made a dozen films for him, including such classics as *Cops*, *The Boat*, and *The Playhouse*.

After Keaton, Virginia worked in another two-reel comedy for Billy Joy, her boyfriend at the time, then starred in a feature titled *Palms* for a short-lived studio called Robertson-Cole. Virginia never made any claims for her acting skills. Mostly, she said, she was obedient: "If I was hanging from an elk's head, and they said, 'Hold it' I held it—even if they went to lunch, I did whatever I was told."

It was good training for the wife of a movie mogul.

When Virginia had been working with Keaton she introduced Mal St. Clair to the comedian, who hired St. Clair to direct his comedies. As a thank-you, St. Clair and his fiancée took Virginia out for a night on the town. She didn't have a date, so St. Clair asked his friend Darryl Zanuck to come along. St. Clair drove, Zanuck and Virginia had the rumble seat, and they all went to the Cocoanut Grove. The next day Zanuck sent her roses and a copy of *Habit*.

It took Zanuck six months to wear her down. At first she wasn't sure she liked this bumptious young man, but she eventually capitulated, mostly because, as she explained, "he was always on the phone, or at the door, or underfoot, or overhead. He would always hire cars. On his salary! There was never a boring moment." Her parents attended the wedding; Zanuck's parents did not, probably because they weren't invited.

They honeymooned at Coronado Beach, near San Diego. John Philip Sousa and his band were on the same train and serenaded the newlyweds with the wedding march. Decades later, Zanuck returned the favor by making *Stars and Stripes Forever*, a biographical film about Sousa.

Virginia was six months older than Zanuck, but usually told people she was the same age or a year younger. She was no pushover, but her new husband was a force of nature, and she couldn't quite get acclimated to the daily hurricane. "Our first year of marriage, I was always going back to mother. I didn't understand him. He used to pull tantrums. One day I said to mother, 'I can't stand this.' She said, 'He's a genius.'"

Virginia's husband leaned toward the autocratic, not to mention the erratic. One day he came home and announced they were moving to a new house that was completely furnished, which was not Virginia's idea of a partnership. They would have three children: Darrylin in 1931, Susan in 1933, and Richard in 1934. Despite the fact that the marriage lasted more than fifty years, it was not distinguished by monogamy on Zanuck's part. Many actresses would have to endure Zanuck's aggressive passes. Among others, Barbara Stanwyck would be chased around Zanuck's desk when they were both at Warner Bros. and left no doubt that she mightily resented the experience.

Zanuck and Mal St. Clair put in some time at FBO, or Film Booking Office, the predecessor of RKO, working on a series of two-reelers called *The Telephone Girl*. Pandro Berman, later to be a producer at RKO and MGM, was working at FBO as a second assistant director. "They hadn't invented the word whiz-kid in those days," Berman remembered, "but if anyone ever merited that description, Zanuck was the one. He was only three years older than I was, and he looked even younger, but he had such an air of authority, such self-confidence, that . . . I found myself looking up to him. He oozed talent and know-how."

Berman said that Zanuck arrived every morning at seven a.m., script in hand hot from the typewriter. After that, Zanuck stayed on the picture all day and into the night, working with St. Clair on set-ups, rehearsing the actors, working out gags. In other words, what-ever was required. On Saturdays, they worked past midnight, because Sunday was the only day off they had, and they could squeeze in more work that way. Of course, there was no such thing as overtime for sixteen-hour days, not at FBO, Warner Bros., or anyplace else in those pre-union days.

The Telephone Girl series was reasonably successful, and Zanuck and St. Clair were called over to Universal to work on a male equiva-lent called *The Leather Pushers*, about a boxer. St. Clair thought a young actor named Reginald Denny would be perfect for the part. Denny was English, but one of the beauties of silent films was that accents didn't matter—only star quality. Zanuck asked Denny to take off his shirt. So far, so good—Denny had a good body. Zanuck then took off his own shirt and began dancing around Denny, slapping him in the chest and neck, but being careful to avoid hitting him in the face.

"Hit me!" Zanuck ordered "Hit me back! Let me see you make me bleed!"

Denny was an amiable man, brought up to be a gentleman, but enough was enough. He finally lashed out with a couple of punches that put Zanuck on the ground. Denny was immediately grief-stricken. "Oh, dear, oh, dear, I say, I am most frightfully sorry. But you did provoke me, you know."

Zanuck turned to St. Clair. "He can do it, Mal. This is our kid. He knocks a bully down and then feels sorry for him. Why, every mother in America is going to love this kid!" *The Leather Pushers* proved so successful that Denny was soon promoted to a series of successful light comedy features at Universal. Sound revealed his English accent, but he continued acting in supporting roles until shortly before his death in 1967.

In April 1924, Zanuck was introduced to Jack Warner by Mal St. Clair. Warner was impressed by Zanuck's youth topped by self-confidence. A few days later he showed up at the Warner Bros. studio on Sunset Boulevard to pitch a script for Rin-Tin-Tin, the amazing German Shepherd who was about to make all the money for the studio that Ernst Lubitsch and John Barrymore didn't.

Where the North Begins was no world-beater, but Jack Warner thought the dog had something special, as indeed he did. Warner wanted Mal St. Clair to direct Rin-Tin-Tin's next picture, and St. Clair suggested that his buddy Darryl could write the script. The two men came to Warner's office and acted out the story. Jack Warner remembered that St. Clair played the two-legged hero, and Zanuck played the four-legged hero. The story was called "My Buddy: the Story of a Doughboy and His Dog," a riff on the dog trainer Lee Duncan's bond with the dog he had found on a Belgian battlefield. Under the title *Find Your Man*, the film was a success, as was *Lighthouse by the Sea*, Zanuck's follow-up script.

"He was the most brilliant bloody animal that ever lived," Zanuck remembered. Looking at the films today proves Zanuck's point. The dog was mostly black, leaner than the modern German Shepherd, able to leap tall walls in a bound, and could complete complicated tasks in a single unbroken take. "He could do anything," Zanuck remembered, while taking time to point out that some of the dog's remarkable set of skills derived from the fact that there was more than one Rin-Tin-Tin. There was a stunt dog who could do stunts deemed too dangerous for the franchise dog, who had a marvelously expressive face.

The Telephone Girl and *The Leather Pushers* had been Zanuck's elementary and secondary schools. Warner Bros. would be his college. He found that the most valuable classrooms were where the editors worked. He was enthralled as they converted a potpourri of shots into coherent dramatic sequences; how they could sharpen and transform the work of a mediocre actor by carefully cutting around them and playing the scene off the reactions of a more skilled performer; how a punchy title could cover up a multitude of sins—flaccid staging, mediocre acting. Mainly, he was startled to discover that it was possible to "turn a turkey into a sleeper, just by cutting, editing, and rejigging."

"I practically lived in the cutting room," he would remember, "and it was a great education. I could see the errors and how to get out of them. I realized that all isn't lost when the script is a dud, the director is a deadhead, and the actors don't know their asses from their elbows. Unless it is a complete and utter disaster, there is no single film that can't be rescued and turned into a seeable movie, even if it doesn't turn out to be an epic."

The editors were flattered by Zanuck's enthusiasm for their work, and they let him have the run of the cutting rooms. He even re-edited a picture that the brothers Warner were very concerned about: *Tiger Rose*, a film version of a David Belasco war horse starring Lenore Ulric. Zanuck spent two days and nights re-cutting the picture. When he was finished he had sharpened the story line and converted a disaster into a something reasonably entertaining.

The cutting room, he realized, was completely creative, even more so than the shooting stage, which often was reduced to programmed lethargy by unimaginative directors: a long shot to introduce a scene, followed by a medium shot, then ping-ponged close-ups of the actors. Lather, rinse, repeat. Anybody could do that, but not everybody could sail into the cutting room and reorganize it into something interesting.

Jack Warner would say that Zanuck "could write ten times faster than any ordinary man." In 1925, Warner Bros. made thirty films, and Zanuck wrote eight of them. Not only that, he could cheerfully devise films that would never actually be made; in that era, the studios would promote a program of titles nine months in advance that often had little relation to what would actually emerge. What was important was that the pictures sound plausibly commercial so that exhibitors would line up to buy the movies in advance. Zanuck proved a master at ad-libbing titles and plots that could be advertised, if not actually made.

He was so prolific that the studio came up with pseudonyms so that it would look like they had more than one writer. When he wasn't credited as Darryl Francis Zanuck, he was Mark Canfield, Melville Crossman, or Gregory Rogers. Zanuck only used his own name on plush prestige pictures such as *Noah's Ark* or *In Old San Francisco*. Gregory Rogers was usually trotted out for comedy, Mark Canfield specialized in melodrama, and Melville Crossman was enlisted for classier projects that were still insufficiently classy for Darryl Francis Zanuck.

Zanuck's energy ran high, and so did the jokes. He shared an office with the director Roy Del Ruth, and the two of them drilled holes in the wall so they could spy on their next-door neighbors on the lot, Michael Curtiz and his screenwriter wife Bess Meredyth. Zanuck and Del Ruth placed battery-powered buzzers on chairs that would emit an electrical shock when sat on. Then there were the non-working telephones they would install on the desks of German emigres such as Ernst Lubitsch and Henry Blanke. The phones would ring, but there was no one on the other end. The Germans would assume that the problem was some form of ignorance about the working methods of American telephones, and grow exasperated, then enraged. Hilarity ensued.

Because Warner Bros. was in the process of an expansion that would eventually result in their adoption and promotion of the Vitaphone, which in turn launched them into the upper tier of studios, Zanuck caught their corporate wave. Besides writing, he worked as an editor, a supervisor, and, in October 1928, Associate Executive in charge of production. The "Associate Executive" title was a sop to Jack Warner's ego—Zanuck was functioning as the head of production. That said, he was still relatively unknown, as was shown when *Film Daily* misspelled his name as "Daryl Zanuck." In 1931, he got the title for the job he had been doing for three years: chief executive in charge of production. Hal Wallis and Lucien Hubbard functioned as his assistants.

The Warner studio was always a contentious place, and the contention started at the top. There were five brothers, but only three really mattered: Harry, Sam, and Jack. Harry and Jack might have emerged from the same gene pool, but in all other respects they were completely different people and never really got along. The bridge between them was Sam, who was loved and respected by both Harry and Jack, but that ended with Sam's early death in 1927, just before the premiere of *The Jazz Singer*, the film Sam had believed in and ramrodded into existence. After that, Harry and Jack settled down to a war of attrition that would last nearly thirty years, until Jack shafted Harry out of his piece of the studio.

"Harry, being president, was prone to jump on Jack for any film that did not come out well," remembered Zanuck. "There was a time I think when they did not see each other. Sam was the bridge between them.

Harry hated Jack. Jack played a role like Louis B. Mayer to a certain extent. It was a gentleman's role."*

"[Jack] could captivate you. Harry was just the opposite. Anyone who got over $2,000 a week he hated instantly, even if he never met him. In Harry's mind, everybody was a thief, including Jack for condoning extravagances. . . . What a boring guy Harry was. Jack was unreliable, but never boring."

Zanuck was an employer's dream: a workaholic with a lot of great ideas and the skill to execute them. Most of his ideas weren't original, but most of them worked. He could write a biblical epic like *Noah's Ark*, and a month later turn out a good script for Syd Chaplin, Warners' main comedy star in the late 1920s. Syd's brother was a genius, while Syd was only a talent, but he was a pleasing talent, although that wasn't the reason Zanuck loved him.

"Sydney Chaplin was the greatest cocksman that ever lived," asserted Zanuck. "Including Errol Flynn. I never saw anybody as ruthless and successful and bold as Sydney Chaplin. He used to stand across the street from Hollywood High School and watch the [girls] come out and he'd approach them—using his real name. Ruthless!"

Zanuck did more than energize the Warner lot; he energized their movies and he energized the audience. After sound rolled silent films into oblivion, Zanuck brought a crew of tough mugs onto the Warner lot who embodied components of Zanuck—his energy, his impatience, his sense of himself. Moreover, they cumulatively redefined movie stardom as something more than beauty. Their presence meant that the films surrounding them had to be consonant with their skill set, which led to a long series of tough gangster films: *Little Caesar, The Public Enemy, Doorway to Hell*. Zanuck broadened the gangster franchise with *I Am a*

* This is the only extant example of anyone calling Jack Warner a gentleman.

Fugitive from a Chain Gang and *20,000 Years in Sing Sing*. For the swells on the high end, he made biographical films with George Arliss. With the exception of the Arliss pictures, Warners product of this period *moved*.

If Zanuck's filmmaking philosophy could be reduced to one sentence, it was this: There's a reason they're called moving pictures.

In January 1933, Zanuck signed a three-year contract as head of production. At the same time, the trade papers began to catch the scent of a potential merger between Fox and Warners. "The feeling around town," wrote the *Hollywood Reporter* in a front-page story, "is that the deal, if and when made, will provide for a substantial cash payment to the Warners, plus a participating interest, places on the board, etc., with [Sidney] Kent heading both groups and Zanuck in charge of production for the joint companies."

The merger didn't happen that year, although the murmurs had more than a touch of truth to them. Fox's problems stemmed from the movies they were making. A merger with Warners would solve that problem, while at the same time opening up the vast Fox roster of theaters, all one thousand of them to Warners, which had about three hundred theaters.

It was a good idea that wouldn't die, as was proved in April 1933 when everybody was shocked but not surprised: "Zanuck Out At Warners."

The partners may have changed, but the dance went on.

CHAPTER SIX

STAND UP AND CHEER

AFTER DISPENSING WITH THE SERVICES OF WINFIELD Sheehan in the summer of 1935, Zanuck decided to hold on to Sol Wurtzel and made him the "Czar" of B movies at the old Western Avenue studio. For the next ten years, Wurtzel made a succession of Charlie Chan, Mr. Moto, and Michael Shayne films on shooting schedules that usually ran under two weeks and budgets that topped out at $200,000.

The Fox Bs compared favorably with those made by the other studios if only because the best of them put the emphasis on pace. In fact, Wurtzel made Fox's first two pictures starring Shirley Temple. *Bright Eyes* cost a very modest $233,000 and made a huge profit of $1.2 million, while *Baby Take a Bow*, released that same year, brought in another $500,000 in profits.

Zanuck spirited Alfred Newman away from United Artists to run the music department and compose. In time, Newman's brother Lionel would join the company and take over the administrative duties of the music department. Harry Brand became head of publicity, and Julian Johnson, an old fan magazine writer from the World War I era, became head of the story department. Lew Schreiber was technically head of casting, but Zanuck usually delegated the running of the studio to Schreiber when he went on vacation.

Where all this left William Goetz is open to question, but then Zanuck neither liked nor respected Goetz. As far as Zanuck was concerned, Goetz's arrival with a certified check from Louis B. Mayer was the beginning and end of his importance.

Zanuck's primary problem was the fact that the new company had very few stars. Besides Shirley Temple and Will Rogers, the contract stars were Warner Baxter, Janet Gaynor, and a promising ingénue named Alice Faye. Baxter was born middle-aged, but Zanuck kept him around for a couple of good pictures. Gaynor had been a huge star in the late 1920s and early '30s as a latter-day Mary Pickford—shy, with an unforced sweetness that made her able to play everything from a betrayed farm wife in Murnau's *Sunrise* to a prostitute in Frank Borzage's *Street Angel*. Sheehan had partnered her with Charles Farrell, a tall, extremely handsome actor who had problems in sound because of his inappropriate voice.

Farrell and Gaynor were both attractive, but oddly sexless—it's no accident that their biggest hits, such as *7th Heaven* and *Street Angel*, invoked a quasi-religious meeting of souls rather than a wrinkling of the sheets. Compared with the sexual pull of stars at other studios—Norma Talmadge in her silent pictures, Gary Cooper and Marlene Dietrich in *Morocco*, Gable and Harlow in anything—Gaynor and Farrell came off like sweetly naïve high school kids, which was just the way their fans liked it. Although Gaynor had been making hits as recently as 1934, she obviously felt uncomfortable with the new regime and soon left Fox to go to Selznick International for *The Young at Heart* and *A Star Is Born*.

Of these contract players, the most valuable were undoubtedly Will Rogers and Shirley Temple. Will Rogers had returned to the winner's circle with *Handy Andy* and John Ford's *Judge Priest*. Between the two pictures, there was a profit of $750,000.

As for Temple, she was born Shirley Jane Temple on April 23, 1928, although the studio changed the year to 1929 so she would seem to be even more of a child prodigy. Temple's pictures cost around $500,000 apiece and would reliably return domestic rentals of more than a million dollars apiece. Add in foreign returns, and two or three pictures a year from Temple could guarantee a clear profit of close to $2 million.

In retrospect, the studio was slow to pick up on just what Shirley Temple represented. She had made some two-reelers for Educational Films, which distributed through Fox. She had a small part in a Fox movie called *Carolina*, then was loaned out to Warners for two films. After that, she returned to Fox for *Stand Up and Cheer*, then had a supporting part in a Gaynor-Farrell vehicle called *Change of Heart*.

Still asleep at the switch, Fox then loaned her out to Paramount for *Little Miss Marker*, but when she returned to Fox she was slotted into another supporting part in *Now I'll Tell*. It was the success of *Little Miss Marker* that made Fox sit up and take notice. Temple's mother had signed her daughter's contract on December 7, 1933, for a salary of $150 a week, not counting $25 a week added for her mother's due diligence. In time, Temple would earn as much as $350,000 a year.

Temple could act a little—mostly via pouting—and could sing and dance quite well. But there is no doubt that she was the greatest child star in movie history. She was the number one box office star in America from 1935 to 1938, and was in the top ten through 1939.

Temple was well-mannered, a pro, and always very smart about her own career. "I class myself with Rin-Tin-Tin," she would say. "People were looking for something to cheer them up. They fell in love with a dog and a little girl." Certainly she was the right little girl in the right place at the right time, but there was more going on than good timing. Watching her tap dance with the great Bill Robinson in *The Little Colonel* or *Just Around the Corner* can put the same smile on your face produced by Fred Astaire and Ginger Rogers. One couple consists of an adult and a child, and the other are both adults, but they're alike in that they're perfect together. And there's one other thing—they radiate a sense of joy in their partnership. "It's like a conversation between an adult and a child," wrote Jeanine Basinger, "in which the adult is patient but uncompromising in the lesson, and the child is precocious and dedicated to showing what she can do."

Will Rogers's pictures had a similar financial structure, but in terms of his personality he was a true one-off. In 1935, Fox's two top box office pictures both starred Rogers. He had flopped in silent pictures because his personality depended on his rambling, shambling way with quietly pointed dialogue. Rogers played a subtle, cagy rustic in an idealized small-town America, casually deflating the pompous, the hypocritical, the prevaricating. In *Judge Priest*, Rogers is at a party where a veteran of the Civil War, still in uniform decades after the war, is orating about his war experiences. He was in a river, surrounded by Yankee gunboats. Rogers passes by and mutters, "Gunboats? Puttin' them gunboats in there is a new touch, ain't it?"

Audiences loved Rogers because, as one reviewer noted, "[Rogers] is what Americans think other Americans are like." So did the people who worked with him, including Joel McCrea, who made several pictures with him as a young $100-a-week male ingénue. "Will and I fell in love immediately, the first day of shooting [on *Lightnin'*] when I asked him how to do a certain Texas skip, and he said, 'You wait until after shooting.' And I said, 'That means I miss the last bus,' and he said, 'You ain't an extra any more, you ride home with me in the LaSalle.' He drove his own LaSalle Coupe."

Rogers proceeded to invite McCrea to dinner with him, Winfield Sheehan, and Henry King. They were at Caliente, where gambling was legal, and Rogers gave McCrea $100 to play roulette. It was all new and thrilling to McCrea. He ended up winning $400, while Rogers had to ask for his $100 back because he'd had a bad day at the tables. After *Lightnin'*, Rogers asked for McCrea again, on his next picture, "and then Fox offered me a contract, just on the strength of Will."

In short, Rogers pretended to be far less complex than he was. He used most of his salary to buy real estate, which meant that his family was land-rich and cash-poor. Despite his most famous remark—"I never met a man I didn't like"—he did indeed meet a lot of people he didn't like;

his son Jim Rogers would reminisce that one sure way to send his father into a towering rage was to abuse an animal—any animal at all.

Tragically, Will Rogers died in an airplane crash on August 15, 1935, little more than a month after Zanuck moved onto the Fox lot. Zanuck tried halfheartedly to replace him with the Kentucky humorist Irvin S. Cobb, but Rogers's good humor proved impossible to replicate—there was no successor to Will Rogers. Not then, not ever.

The fact of the matter was that the merger happened at a time when both Fox and Twentieth Century were catching an upward draft. Fox's profits for the year 1935 amounted to $5.9 million, an increase of nearly 20 percent over 1934. That said, Sheehan's last personal productions, including a remake of D. W. Griffith's *Way Down East*, were big commercial losers.

Zanuck's first batch of pictures began rolling out at the end of 1935, but the outlines of his studio policy didn't become clear for another few months. Basically, his pictures at 20th Century had been a preview of his work at 20th Century-Fox. The tough, streetwise pictures that had filled Zanuck's roster at Warner Bros. seemed to be more of a response to the social and political moment than a reflection of Zanuck's own personal tastes. When the urban thread reappeared, it would be years later, transmogrified into smoky noirs such as *Cry of the City*.

1936 brought three Shirley Temple pictures, a couple of musicals, a costume extravaganza titled *Lloyd's of London*, and a war picture called *The Road to Glory* with Warner Baxter and Fredric March that was efficiently built around battle scenes lifted from the French picture *Les Croix De Bois*. It was a roster of pictures indicating an evolution of Zanuck's production policy. He avoided the often brutal ripped-from-the-headlines approach of much of the Warner product in favor of romantic, nostalgic evocations of American and English history. The joke about 20th Century-Fox being more accurately called "19th Century-Fox" quickly became current. One historian estimated that nearly 25 percent of Zanuck's pictures at his new studio were set between 1865 and 1920.

Zanuck's production policy was immediately successful—the operating profit for 1936 was $7.9 million after taxes, a sizeable increase over 1935. The two years following 1936 also showed increased profits. And he began creating stars of his own. Tyrone Power was a stunningly handsome twenty-four-year-old third-generation actor appearing with Katherine Cornell on Broadway when he made a screen test for Zanuck. He didn't like it. Power had a low hairline, and his eyebrows nearly grew together. "Take it off!" ordered Zanuck. "He looks like a monkey."

Providentially, Virginia Zanuck was sitting there watching the test with her husband, and she countermanded him. "Shave his eyebrows," she said. Power had a small part in his first picture, *Girl's Dormitory*, starring Simone Simon. It was a nothing part in a nothing movie, but Zanuck could feel the audience quicken at Power's close-ups. In 1936, Zanuck gambled that Power could headline *Lloyd's of London*, the studio's biggest production of the year. Just like that, he had the romantic leading man who would anchor the studio's major films for more than fifteen years.

Power set hearts fluttering off-screen as well as on. Evie Abbott, who would later marry both Keenan Wynn and Van Johnson, had been appearing with Power in the Katherine Cornell production of *Romeo and Juliet*, which featured Cornell as Juliet, Maurice Evans as Romeo, Ralph Richardson as Mercutio, and Power as Benvolio. It must have been an interesting evening in the theater—the dances were by Martha Graham and the scenery by Jo Mielziner.

"Ty was my first lover," said Evie Abbott Wynn Johnson. "He was a very gentle man, which is why I fell in love with him. He was a gentleman's gentleman—so sweet, so nice, so caring. We broke up because Ty was going to California to go into the movies and I was still doing plays in New York."

A flukier success came when Zanuck looked at some film of a Danish ice-skater named Sonja Henie, who had an ingenuous smile and charming dimples. Zanuck took a flyer, and the result was *Thin Ice*, which brought in a startling $1.3 million in America alone. Henie didn't have a lengthy career, but her example brought forth other stars such as Esther Williams—attractive female athletes with a pleasing personality who could be transformed into movie stars.

As he had at Warners, Zanuck preferred creating stars rather than buying them. For one thing, it was cheaper. For another, homegrown talent tended to be more grateful than freelancers, who tend to be loyal only to their own careers.

Zanuck did his best to compose variations on a theme, and sometimes even introduce a new theme entirely. The Shirley Temple formula of a lovable little waif bringing her parents—or prospective parents—together had to be varied. Zanuck wanted the Kipling adaptation *Wee Willie Winkie* to be something different, and he instructed the writers that they had to "disregard the formula of all the previous pictures Shirley Temple has appeared in to date. . . . My idea about doing this picture is to forget that it is a Shirley Temple picture. . . . Write the story as if it were a *Little Women* or a *David Copperfield*. . . . All the hokum must be thrown out. The characters must be made real, human, believable. Only then can we get a powerful, real story. . . . And it must be told from the child's viewpoint, through her eyes." Zanuck gave the project to John Ford, whose initial response was a large roll of the eyes, but who grew very fond of the little girl and responded with a heartfelt job of direction—Temple's best picture.

Ford and Zanuck were both alpha males and had an interesting, predominantly productive relationship based on mutual, wary respect. One of their few open disagreements occurred on *The Prisoner of Shark Island*. Zanuck took exception to Warner Baxter's southern accent, whereupon Ford snapped, "If you don't like it, get someone else [to direct]."

"Goddam it to hell, don't threaten me!" snapped Zanuck right back. "People don't threaten *me*. *I* threaten them!"

Parameters thus established, the two men worked more or less in harmony for the next fifteen years. Near the end of his career, Zanuck paid Ford the ultimate compliment. "I have finally come to the conclusion that John Ford is the best director in the history of motion pictures. . . . Ford was unique in that he visualized motion pictures in purely visual terms and I believe any director . . . would agree that Ford could get more drama into an ordinary interior or exterior long shot than any director and that his placement of the camera almost had the effect of making even good dialogue unnecessary or secondary. . . . He makes the camera act. . . . He was an artist. He painted a picture—in movement, in action, in still shots. . . . You would look at the set and think, maybe you need a closeup, but you didn't. He was a great, great pictorial artist."

There was never any doubt who ran the studio. Zanuck often walked through the lot wearing jodhpurs, wielding a riding crop, and smoking a cigar. He oversaw every A picture the studio made, from the initial script conference after the story was purchased, through the various drafts. Then came casting, followed by careful observation of the rushes, finally taking personal charge of the final edit with the help of his favorite editor, Barbara McLean. It was McLean—"Bobbie" around the lot—who was Zanuck's right arm.

McLean had worked as an assistant to Raoul Walsh on *The Bowery* and had never met Zanuck during the shoot, but sat in on his late-night editing sessions. A few films in, Zanuck noticed that only McLean's cutting notes resulted in his suggestions being implemented exactly as he intended. Along with Anne Bauchens, Cecil B. DeMille's trusted editor for forty years, and MGM's Margaret Booth, McLean became one of the industry's most valued editors. "You loved [the people] and you wanted the picture to be great, and you didn't mind how hard you worked," McLean recalled. "And that's the faculty that Zanuck had.

"With Zanuck, when you'd run pictures in the projection room, nobody made a sound. Even if you had a cigarette packet with that cellophane on it, you'd take it off before. His powers of concentration were terrific. The editor sat next to him and when he didn't like something, he'd just touch you on the arm. I'd write it in the dark. . . . You almost are reading his mind, you almost could tell what he would want done. It was amazing, because look how many pictures he was working on. It was not only one picture, but he had to divorce himself from one to the other. He could. He could remember."

Because the studio was both creatively and financially successful immediately, there was nobody around to voice any doubts about Zanuck's methods. Writers are notorious complainers and resistant to meddling, or, as it's usually called in Hollywood, supervision, but the writers at Fox all recognized that Zanuck was not their enemy, but rather their friend.

Besides the normal couple of pictures from Shirley Temple, 1938 brought *In Old Chicago*—a good spectacle about the Chicago fire that was clearly inspired by MGM's *San Francisco*—and some more musicals. 1939 was a step up, not in design, but in execution. There was *The Rains Came*, expertly directed by Clarence Brown in his only loan-out from MGM (L. B. Mayer was determined to have his investment in 20th Century-Fox turn out well), John Ford's *Drums Along the Mohawk* (in Technicolor), *Stanley and Livingstone*, *The Story of Alexander Graham Bell*, and Ford again with *Young Mr. Lincoln*. The nineteenth-century epics were returning profits and proved that David O. Selznick wasn't the only game in town when it came to romanticizing the past.

1940 would prove conclusively that Zanuck didn't think in terms as programmatic as other moguls, perhaps because the audience was always in the process of evolving, and they didn't always evolve in the way a movie mogul might wish. (For a business as attached to popular taste as the movies, it's always adapt or die.) For one thing, Shirley Temple was no longer a sure thing. *Susannah of the Mounties* had only earned domestic rentals of $800,000, a precipitous drop from her usual returns.

The truth is that the only enemy a child star has is puberty, as everyone from Jackie Coogan to Macaulay Culkin eventually discovered. Zanuck decided to roll the dice on a spectacular production of Maeterlinck's *The Blue Bird* in Technicolor as a make-or-break vehicle for Temple. The result was a serious financial disappointment. Temple's last picture at Fox was a modest black-and-white picture titled *Young People*, after which she left Fox and went to MGM. Despite the best efforts of filmmakers as skilled as David O. Selznick and John Ford, Temple never did manage to transfer her childhood success to adulthood. Zanuck understood that Temple had been a glorious exception; other than some pictures with Jane Withers, he didn't attempt to duplicate her success. He had to compensate in other ways.

He took a considerable risk by making a movie of *The Grapes of Wrath*, John Steinbeck's landmark novel of the Depression's dispossessed. Zanuck knew he couldn't spend a lot of money on such a downbeat story, so he asked John Ford to direct, which meant that the picture would be made beautifully but also expeditiously—Ford didn't shoot a lot of takes, or a lot of coverage. After some loose talk involving Tyrone Power for the part of Tom Joad, Zanuck capitulated to Ford and cast Henry Fonda, who responded with one of the great performances in American movies. To get the part, Fonda had to sign a contract tying him to Fox for seven years, and he never got over his disgruntlement at Zanuck's ruthless leveraging—to the end of his life, Fonda usually referred to his boss as "Darryl F-for-Fuck-It-All-Zanuck."

Zanuck went over Nunnally Johnson's adaptation of the Steinbeck novel carefully, giving the writer detailed notes. Between Zanuck, Ford, and Johnson, Steinbeck's steely, Socialist portrait of an entire generation rendered disposable by social and economic oppression was subtly transformed into a compassionate family drama. Ford and cinematographer Gregg Toland keyed their visual approach to the Depression-era photographs of Dorothea Lange and Walker Evans. Toland used no diffusion, kept the focus razor sharp. Coming at the height of the Hollywood Dream Factory, *The Grapes of Wrath* emerged as a visual poem with a brutalist specificity.

For the climactic farewell scene between Tom Joad and his mother, Zanuck told Johnson that "[in the current script] we get the impression Tom is running away, whereas it should be plain that he is making a sacrifice. He should tell Ma that he is going away and the reason is that he's just heard that somebody has come around and is looking for a fellow with a scar. Even if he got by with it this time, it would only be a matter of time that he'd be getting them all in trouble, etc." Johnson's polish transformed the scene.

Made for a reasonable $850,000, *The Grapes of Wrath* surprised everybody by earning $2.5 million in rentals. This should have catapulted

Fonda to an equivalent status with Tyrone Power, but that was never going to happen. Power was a docile team player, a description that nobody could ever apply to Fonda. Besides that, Fonda and Zanuck disliked each other. Fonda hated taking orders from anyone, while Zanuck thought Fonda was bereft of sex appeal for the female audience. With the exception of *The Ox-Bow Incident*, a personal project for director William Wellman, Zanuck tended to cast Fonda as an amiable hayseed. This didn't mean the picture was necessarily bad (*Chad Hanna* is a real charmer), but it was inevitable that it would further alienate Fonda.

The Grapes of Wrath was the beginning of a protean decade for Zanuck, and profits followed. In 1939, the studio had a net profit of $4.1 million, which was followed in 1940 by a loss of $517,336. But 1941 produced a profit of $4.9 million, and the numbers would grow even larger during World War II when the studio's profits surged to between $10 million and $12 million yearly. In 1946, Fox's profits skyrocketed to $22 million and change, while the stock price rose to 63⅞.

Between 1940 and 1950, Zanuck's studio would win the Best Picture Oscar three times—for *How Green Was My Valley*, *Gentleman's Agreement*, and *All About Eve*. And he once again assumed his 1930s role as the industry trendsetter by making movies about anti-Semitism, racism, and a dazzling series of noirs that included *Laura* and *Night and the City*—more or less the social problem pictures that Zanuck had made at Warners transposed to a new place and time. In 1950, he made the cover of *Time* as "the preeminent Hollywood executive of his generation."

To front the noirs, he developed new stars that were less conventionally romantic than Tyrone Power—Dana Andrews, Victor Mature, and Richard Widmark. Mature was a big, easygoing charmer who always followed his father's advice: "As long as people think you're dumber than you are, you'll make money."

Mature was invariably best when working for a director who scared him and refused to settle for anything but the actor's best: John Ford (*My Darling Clementine*) or Henry Hathaway (*Kiss of Death*). "I took acting five times as seriously as anyone else," Mature would say years after leaving Fox. "I just couldn't show it. Some kind of complex, I guess. In the car, driving to a premiere, I used to be scared to death. Then the door opened and I would leap out, going like apeshit."

Mature had studied acting at the Pasadena Playhouse, but any thoughts of High Art were dispelled on the set of *One Million B.C.* "when Hal Roach would turn to his assistant director and say, 'I don't want to miss the second race at Santa Anita. You direct this.'"

"Fox was like a country club," Mature remembered. "At Fox, there was no pressure and only one boss—Darryl F. Zanuck. There was no room for two geniuses there. They turned pictures out like crackerjack. *Kiss of Death* got made because Fox was one black-and-white picture short on its schedule. . . . I wasn't pampered the way a Tyrone Power was. . . . Tyrone Power was the king. One director of mine got so nervous when Ty Power came on to the set to watch that he forgot where he told me to walk in a scene. . . . Zanuck would say to the producers, 'If you're not careful, you son of a bitch, I'll give you Mature for your next picture.'"

What set Zanuck's pictures apart in this era was their dramatic clarity, which derived entirely from the clear line of power that extended from the office in the Administration building that was painted what became known as Zanuck green. "Fox pictures were like Darryl F. Zanuck," said David Brown, who worked at Fox as a story editor. "Clean and sharply focused. They weren't like Metro pictures. Those were fuzzy and lush."

The Ox-Bow Incident was a passion project for William Wellman, who had personally optioned the book but couldn't find a single studio that would let him make a western about a lynching of three innocent men. In desperation he went to Zanuck, despite the fact that the two men had had a fistfight years earlier and hadn't spoken since. The brawl hadn't really affected Wellman's affection for the producer: "I was as fond of him as a director can be fond of a producer. I admired him for his guts . . . [and for] generating the speed and enthusiasm all down the line to make a good picture quickly—at that he was a master, and the hardest-working little guy you have ever seen in all your life."

Zanuck listened to Wellman's pitch, sighed, and said, "It won't make a dime, but I want my name on it." He told Wellman he could make the picture on a limited budget of $500,000 as long as Wellman agreed to make two other pictures of Zanuck's choosing. Wellman swallowed and agreed. Wellman thought the two pictures Zanuck chose for him were hopeless stinkers—*Thunderbirds* and *Buffalo Bill*—but a deal is a deal.

When Zanuck read Lamar Trotti's script for *The Ox-Bow Incident*, he was the one who was swallowing hard. "I read the novel before publication, more than two years ago," he wrote in a memo, "and even then its material seemed too bitter and sunless to be good box office. . . . As a prestige picture, yes, definitely, provided it is well cast and well directed. But in my opinion, this is certainly not entertainment for these times."

The Ox-Bow Incident returned rentals of $750,000, justifying Zanuck's estimation of its commercial potential. On the other hand, when the film began appearing on TV in the 1950s, it earned a popularity it has never lost. It's a quietly savage film, made more so by Wellman's audacious casting of Jane Darwell, Ford's beloved, indomitable Ma Joad, as a bloodthirsty member of the posse. "Keep your chin up," she tells Dana Andrews shortly before he's lynched. "You can only die once, son."

John Ford was not an effusive man, but he wrote Wellman a fan letter about the movie—as he should have.

━━━━━━━━━━━━━

The outbreak of World War II brought waves of refugees to Hollywood, a situation that Zanuck took full advantage of. Fritz Lang turned out three successful pictures for Fox, including *The Return of Frank James* and the superb *Man Hunt,* before going on to make twenty-one more pictures for other studios in the next twenty years.

A less felicitous pairing came with Jean Renoir, despite Zanuck's enthusiasm for Renoir's film *Grand Illusion,* which he called "the most magnificent picture of its type that I've ever seen." When John Ford suggested an American remake, Zanuck's instincts told him it was a bad idea: "I think it would be a criminal injustice to attempt to remake the picture in English. The most wonderful thing about the picture is the fine background, the authentic atmosphere, and the foreign characters, who actually speak in the language of their nationality. Once you take this away, I believe you have lost 50% of the value of the picture."

The relationship between Zanuck and Renoir was never comfortable. Renoir seemed to have no particular handle on what kind of picture he should make for his American debut; at one point he expressed enthusiasm for the script to *I Wake Up Screaming*, which was actually announced as his first American film, but that was soon displaced by a Nunnally Johnson script called *Venezuela,* which Renoir wanted to make with Jean Gabin, also newly arrived in Hollywood.

Zanuck thought these were terrible ideas: "I have come to the conclusion that you should not direct [Gabin's] first American film and that you should direct an American cast in your first American film and that [Gabin] should have an American director for his first American film."

Zanuck decided to take the project that became *Swamp Water* away from Fritz Lang and give it to Renoir. The director became enthused about the possibilities of shooting the picture on location in the Okeefenokee swamp, a thought that horrified Zanuck. "This is a film that must be made for an economical price," he informed Renoir in a memo. "It will have a tight budget and tight shooting schedule. There is nothing surefire about it from a commercial standpoint."

Renoir hoped to change that by casting Tyrone Power in the lead, but Zanuck had no intention of sticking Power into a backwoods part for an untried director: "In the first place, [Power] is not available," he wrote Renoir, "and in the second place, I am sure when you learn more about this work you will realize that he has a voice that would never be adapted to this locale." Zanuck suggested Dana Andrews for the lead and Renoir grudgingly agreed. Zanuck compromised to the extent of allowing Renoir his choice of Anne Baxter for the leading lady instead of Zanuck's preferred choice of Linda Darnell.

Zanuck also allowed Renoir to shoot for a week in the swamp, but the only principal to go on location was Dana Andrews, and most of the footage was utilized for rear projection. More damaging was Zanuck's decision to assign Irving Pichel as a dialogue director alongside Renoir. Pichel was a competent but unremarkable director-for-hire whose main claim to fame was codirecting *The Most Dangerous Game* with Ernest Schoedsack and narrating John Ford's *How Green Was My Valley*.

Renoir's English was rudimentary at this point, so he needed someone to translate for him, but it seemed to many onlookers that Pichel was standing by in case Renoir was unequal to the task of making the movie on time and on budget. Renoir's preferred moviemaking method was antithetical to Zanuck's. Renoir made accomplices of his actors and crew—friendship led to laughter and pleasant dinners. With any luck, in eight weeks or so a movie would result.

This was anathema to Zanuck's business-oriented approach. "It's really a factory," Renoir wrote to a friend. "It doesn't feel like working in film, but like being in school. We have a very nice, very friendly teacher who, instead of using the right method, which consists in developing the personality of each student, keeps on practicing the bad one, consisting of modeling the mind of each student after his own."

A week after the film started shooting in July 1941, Renoir wrote to his brother Claude, "There's no pleasure in my trade. It consists of being seated in a comfortable chair, smoking cigarettes and saying 'action' and 'cut.' I've understood the futility of trying to do something personal."

Among other things, Zanuck was unhappy with the pace Renoir set. Two weeks into the shoot, he wrote to the director: "You are going entirely too slow. . . . We have changed the cameraman and now you have a photographer who can keep up a fast pace, yet we are getting no more film than we did with the other cameraman." Zanuck also thought there were too many dolly shots, too much atmosphere, and scenes were being shot with shifting approaches rather than with firm intent. Zanuck also took umbrage at Renoir's habit of waiting until morning to decide on the day's first setup, as opposed to the Hollywood tradition of the director deciding the next day's first shot the night before.

The result of all this was a thoroughly demoralized Renoir. "Never would I have believed that you could come to detest your profession the way I detest it now," he wrote to the art director Eugene Lourie. The day after the shoot ended, Renoir found out that his presence in the cutting room was neither welcome nor necessary—Zanuck would edit the film.

The result of all this was a film that cost a modest $601,000, got decent but unspectacular reviews, and returned domestic rentals of $1.5 million—a solid commercial success. Despite that, Zanuck and Renoir parted ways; Renoir would make four more films in Hollywood, but the only one he liked was *The Southerner*, a movie he made independently in 1945.

Near the end of his life, Renoir would return to the problem of his difficulties with the systemized production he found in Hollywood. "It was not the filmmaking system itself that was bad," he told me. "It was the whole machinery. What was wrong was that the aim of an industry is to make money. I always felt that there was something more, something which I always struggled to achieve: the desire for planned perfection.

"I believe in spontaneity, in the personality of the artist; not the final product, but the heart of the artist. Perfection comes before money, at least I always thought so. I feel that the studios were ruined looking for the impossible perfection of the perfect money-making machine.

"Zanuck was mostly quite helpful. He really gave me trouble about one thing only. I was working in long sequences, without a cut. This was not liked. They wanted what they called 'protection' for the cutting room, so it would be easier for them to re-edit the way they wanted. They did not understand that I did what I did out of style, not out of a desire to sabotage their editing. I simply felt that this was the most harmonious way of exploring the characters."

―――――――――――――
―――――――――――――

As with most moguls, Zanuck had getaways, predominantly a three-story, thirty-room house on the beach designed by Wallace Neff. Then there was a house in Palm Springs, purchased from Joe Schenck and called Ric-Su-Dar, after his children.

When Darryl Zanuck woke in the morning, his wife would call the studio and tell them to "send Sam down." That meant that Sam Silver, the studio barber, would drive his Pontiac down Olympic Avenue to the sea and give Zanuck his morning shave. After that came breakfast, which Zanuck would eat while reading the *Los Angeles Times*. Then came the drive to the Fox lot in Westwood—before the war he drove with Silver; after the war he usually drove himself. The car was painted Zanuck green and bore the license number 13—his lucky number. As with everything else in his life, speed was of the essence—Zanuck drove fast. In later years, his companion on the ride was usually his French tutor, a man named Edward Leggewie, who attempted to instruct him in the proper accent, to no avail. Zanuck's French always emerged with a strong Nebraska twang.

By the time he got to the office it was around eleven in the morning. He would eat lunch at the Café de Paris, the Fox commissary, and he often ate dinner there as well, with Nick Janios, who ran the commissary.

His office had four rooms: an outer area for secretaries and supplicants to cool their heels, the inner sanctum featuring his desk—a prop replica of George Washington's—a back room for his hunting trophies, and a small bedroom adjacent to the trophy room. All of the walls were painted Zanuck green.

The office was designed to be large and intimidating, with a long walk to get to his desk. "It was the same kind of setup Mussolini had," said the scenic designer Walter Scott. "It made you feel very small and powerless." If the size of the office was insufficiently indicative, the profusion of hunting trophies and zebra skins provided further confirmation that this was not a man to be trifled with.

During the day Zanuck would have meetings with writers and producers. Unless there was an emergency, he rarely went on sets, believing it was the director's preserve. Many days at four o'clock all activity around the Executive building would stop while Zanuck entertained one of the chorus girls or contract actresses for a half hour or so, his particular version of the *droit du seigneur*. June Haver, who worked at Fox as a sort of Betty-Grable-in-training, told a story about walking into his office. Zanuck was sitting behind the desk and rose politely to greet her, revealing an unzipped erection that he presumably hoped would be appreciated. She believed that every young actress on the lot had to endure the same ritual of greeting—Corinne Calvet reported that he pulled the same stunt on her in the early 1950s. Patricia Morrison would advise female newcomers to the lot to get out of this initiation by quickly telling Zanuck they were having their period, which deflated his ardor, among other things.

Zanuck certainly miscalculated with Haver; she would eventually quit the movies to become a nun, still later realize her mistake and marry Fred MacMurray. Similarly, a woman named Marcella Rabwin applied for a job as Zanuck's secretary and said that she was "nearly paralyzed with fright" by Zanuck's sexual demands during the interview. "When I refused he started screaming." Rabwin eventually became secretary for David Selznick, who, by comparison, was "a gentleman and a talent," said Rabwin.

As far as the public was concerned, Zanuck's four p.m. appointments were described as daily naps, but there was little sleeping involved. He was never serious about any of the women; they were conveniences. Some of them had professional success, while others were just passing through.

Even by the lenient, boys-will-be-boys standards of the time, this was outrageous behavior, but Zanuck indulged in it with impunity. And in truth it was nothing new. Myrna Loy said that Zanuck always gave her the cold shoulder because when she had been a starlet at Warners she had opened a door to find "a sort of half-star at Warners sitting on his lap. . . . Maybe he never forgave me for that. I used to tease him about it, which didn't help matters. He had enough trouble on that score. His wife, Virginia, used to invade his office wielding a pistol."

The casting couch was probably invented by the ancient Greeks, but it was also a nominal part of the Hollywood culture. "Zanuck was a very complex man," said Evie Johnson. "A very difficult man to judge. He certainly did things that you wouldn't expect a man in his position to do.

"But this is the way it was. I thought Virginia was wonderful, a lot of fun and a wonderful hostess. She loved to have parties and show people a good time. And she had to put up with a lot from Darryl. But that was part of the deal. What were these women going to do? They're up against the most beautiful women in the world. Were they going to take their clothes, leave Bel-Air and go home to mother? I don't think so.

"The worst part of it was that a man could do it, but a woman? It was not a good idea. Word got out real fast, as it tends to. There wasn't much a wife could do about it. When it came to sex, Hollywood was a very male-oriented place."

This attitude permeated Hollywood. Joe Schenck, the chairman of Fox, had been married to Norma Talmadge, but after she divorced him because she had fallen in love with Gilbert Roland, Schenck became Uncle Joe to a lengthy procession of beautiful women. In July 1947, the screenwriter and biographer Gene Fowler wrote a letter to Schenck, ostensibly about selling his most recent book to Fox, but he soon digressed: "When I think of women, it interferes with everything else. My doctor says it is very dangerous for me to do this. As soon as I am able to get out of the house, I am coming right over to Fox with a police escort to discuss matters of sex with the world's greatest expert."

Schenck replied with a touch of coyness: "Just one word of advice. When you reach a certain age, and you are very much younger than I am, we must not think of any one thing too much. Your observation about a certain thought being likely to interfere with everything else is quite correct. When you sort of spread your emotions thinly you can enjoy them better and for a longer period of time."

Zanuck's devotion to his particular corporate perk led Irene Mayer Selznick to declare, "Thank God [Zanuck is] a gentile. Otherwise he'd give the Jews a bad name."

At 6:30 p.m., Zanuck would head for the barbershop, where Sam Silver would shave him again, and then it was off to the steam room. After that there was a plunge in the pool and a massage, followed by a quick nap, then dinner. About nine p.m. he would go into the projection room and watch rushes from the six or seven films being shot on the Fox lot, giving notes to Barbara McLean about favored takes. After that, he'd watch a movie or two made by other studios, in order to keep an eye on the competition. If the movies were good, Zanuck was attentive. If he got bored, he'd drop off into a sound sleep or look around for something to distract him. This was the cue for a practical joke, as in switching a different set of false teeth with the ones that a regular projection room attendee liked to pop out of his mouth when watching a movie.

Then came late-night story conferences with writers that could begin as late as midnight and go till three or four in the morning. It was difficult for the writers, most of whom came to work at nine or ten in the morning, but they had to acclimate themselves to Zanuck's particular work habits. After that, it was time for the ride home.

Surrounding him at all times was an almost palpable electric hum amplified by short man's disease—Zanuck acted as if he were six feet four. He played polo aggressively, but then, he did almost everything aggressively.

Polo occupied him three times a week. Although he had been riding since he was a child and felt comfortable with horses, he was not a great player, but he made up in courage what he lacked in skill. "I used to plow into him on the polo field," said the writer-producer Sy Bartlett. "He would come back at you—hard! He was a tiger, a scrappy bulldog."

Zanuck's obsession with polo began in 1932, and before long he was playing with Will Rogers and Raymond Griffith, who had both been playing for years. Rogers and Zanuck were only rated as one-goal players, but Zanuck meant to get better fast. He began timing vacations so he could go to Europe with Laddie Sanford, a polo champion and Palm Beach scion who had married the Fox leading lady Mary Duncan.

Zanuck's obsession with polo began a strange habit of hiring athletes at Fox, perhaps hoping that some of their physical expertise would rub off on their employer. Aidan Roark, an Irishman who played polo on Zanuck's team, was put on the studio payroll. The screenwriter Philip Dunne observed that Roark's "function was to hit the ball up to Darryl so that the boss, an aggressive but only average performer on the field, could score a lot." Sometimes these men would be rewarded with jobs that raised eyebrows—Otto Lang, Zanuck's ski instructor, became a producer, although he was invariably assigned to pictures with a strong director, more or less negating the need for a producer.

Similarly, Zanuck sparred with a Stanford graduate named Fidel la Barba, a flyweight champion who habitually pulled his punches when sparring with his boss. Otherwise, Philip Dunne observed, "Zanuck wouldn't have survived to produce any movies."

By common consent, the most pointless of these hires was Aidan Roark, the ten-goal man. It soon became obvious that, despite his skills on horseback, Roark was quite stupid. Zanuck managed to convince himself that Roark was still a plus. "If Aidan understands a script, it should be crystal clear to a ten-year old kid in the front seat of a movie," he told one assistant. "Anyway, think what it means to our prestige, having a ten-goal man on our payroll."

Roark lost his job because of a memo he sent to Zanuck regarding a script. "This is a machinegun-paced comedy that seems to drag a little," Roark wrote.

"Jesus," said Zanuck, "that's the first time I've ever seen anyone do a U-turn in the middle of a sentence."

Despite its reputation as a rich man's plaything, polo is a genuinely dangerous sport. In December 1941, Zanuck's carefree days with the sport ended. It was only a practice game, but the ball came flying at Zanuck's head. To protect himself, he raised his mallet to block the missile. The ball struck his hand, breaking it, and the mallet bounced back and hit Zanuck in the face, breaking his nose and gashing his face. Richard Zanuck remembered coming into the bathroom to find his father bending over the tub, thick clots of blood dripping from his face onto the white porcelain. "It was like a slaughterhouse," the younger Zanuck said.

Zanuck tried to laugh it off until a doctor who was providentially visiting the house told him medical attention was mandatory. The doctor set the nose, taped up his face, and left slits in the bandages for Zanuck's eyes and mouth, making sure to leave enough room for a cigar.

Virginia Zanuck's response can be imagined, and her reaction was duplicated by the Fox board of directors. Shortly afterward, Zanuck donated his twenty Argentine polo ponies to West Point, taking $1 for each of them as token payment. After the war, he again took up polo, but in a less aggressive spirit. He ultimately drifted away from the sport.

After polo, he took up the less dangerous game of croquet, but his style remained cutthroat, which is pretty much the norm in a game widely misinterpreted as an overly genteel activity for garden parties. He converted the lawn of his Palm Springs house into a world-class croquet court, and it quickly became the acknowledged center of California croquet.

The Palm Springs property contained two houses—the main house and a large guesthouse in the back, by the swimming pool. The living room of the guesthouse featured a bountiful display of Zanuck's hunting trophies, which rather presupposed that none of his guests were anti-hunting.

The most frequent croquet players included Moss Hart, who had been part of the East Coast croquet contingent that included Harpo Marx, Alexander Woolcott, and Herbert Bayard Swope. It was Moss Hart who introduced Zanuck to the sport.

"Until then," Zanuck said, "I always thought of it as a kid's game. I was soon to realize it was one of the most difficult and scientific sports in the world. Strategy is much more important than accurate hitting. It's like chess. The game is not just to go through the wickets but to cripple your opponent." Actually, the way that Zanuck played the game centered on crushing his opponent's spirit.

The croquet court was cut every other day and watered with a roving sprinkler until it played like a putting green at Augusta. Balls were imported from England, and the best players all had custom mallets. (Zanuck's mallet had his initials carved on top of the grip.) For games that stretched into the night, Zanuck first lined up cars with headlights directed onto the field, but he eventually installed floodlights. Tyrone Power, Mike Romanoff, Howard Hawks, Jean Negulesco, and Sam Goldwyn all became quite expert at the sport, although there was general agreement that Louis Jourdan was the best overall player.

The arguments about croquet were ferocious and could threaten to get physical. "I saw more than one friendship broken," said Zanuck. "People would pick up in the middle of a weekend and leave. I remember Jean Negulesco being so violent—more than once. Jesus, he was cunning—like all Rumanians. He was always complaining that a foul was committed on his ball. Sam Goldwyn and Mike Romanoff practically broke with each other over croquet. I've seen players break a mallet in anger."

Zanuck and Moss Hart generally got along, but not on the croquet court, and their wives were always prepared to get in the middle in case things got murderous. Hart and his wife Kitty Carlisle left a record of their weekends at Ric-Su-Dar in the guest book:

"This is a roundelay, this is a song
Of lunches late and dinners long
Of bitter croquet and games at the table
Of hitting the ball when you're hardly able
To see your partner, much less the wicket,
Of hiding from Darryl way up in some thicket
Of starting at noon and playing all night
Of knowing your strategy never is right."

There was much *sotto voce* conversation about cheating, and there was general agreement that if cheating ever became generally accepted, Sam Goldwyn would win the tournament—a charge Goldwyn strenuously denied. Zanuck refused to acknowledge that such a thing was possible—not on his court. "People would not really cheat," he said, "but they would take terrific advantage of someone else."

Olivia de Havilland came one weekend and found it a very educational experience. "I watched Zanuck play croquet and I learned all about him. He was the strategist. He was not only superb in terms of strategy, he was awfully good as an individual player. He ran the game like a military operation. He took the initiative, the responsibility. As he saw it, he had an absolute right to his position. He knew where every ball was.

He would outwit his opponents in advance. As I watched him I saw the whole shape of the man.

"He had no magnanimity towards anyone he had beaten. In Hollywood it was often a done thing to lose to your boss, and let him feel superior. But anyone who did that with Zanuck—in bed or on the croquet lawn—won nothing but his patronizing contempt."

A natural bent toward competition and winning couldn't be turned off once the players left the court. When Richard Zanuck was a child, Zanuck would play checkers with him, and took some pleasure in beating his son. Similarly, he never gave his son any points at badminton until the boy grew skilled enough to ram the shuttlecock down his father's throat.

Sunday nights were reserved for screenings at the house, usually two or three pictures. If the movie was any good, Zanuck was attentive. If he got bored, he'd reach for his son and start wrestling. "He always won," said Richard, "until the last time. I was about fourteen and I got him in a neck lock and that was the end of the wrestling."

Given Zanuck's workaholic traits, he wasn't around the house a great deal except on weekends, and then croquet and reading scripts could take up a lot of his time. "So far as I was concerned, he was an absentee father and a distant figure during my childhood years," Richard Zanuck would remember. "He was never there when I needed him. It was hard for me to go to him and have a father-son conversation on the most basic levels because his working habits were so strange. Weeks would go by where I would never see him, even though we lived in the same house. I would go to school in the mornings and come back and he would still be sleeping because he had been out late the night before. On weekends he'd leave on Friday night right from the studio and go down to the house at Palm Springs, and we would be left on our own for the weekend. If I had to see my father, I'd come to the office after school."

On rare occasions, Richard remembered throwing a football around with his father, and swimming together, but, he said, "we didn't really have in that sense a family, a normal kind of family, things where parents are there for dinner, and have breakfast together. We didn't operate that way."

Richard Zanuck put the familial pecking order this way: "Darrylin was my father's pet, Susan was Mother's pet, so I was kind of left out, being third. But I had Alma." Alma was Alma Schlatter Diehl, the governess/nurse and designated point person for all things relating to the Zanuck children. They responded with an appropriate level of devotion; at the end of Alma's life—she died in 1989 at the age of ninety-eight—Richard Zanuck would make weekly trips to visit her at her residence in Placentia, California, a three-hour round trip.

Zanuck's expectations for his son were obvious—he wanted a boy in his own image. His ambitions for his girls were, by comparison, nebulous. He seemed to have no particular ambitions for them whatever; if they grew up to be Hollywood wives like his own wife, that would have been fine with Zanuck. Go to high school; go to parties; be pretty; get married.

Everybody agreed that Virginia ran a beautiful house. She was a relaxed hostess, didn't hover, and kept her expectations of her guests to herself. She took sufficient satisfaction in that and in keeping abreast of all the latest gossip. She even went so far as to occasionally host her husband's girlfriends, explaining to one friend that if she didn't it would considerably reduce the list of acceptable guests. "She loved being in on the adventures and misadventures of Hollywood stars," said John O'Grady, a Hollywood detective who worked for Virginia from time to time.

She was naturally adept at responding to the fevered mating habits of stars. One weekend Tyrone Power brought his wife Annabella to

Ric-Su-Dar, and the following weekend he brought his girlfriend Linda Christian, who would become his second wife. Virginia smiled and never gave away the game.

The result of this unusual domestic environment was that Darrylin and Susan became indulged girls around town. "Both of the girls would climb up over the wall of the house to get out late at night and meet boys on the beach," said Martha Newman Ragland, the widow of Alfred Newman. "They were pretty wild."

Virginia Zanuck backed up her husband in almost all things. "Your father comes first, your father comes first, your father comes first," remembered Darrylin Zanuck. "If I heard it once, I heard it 20 times a day." "She scared him a lot of the time," said Richard Zanuck of his mother. "She was about the only person who could. Not because she was so tough, but she knew a lot and put up with a lot."

Whatever frustrations Virginia had because of her husband's unorthodox private life were well hidden; she plunged into the Hollywood social whirl and was close with Edie Mayer Goetz, Louis B. Mayer's daughter and the wife of William Goetz. The two would talk on the phone every morning and at least once more every day, discussing menus, guest lists, and fashion tips along with gossip.

Darryl Zanuck kept tabs on his kids more or less the same way he kept tabs on his employees: through memos. He would write quick appreciations of good grades or castigations of bad grades and leave the notes for the kids, signing the notes "Z." When the kids got home from school, they would read his notes and reply via other notes, and he would read them when he returned in the middle of the night.

"He was a very frightening person a great deal of the time—not just to me, but to everybody—until I had a little age on me," said Richard Zanuck. "He was really intimidating. We were all kind of a little scared of him. He had a quick temper and would get very irritable if we were making too much noise or that kind of thing."

Richard remembered his father hitting him only once. Richard was on the roof of the beach house and was using a curtain rod as a bean shooter. He hit a car on the Pacific Coast Highway; the car swerved and came to a stop. The driver got out and happened to be a police officer. "DZ beat the bejesus out of me with the curtain rod," said Richard.

One of Richard's childhood chums was Irving Thalberg Jr. Richard remembered that he and Thalberg tied Elizabeth Taylor, who was just getting started at MGM, to a beam in the basement of the Zanuck house. Taylor started screaming because she was afraid she was going to be locked in the basement, which brought her nurse into the fray. The nurse slapped Thalberg Jr., which led him and Richard to tie the nurse to another beam.

If Richard was an entitled brat, it was because his father wanted him that way. Richard began selling the *Saturday Evening Post*, hiring four classmates from school to assist in his endeavors. Zanuck's chauffeur would pick up Richard and his friends and drop them at the street corners, while the younger Zanuck kept the studio itself as his territory. He would stand outside the cafeteria and sell magazines. Richard estimated he moved about nine hundred copies per issue. Everyone who passed by bought a copy, if only to curry favor with his father.

"What he did," said Richard, "was instill a certain appreciation for my position and, thanks to his position, a certain recognition and an inheritance of privilege and power. He instilled in me the realization that I had many advantages and that I had a certain responsibility to other people because of my position in the world. . . . He did see me as someone in his own image. He always emphasized . . . that because I was his son I had special talents, I could go 'all the way.'"

Darryl would ask his son for his opinions about scripts as well as finished pictures, and Richard would announce, "It stinks!" in the presence of the men and women who had made the movie. The adult Richard Zanuck was mortified by his behavior as a child, but his father wanted the boy to be definitive. If Richard was going to make movies—and Darryl Zanuck gave every indication that was what he expected the boy to do—he was going to have to be comfortable with the assertion of authority.

Richard Zanuck believed that his father "cared ferociously about his children," but Richard's producing partner David Brown, who also served as the Fox story editor for years, believed that "Darryl was *very* proud of Dick as long as Dick was the kid, because Darryl saw him as an extension of himself. The problems came later."

Zanuck intended that his son should grow up to be the same kind of man as his father. When Richard was fourteen, Sam Silver, the studio barber, showed up at the beach house and told Richard they were taking a ride. They drove to the Fox lot and went to the apartment of Nick Janios, the manager of the commissary. Inside the apartment was what Richard recalled as "this gorgeous dame. And I was scared to death."

Richard wasn't sure what was supposed to happen, so Sam Silver suggested that he just talk to her for a while. The conversation didn't last long. "That was my first experience," said Richard, "and on the way home I was kind of shell-shocked." Finally, Richard asked if Sam was going to get in trouble with his father for what had just happened.

"Jesus," Silver snorted, "you don't think I'd do a thing like this without his instructions." Zanuck never asked his son about the event he had arranged.

Zanuck had been a writer and took pride in his ability to diagnose what would make a given story or script work as a movie. There was an inner circle of writers he trusted—Nunnally Johnson, Philip Dunne, Lamar Trotti—as well as directors—John Ford, Henry King. Nunnally Johnson was a courtly, witty Georgian who had come to Hollywood from journalism, as had dozens of other writers in the early days of sound. Zanuck began working with Johnson at Twentieth Century Pictures, and they quickly grew to respect one another.

"Darryl always thought of himself as a writer," Johnson would say, "although he wasn't. He could hardly spell *cat*. He was an ideas man, pure and simple. We would go to the Brown Derby at two in the morning and look through the early editions of the papers, and he would tear out a story and say, 'How about that?' . . . And by the next morning he would have an outline ready to be turned into a script and handed to a director." With a few years out for starting his own production company, Johnson would work for Zanuck for the majority of his career, gradually assuming more responsibilities—producing successfully, directing less successfully.

Despite Zanuck's high opinion of Ford, he was quite aware of Ford's particular dodges and noted "the kind of thing John Ford does when he is stuck and has run out of plot. In these cases, somebody always sings and you cut to an extreme long shot with slanting shadows." With other directors that he didn't respect as much, he could be peremptory, sometimes savage.

Next to story structure, Zanuck prided himself on his abilities as an editor and was highly respected for his skills. "He cut every picture," said Nunnally Johnson, "[but] it was never without cooperation though. There were very few disputes I ever heard of . . . and there was no question as to who was the man doing the cutting. That was Zanuck."

Even actors, invariably the neediest people on any lot, respected Zanuck. "Brilliant," was the estimation of Ida Lupino, who rarely played nice. "That man could, *had* read every script on the lot; he watched every wardrobe test of every male star, every female star; he could remember— with all the people under contract—that he didn't like a spotted tie on a man in test number three, or he didn't like the cut of a skirt on me in test number four."

Zanuck had enough confidence in his abilities that he didn't feel the need to preview a drama after he cut it—he was particularly proud of the fact that pictures as varied as *Call Northside 777* and *Boomerang* were never previewed at all. Comedy was a different matter. When it came to comedy, he believed that "a sneak preview is practically essential." Zanuck would intentionally let a rough cut of a comedy run long. "We go to a preview expecting the picture to drag and not to screen anything resembling a finished product."

His signature quality was enthusiasm. "I would think that Zanuck, at age two, thought he'd be great," said the writer/producer Samuel Engel. "I don't think he ever had a doubt in his mind about his own capabilities. . . . He wasn't just an optimist, he was completely and totally without fear."

Zanuck liked his cronies. People like George Jessel and Gregory Ratoff were promoted to the rank of producer in the case of the former, and director in the case of the latter. Their real job was to play cards with Zanuck and make him laugh. The through line of all this was a confidence impossible to separate from arrogance and intelligence.

This was the life at 20th Century-Fox before and after World War II, when Zanuck was consistently successful and full of the confidence bred by success. "I think he had high aspirations, but they weren't on any intellectual levels," said Nunnally Johnson. "He had plenty of courage— all the courage in the world—physical and commercial.

"I suppose he had weaknesses, but they were inconsequential."

With all his attention to specific scripts and their attendant problems, Zanuck had unyielding ideas about what made a good movie. "We pay entirely too much attention to good scripts—and not enough attention to good *subjects*. . . . It may sound stupid to say so, but I would rather have a bad script on a great subject than a great script on an ordinary subject. . . . Star power is valueless no matter how big the personalities . . . unless the subject matter in the story stands the test.

"What do I mean by subject matter? I mean stories that are about *something* . . . stories that deal with something more than the usual formula output of most studios."

———

By 1940, Zanuck understood that he needed to broaden Tyrone Power's appeal to include men, so he began alternating Power's romantic comedies with man-of-destiny movies such as *Lloyd's of London* and *In Old Chicago*. Those pictures worked, so Zanuck went further, casting Power as Jesse James opposite Henry Fonda's Frank James. Then came a gangster picture, *Johnny Apollo*, and swashbucklers—a remake of Douglas Fairbanks Sr.'s *The Mark of Zorro*, followed by *Son of Fury* and *The Black Swan*. As career building goes, Zanuck's crafting of Power's rise is a prototypical example.

Power was believable in all of these quite different movies, and his essentially gentle personality made it possible for him to believably play in costume pictures, unlike Clark Gable, whose brusque masculinity made him slightly incongruous in ruffled shirt costume pictures. (Yes, there was *Gone with the Wind*, and he got away with *Mutiny on the Bounty*, but it's Charles Laughton's movie. Gable's turn in *Parnell* was panned, and justifiably so.)

Power's opposite numbers in the Fox pantheon of stars came down to two: Linda Darnell and Gene Tierney. Darnell had begun working at Fox as a teenager and matured into a stunning beauty and a competent actress whose stardom was maintained by careful casting. Starting out in decorative but undemanding parts in *The Mark of Zorro* or *Blood and Sand*, she graduated to bad girl parts in *My Darling Clementine* and *Forever Amber*.

Darnell's best performance came in Joseph L. Mankiewicz's *A Letter to Three Wives*, where she plays a manipulative, much-traveled woman who wants to move onto easy street by marrying the gruff businessman Paul Douglas. Darnell more than holds her own in a difficult part. Darnell's career went into decline when she left Fox in the early 1950s, which was accompanied by a weight gain that is the invariable sign of an actor or actress grown tired of the demands of stardom.

Darnell was an earthy actress, but Gene Tierney personified an ethereal, slightly feline femininity that existed in some rarified realm of her own. She was born in 1920 into a well-to-do family and was educated in private schools in Switzerland and Connecticut. She made her Broadway debut at the age of nineteen and was signed to a contract by Zanuck a year later.

She made an impact in *Tobacco Road* and Josef von Sternberg's *The Shanghai Gesture* and solidified her stardom with Lubitsch's *Heaven Can Wait* and, in 1944, *Laura*. That was followed by a startling turn as a murderess in *Leave Her to Heaven*, Fox's greatest commercial hit of the entire decade; a good performance as a spoiled debutante in *The Razor's Edge*; and a beautifully modulated characterization of longing and loneliness in *The Ghost and Mrs. Muir*. Tierney's quality of being slightly removed enabled her to carry off parts that were often lacking in specific emotional background, as in *Leave Her to Heaven*.

Murdering potential human diversions in order to monopolize your husband might be understandable if the man in question was Tyrone Power. But for Cornel Wilde?

For all of her professional success, Tierney's life was marked by tragedy. Her marriage to the fashion designer Oleg Cassini in 1941 resulted in the birth of a disabled daughter when Tierney contracted German measles from a fan on a publicity tour. (The incident was used, somewhat crudely, as a plot point by Agatha Christie in her novel *The Mirror Crack'd*.) It was an emotional catastrophe from which Tierney never fully recovered. The marriage to Cassini broke up, and Tierney entered into a series of unsuccessful relationships (Spencer Tracy, Ali Khan) interspersed with sanitarium stays.

Robert Wagner, who arrived at 20th Century-Fox in 1950, said that Tierney was his first experience with a performer perennially on the emotional precipice. Tierney still walked like a dancer, as if suspended by invisible wires under her shoulders. Everybody at the studio liked her, and everybody watched her for signs of another breakdown. Darryl Zanuck remained intensely loyal to Tierney and kept her at the studio until 1955, shortly before his own retirement as production chief. She made only three more movies after leaving Fox. A 1960 marriage to a Houston oilman gave her some of the security her personal and professional lives had lacked.

When World War II arrived, many Fox stars signed up. Tyrone Power enlisted in the marines and became an expert pilot in the South Pacific. Henry Fonda enlisted in the navy and also spent most of the war in the South Pacific.

Zanuck was not about to miss all the fun. In January 1942, right after Pearl Harbor, he applied for overseas duty. In September 1942, Zanuck took a leave from the studio to devote his full time to the military.

William Goetz was delegated to run the studio in Zanuck's absence. It was a curious decision on Zanuck's part, if only because he termed Goetz "a thumbtack" (i.e., a bureaucratic functionary). As soon as Goetz moved into his boss's office, he had all the accessories removed—the hunting trophies, the white piano, the George Washington desk. Then he had the characteristic Zanuck green painted over.

Creatively, the first thing Goetz seems to have done was try to cancel *The Ox-Bow Incident*, but William Wellman got word to Zanuck, who instructed Goetz that a deal was a deal, and his agreement with Wellman had to be honored. Goetz grudgingly let the picture proceed.

Initially, Zanuck served as a military attaché to the American Embassy while living at Claridge's during the Blitz. Later he was assigned to Lord Mountbatten's commandos as an observer, and went along on a night raid to France. He was sent to the Aleutian Islands, where he established a unit of combat cameramen. Still later he went to England and Gibraltar. Zanuck kept a diary of his time in battle and out, and published it as *Tunis Expedition*, which got good reviews and remains worthwhile reading, as Zanuck sees battle as an extended 4th of July fireworks display:

"The sky is alive with colored tracer bullets," he wrote. "A Nazi plane crashes nearby. Another explodes in the air and floats down, a mass of brilliant yellow and scarlet flames. . . . [This] is really a battle and I am in it. The excitement of it was like the thrill that possesses one who looks at a dangerous polo spill or a thrilling bullfight."

"We were confident he would be rank-happy and obnoxious," remembered Robert Gordon Edwards, a staff sergeant in Zanuck's Signal

Corps unit. "He turned out to be neither. He was dynamic, aloof, full of nervous energy, and anxious to get into battle. One got the impression these were the most exciting days of his life until then, and he was determined to live them at the utmost pitch. . . . Zanuck was a man of considerable personal courage. Now it is one thing to be brave at twenty, and quite another to be bold at forty, which was Zanuck's age. . . . I never saw him run, break, hesitate or even show signs of deep concern."

For Zanuck, the war was as close as he would ever get to the pioneer experiences of his grandfather, and he was determined to live up to Henry Torpin's example. By the time he emerged from the service, he was a colonel and had been awarded the Legion of Merit. He served with distinction, allowing for a minor kerfuffle that erupted after he returned to the movie business.

Zanuck had asked that his studio salary of $5,000 a week be discontinued while he was in the service, but the board of directors at Fox didn't get around to it for four months while his salary continued, as did the payout from his stock dividends. Those months when he continued to draw his salary and dividends got him investigated for war profiteering. On the other hand, Zanuck never took a salary from the government for his service, ignoring the pay vouchers they sent him.

Zanuck returned to the studio, and there were soon varying stories about the confrontation that led to William Goetz leaving the studio. The most likely has Zanuck returning to his desk and sweeping all of Goetz's scripts onto the floor, declaring them dead on arrival. Whatever happened, Goetz again enlisted the help of his father-in-law and formed International Pictures, which eventually merged with Universal.

When the war was over, Tyrone Power returned to the studio for a lavish welcome home, an adaptation of Somerset Maugham's *The Razor's Edge*. Power plays the seeker of truth Larry Darrell, and Zanuck gives him the finest in luxury surroundings—Gene Tierney as costar, Clifton Webb as a society queen, a gorgeous, surging score by Alfred Newman. It's a strange, haunting novel, and it's a strange, haunting movie as well, despite a sense of strain in the script because of Larry Darrell's inability to articulate just what it is he's after.

The Razor's Edge was expensive but returned a profit, and Power decided to call in his chits and demand a personal project. His choice was *Nightmare Alley*, a scabrous novel by William Lindsay Gresham about a con artist who descends into alcoholic carny squalor. Zanuck could see financial disaster moving toward him, but Power believed Zanuck owed him one, and Zanuck grudgingly agreed. He struggled to find a way to make Power's character at least slightly sympathetic. "Nobody is all good or all bad," Zanuck noted in a script conference, "and there must be a shading in Stan's character so that once or twice in the script we see him do a decent thing."

The result was a fascinating downer that showcased all of Power's charm as well as latent self-loathing that would become part of his acting repertoire—"The secret of charm," Power once said, "is bullshit." The problem was that Power's audience didn't want to see him playing a man who ends up as a drunken geek. The picture showed a dead loss of $500,000, but over time it has become one of the actor's signature pictures, and it pointed the way to his other gem of unreliable sleaze, *Witness for the Prosecution*.

The flop of *Nightmare Alley* didn't affect the most-favored-nation status that Power had with his boss. "Ty liked Zanuck," said Evie Johnson. "But Ty liked everybody." With that beau geste out of the way, Zanuck went back to showcasing Power as the audience wanted to see him, primarily in a series of luxurious swashbucklers: *Captain from Castile, Prince of Foxes, The Black Rose*. These were all well-produced, entertaining movies, but as the 1940s segued to the 1950s, Power's commercial appeal began to slowly decline in the wake of younger, more *au courant* actors such as Marlon Brando and Montgomery Clift.

Power was also having off-screen troubles, largely brought on by a disastrous marriage to Linda Christian. "She was a piece of work," said Evie Johnson. "Kind of wild, but definitely fun. Wonderful looking, a very exciting woman. But she was terrible for Ty. I think she was madly in love with him, and he was madly in love with her . . . for a while. Then he cooled off. She had Edmund Purdom, and he had someone else as well."

Unbeknownst to their respective spouses, Power and Evie Johnson had continued their occasional affair. "I always had the urge with Ty. And I followed that urge. We were very good friends and lovers over a period of I don't know how many years. Between marriages and during marriages."

Power's divorce from Linda Christian drained him of most of his cash, and he left Fox in the early 1950s to take on serious stage roles and more lucrative profit-sharing movie deals than Zanuck would allow. Power gradually found his sea legs as an independent star in such huge hits as *The Eddy Duchin Story* and the aforementioned *Witness for the Prosecution*. He was only forty-four years old when he died of a heart attack on the set of *Solomon and Sheba*—a great star who wanted to be a great actor.

Zanuck invariably trended toward a varied program, but he always made sure to produce musicals. Between 1940 and 1949, the studio turned out over sixty of them, many starring the studio's cute blondes—Betty Grable, Alice Faye, June Haver. They were almost always profitable, sometimes wildly so, but Zanuck seemed slightly embarrassed by them—he made sure that none of his personal productions were musicals. There was a sense that he regarded movies such as *Boomerang, Panic in the Streets,* and high-minded personal productions such as *The Grapes of Wrath* and *The Razor's Edge* as penance for making so much money on musicals.

The formula for a Fox musical was 180 degrees from the equally successful MGM musicals, which tended to be redolent of sophisticates standing on balconies overlooking Park Avenue. Besides the Fox blonde, the score would be full of hummable tunes by the severely underrated Harry Warren. The leading man would be someone like Don Ameche or John Payne and, later, Dan Dailey—competent and charming, but never so overwhelming that they might distract from the leading lady. And the setting would be someplace exotic: Rio, Argentina, Miami, Sun Valley. (The location footage would derive entirely from the second unit, but it would be there nonetheless.)

Along the way there would be what can only be termed a profusion of high-end specialty acts: the Nicholas Brothers, Charlotte Greenwood and her high kick, Edward Everett Horton's nervous wreck, the uncategorizable side show of Carmen Miranda. Then there was the occasional radio favorite whose fame had a limited shelf life: Phil "Take It or Leave It" Baker, one of the stars of the certifiably insane *The Gang's All Here,* was the host of a then currently popular radio quiz show, which meant that Baker's presence has had viewers scratching their heads ever since, say, 1955.

In posterity's eyes, the Nicholas Brothers are particularly spectacular, with dance moves that combine tap, acrobatics, and leaps that approach parkour. After years playing at the Cotton Club and appearing on Broadway in "Babes in Arms," the brothers made *Down Argentina Way* and two other Fox musicals the same year and were placed under contract. It was a good deal for Fayard and Harold Nicholas because they had plenty of free time for club dates when they weren't needed at the studio. When Fayard got drafted, the studio rushed *Stormy Weather* into production so there could be one more Nicholas Brothers movie before the act got broken up.

The brothers came by their acrobatics naturally—Harold Nicholas was named after Harold Lloyd. For the most part, the brothers did their own choreography, although they worked closely with Nick Castle, a tap specialist and the dance director for most of their films. It was Castle who staged and directed their sequences to emphasize the brothers' close floor work and amazing athleticism. "Nick Castle *presented* them," said Bruce Goldstein of the Film Forum, a friend of both of the brothers. Castle became a good friend and was the only white person invited when Harold married Dorothy Dandridge.

The brothers displayed a free-flowing virtuosity that simply doesn't exist anymore. One move in particular astonishes modern dancers: their shared ability to rise from a complete split without using their hands. "You can't rise up from a split *on ice*," Gregory Hines told Bruce Goldstein with a touch of wonder.

After the war, the brothers broke up. Fox had made them cabaret stars and they toured throughout Europe and South America. As with many Black musicians, Harold found that he loved Europe because he was treated, not as a Black artist, but as an artist. He wanted to live there and Fayard didn't because he had a family in America. The result was that they stopped working together for seven years.

Fox's showcasing of Fayard and Harold Nicholas, as well as producing movies such as *Stormy Weather* and *No Way Out,* marks Darryl Zanuck as an early progressive in terms of the movie industry's attitude toward race relations, which could be characterized as deeply hesitant until the subject became safe in the late 1950s.

The single most important ingredient of the Fox musicals was Technicolor, so bright it could scald the optic nerve. The title of one of the great Fox musicals aptly sums up their anything-for-a-good-time charm: *The Gang's All Here*, i.e., something for everyone.

If a Fox musical wasn't set in some exotic city where nobody in the audience had actually been, it was likely to be set in the past. For Zanuck, nostalgia sold. *Hello, Frisco, Hello*; *The Dolly Sisters*; *The I Don't Care Girl*; and many others were all set in the past. George Custen did the math and totaled 81 of 371 20th Century-Fox films made in the 1940s—a full 22 percent—were set in the era between the wars, or earlier. A third of these movies were musicals. This compared with a mere 12 percent of similar vehicles at Warner Bros., of which only 15 percent were musicals.

But there were some films that were completely up to date—*Sun Valley Serenade* and *Orchestra Wives* both starred Glenn Miller and his orchestra. These were essentially jukebox movies featuring Miller's great hits, but Zanuck made sure to add a little something to the mix, extra value in the forms of the Nicholas Brothers and Dorothy Dandridge dancing to "Chattanooga Choo-Choo." Each of these films earned more than $2 million in domestic rentals on very reasonable costs.

Zanuck also took pains to upgrade his product by hiring Rodgers and Hammerstein shortly after the Broadway opening of *Oklahoma!*. Their assignment was to write a musical version of *State Fair*—the only original score they wrote for a movie. It did well when it was released in 1945, but it didn't make any more money than the homegrown, entirely typical Fox musical *The Dolly Sisters* did that same year. *State Fair* may have had Rodgers and Hammerstein, but *The Dolly Sisters* had Betty Grable *and* June Haver.

Hammerstein was still in the fold a year later, setting the lyrics for Jerome Kern's last original score for the ambitious *Centennial Summer*,

FROM TOP: William Fox, née Wilhelm Fuchs, born in Hungary and raised on the Lower East Side of New York, ran his studio as an act of belligerent revenge on a world that didn't take him or his ambitions seriously. • Theda Bara may not have been subtle but her huge eyes and willingness to appear in outre costumes made her undeniably effective. She made a great deal of money for William Fox.

FROM TOP: Pearl White became famous by starring in serials such as *The Perils of Pauline* (1914) and *The Exploits of Elaine* (1915), but signed with Fox to get away from typecasting. She spent a few years with Fox making features, then returned to serials until her retirement in 1924. • Tom Mix and his horse Tony were two of the primary building blocks with which William Fox constructed his studio. Mix was short but well proportioned and handsome, and he moved well. His Fox westerns enthralled adolescents of all ages for more than a decade.

FROM TOP: George O'Brien in John Ford's *The Iron Horse* (1924), made on location in Nevada in largely frigid conditions, proved an enormous financial success for the Fox studio as well as an early marker of Ford's greatness as it told the story of the uniting of America through the transcontinental railroad. • William Fox and Mary (Mrs. John) Ford attending the premiere of *The Iron Horse*.

ABOVE: Buck Jones in Frank Borzage's *Lazybones* (1925), one of the silent films that began the director's reign as the great romanticist of his era.

OPPOSITE FROM TOP: William Fox brought F. W. Murnau to Hollywood and gave him carte blanche to make *Sunrise* (1927). Here, Murnau (knickers, sitting in front of the cameras) is shown with his camera crew. Cinematographers Karl Struss (glasses, standing by camera on far left) and Charles Rosher (wearing a hat and vest next to Struss) won the first Academy Award for cinematography. • The late 1920s proved to be the period of William Fox's greatest commercial and critical successes. Here, Victor McLaglen and Edmund Lowe play a couple of carousing marines in Raoul Walsh's *What Price Glory?* (1926), a huge success that spawned several sequels.

RW-20 60

ABOVE: Star-crossed lovers provided Fox with one of the decade's great hits in *7th Heaven* (1927), propelling Janet Gaynor and Charles Farrell into a long series of costarring efforts that helped the studio compete with Paramount and MGM.

OPPOSITE FROM TOP: The now-lost *4 Devils* marked the end of the honeymoon between Murnau and William Fox, as the studio added talking sequences by other hands ("Staged by A.H. Van Beuren & A.F. Erickson") to Murnau's silent footage • Charles Farrell and Mary Duncan play one of Murnau's most rhapsodic love scenes in *City Girl* (1930), a silent film that was barely released, a casualty of sound.

The Picture of a Thousand Thrills!

4 Devils

WILLIAM FOX PRESENTS

A JANET GAYNOR
Talking Picture

4 DEVILS

with

MARY DUNCAN   NANCY DREXEL
CHARLES MORTON   BARRY NORTON
FARRELL MACDONALD

All talking their parts on Fox Movietone ~

Directed by ~ F.W. MURNAU

Adapted by ~ BERTHOLD VIERTAL
from the novel by ~ Herman Bang
Staged by ~ A.H. Van Beuren & A.F. Erickson
Dialog by ~~ John Hunter Booth

On the poster:

$5,000.00 REWARD!

"The Cisco Kid"

HOLDUP AND ROBBERY
of
POSTAL STAGE

This reward will be paid
for the capture of this bandit
DEAD or ALIVE

ABOVE: Raoul Walsh began directing as well as starring in the fanciful western *In Old Arizona* (1929), but had to leave after an accident cost him an eye. Irving Cummings took over direction and Warner Baxter took over the part of the Cisco Kid with a spectacularly bad approximation of a Mexican accent. It was a great hit in the early days of sound and Baxter got an Oscar for Best Actor. Go figure.

OPPOSITE FROM TOP: In the early 1930s, Fox's biggest stars were Janet Gaynor and Will Rogers. Here, on the set of *Judge Priest,* are Rogers (in white suit) with director John Ford (left), humorist Irvin S. Cobb (right), and visitor Dorothy Arzner, the only woman director in American movies in the 1930s. • Anne Shirley and Will Rogers in John Ford's *Steamboat Round the Bend* (1935), Rogers's last film before the plane crash that took his life.

OPPOSITE: The two founders of Twentieth Century Pictures: Joseph Schenck and Darryl Zanuck.

FROM TOP: Darryl Zanuck just about the time he merged Twentieth Century Pictures with Fox to form 20th Century-Fox. • Before she developed a genuine dislike of Darryl Zanuck and everything he represented, Alice Faye was one of the most radiant stars of her era. Here she is at the height of her career.

OPPOSITE FROM TOP: Gregg Toland's unadorned photography of John Ford's *The Grapes of Wrath* (1940) was modeled on the Dust Bowl photographs of Dorothea Lange, and the result was a classic that gave Henry Fonda the part of a lifetime. • Alice Faye—determined—and Carmen Miranda—an explosion in a wax fruit factory—in *Weekend in Havana* (1941), one of the wildly colorful Fox musicals set in an exotic setting but made on a soundstage.

ABOVE: John Ford lining up a shot on the huge set of *How Green Was My Valley,* with cameraman Arthur Miller leaning over him.

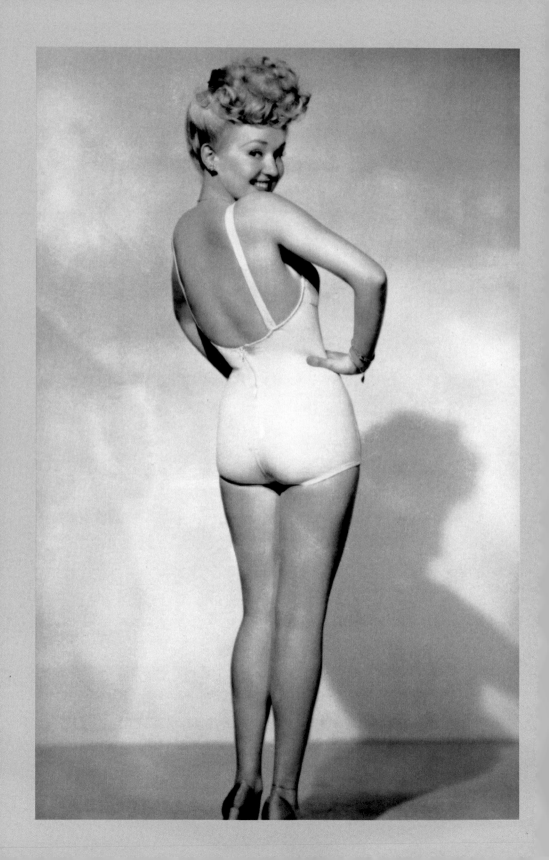

OPPOSITE AND LEFT:
Everybody knows Betty Grable, if only for this publicity still that defined what American soldiers thought they were fighting for. But most stars are made, not born. As proof, here is a considerably different Grable in 1930, in a Fox picture called *Let's Go Places*.

BELOW: Beginning in World War II, Darryl Zanuck produced a series of tough, innovative noirs with stars such as Victor Mature, Richard Widmark, and Dana Andrews. Here, Mature looks properly bedeviled by the casting of Betty Grable in *I Wake Up Screaming* (1941), her only drama for 20th Century-Fox.

ABOVE: Genuine candids of stars are rare, but this one is authentic: During World War II, Tyrone Power enlisted in the marines as a pilot. Here he is relaxing between flights in a tent on Okinawa.

FROM TOP: A rogue's gallery of high society reprobates, including Clifton Webb and Vincent Price, a stalwart detective played by Dana Andrews, and an enigmatic beauty played by Gene Tierney. It could only be *Laura* (1944). •
The highest grossing Fox movie of the 1940s was a Technicolor noir about a psychotic murderess played by Gene Tierney. John Stahl's *Leave Her to Heaven* (1946) made up in intensity what it lacked in credibility. Here, the icy Tierney prepares to bump off her husband's little brother, played by Darryl Hickman.

OPPOSITE FROM TOP: In his youth a Broadway dancer regarded as competition for Fred Astaire, Clifton Webb became an accidental movie star with *Laura*. Darryl Zanuck cemented Webb's stardom by crafting a series of vehicles in which Webb played a series of sniffy, persnickety snobs ranging from Elliot Templeton in *The Razor's Edge* to *Mr. Belvedere*. • Darryl Zanuck believed that a movie that worked once would work two or three times. *Three Little Girls In Blue* (1946) starred Vivian Blaine (left) and June Haver in a pleasant musical about three sisters out to get wealthy husbands. Sound familiar? It's a remake of *Moon Over Miami* and still later was modified as *How to Marry a Millionaire*.

ABOVE: Darryl Zanuck brought Ernst Lubitsch to 20th Century-Fox in 1942, and he responded with *Heaven Can Wait* (1943), one of his best films. A serious heart attack sidelined Lubitsch for a time, but he made a welcome comeback with *Cluny Brown*. He died shortly after beginning production on *That Lady in Ermine*, which was completed by Otto Preminger. Betty Grable didn't really fit into the director's stylized never-never-land aesthetic and the film failed.

FROM TOP: A glum Alice Faye with Dana Andrews in *Fallen Angel* (1945), the movie that sent her out of 20th Century-Fox in a fury at Darryl Zanuck's cutting some of her scenes in order to make room for Linda Darnell. • *The Ghost and Mrs. Muir* (1947) was a romantic love story about a lonely widow and a ghost that succeeded because of Joseph L. Mankiewicz's subtle direction, a stunning musical score by Bernard Herrmann, and restrained performances from Rex Harrison and Gene Tierney.

FROM TOP: Tyrone Power was the king of the Fox lot, adored by his coworkers and certainly one of the handsomest men to ever appear before a camera. Here he is with Jean Peters in *Captain from Castile* (1947), one of the lavish swashbucklers that constituted a primary pillar of his career. • Preston Sturges, outfitted in a fez and an incomprehensible sport coat, directs Rex Harrison in *Unfaithfully Yours* (1948). Sturges lost Fox a great deal of money with this film and *The Beautiful Blonde from Bashful Bend*, but Darryl Zanuck didn't seem to mind—Sturges was a flamboyant character who amused his employer.

ABOVE: Darryl Zanuck looking quietly fierce while holding the Best Picture Oscar for *All About Eve* (1950).

OPPOSITE FROM TOP: Robert Wagner (far left), Barbara Stanwyck, and Clifton Webb in *Titanic* (1953), Fox's first spin with the story and a good picture in its own right. • Zanuck squeezed one more hit out of Betty Grable by pairing her with younger stars Lauren Bacall and Marilyn Monroe in *How to Marry a Millionaire* (1953).

OLD STANDARD SCREEN

CINEMASCOPE

FROM TOP: *The Robe* (1953) was the first film in CinemaScope, which helped 20th Century-Fox survive the very difficult period of the 1950s. The film also confirmed the stardom of Richard Burton and gave Victor Mature's career a fresh burst of oxygen. • A publicist's rough approximation of the difference between the screen ratio of the standard screen and CinemaScope, which actually understates the width of the latter.

FROM TOP: Director Leo McCarey working on a scene in *An Affair to Remember* (1957) with Cary Grant and Deborah Kerr (producer Jerry Wald is on the right), and a close-up from the film's final scene.

OPPOSITE FROM TOP: Joseph L. Mankiewicz struggled through a year of production to breathe life into *Cleopatra* (1963). The result was a four-hour slog that nearly bankrupted 20th Century-Fox and brought Darryl and Richard Zanuck riding to the rescue of the studio, if not the movie, which was beyond help. • Darryl Zanuck on the set of *The Longest Day* (1962) with Robert Mitchum, who seems much less amused than Zanuck.

ABOVE: Julie Andrews in *The Sound of Music* (1965), the musical that caught the last wave of Hollywood tradition and convinced the industry that what the public wanted was more musicals. It didn't work out that way.

FROM TOP: Rex Harrison in *Doctor Dolittle* (1967), another would-be musical spectacular for the family trade that failed miserably. • Julie Andrews in *Star!* (1968), a slightly off-key musical that lost much of the money that *The Sound of Music* had earned.

FROM TOP: George Roy Hill's spirited direction of William Goldman's funny, occasionally cutesy script for *Butch Cassidy and the Sundance Kid* (1969) made the film one of the last westerns to prove an across-the-board critical and commercial success. The stars, a couple of aspiring kids named Newman and Redford, didn't hurt either. • Alan Ladd Jr., the studio head who returned 20th Century-Fox to its status as a leading Hollywood studio.

FROM TOP: Fred Zinnemann directed *Julia* (1977) with all his usual attention to behavioral nuance that made his films compelling, and drew convincing performances from Jane Fonda and Vanessa Redgrave. • *The Turning Point* (1977) is a sisterhood-is-powerful movie about two ballet dancers, one retired (Shirley MacLaine), one hanging on (Anne Bancroft). Great conflict, a young Mikhail Baryshnikov, and a moving ending that almost makes you forget a ridiculous catfight that precedes the ultimate reunion.

FROM TOP: Seventy years after *7th Heaven*, another set of star-crossed lovers, this time played by Leonardo DiCaprio and Kate Winslet, once again provided a huge success for Fox in James Cameron's *Titanic* (1997). • One of the last films made by 20th Century-Fox as a free-standing corporation was *Ford v Ferrari*, a taut throwback about racing and the men who live within it. Tightly written, performed with commitment by Christian Bale and Matt Damon, and directed for maximum physical and emotional impact by James Mangold—Darryl Zanuck would have loved the film.

a fairly obvious attempt to replicate the success of MGM's *Meet Me in St. Louis*. The close association with Hammerstein would bear great fruit a decade later when Fox produced the successful film versions of such classic Rodgers and Hammerstein shows as *The King and I* and *Carousel*.

Zanuck might have been embarrassed by musicals, but he spent nearly as much time on them as he did *How Green Was My Valley*. In September 1940, he fired off a memo for the film that became *That Night in Rio* which outlines what became Carmen Miranda's primary schtick when not singing or dancing. "Your handling of Carmen [Miranda] was good except that she does not need to talk nearly as much as she does in English. You should confine her English to one or two line speeches and if she has to explode, she should go into Portuguese—ending up with a denunciation of one or two words in English."

These pictures could generally be made for just under or just over a million dollars, although some of them, such as Busby Berkeley's *The Gang's All Here*, ran over $2 million. They could return double their costs in America alone.

Zanuck was probably too attached to action and melodrama to be equally attached to the mistaken identities and cross-purposes that constitute the plots of most musicals, but he didn't slough them off. Zanuck's story notes for Charles Lederer's first draft script for *Gentleman Prefer Blondes* are revelatory. The other people in the meeting included director Howard Hawks, producer Sol Siegel, and Lederer, but Zanuck seems to have done all the talking and all of the thinking.

"We are going to eliminate the first 23 pages of the script," announced Zanuck at the start of the conference. "Our story will start, then on the dock, scene 14, page 24. . . .

"I want to say that I think this is some of the best dialogue I have ever read in any script, and I hope you will be able to retain most of it in the final version. . . . This is not a satire. It is a solid and honest comedy in the same terms as *I Was a Male War Bride*, for instance. In *War Bride*, the audience knew that our people had a very real problem, and they never lost sight of that no matter how ludicrous the comedy seemed at times.

"Therefore, these two things, Dorothy's romance, and her genuine affection for Lorelei must be solidly grounded in our story. . . . In order to accomplish these two things we must be willing, if necessary to sacrifice comedy in these particular scenes. . . .

"Opening: After the 20th Century-Fox insignia but before any titles come on we should see the following scene:

"We are on the deck of the boat, shooting down to the dock. We see passengers milling around, etc. Camera comes down to the Olympic team standing in line, being checked in.

"One guy, staring off as though hypnotized, nudges the man next to him; he turns, looks off, gets that hypnotized look, nudges the man next to him. This routine continues to the end of the line, so that we have a line of guys all staring off in the same direction. When the last man turns and looks off we cut to what they are looking at: Lorelei and Dorothy coming down the dock, heading for the passport officials. One Olympic says to another, 'Suppose the ship hit an iceberg and sank, which one would you save from drowning?' The other Olympic replies, 'Those girls wouldn't drown. Something about them tells me they can't sink.'

"From this we go to the Titles. . . . At the end of the titles we should be at Scene 17, Page 26."

Zanuck's opening scene was replaced by an even better idea—the splashy musical number "Little Girls from Little Rock," which led into the titles. Aside from cutting the first twenty-three pages of the script and rewriting the beginning of the picture, Zanuck also chose which musical numbers would be included and a multitude of other details that made the movie what it was. The fact that the main title proclaims the film to be "Howard Hawks' *Gentlemen Prefer Blondes*" has led many ardent auteurist critics to ignore the fact that Zanuck—and choreographer Jack Cole, who directed the musical numbers—had at least as much to do with the film as Hawks.

———————————

Alice Faye often seemed slightly depressed, or maybe it was just the deadpan that seemed to synch up so perfectly with her throaty contralto. What was certain was that she didn't get along with Darryl Zanuck. In later years, she referred to the studio as "Penitentiary Fox" and her boss as "Mister Zanuck." She had been the reigning queen of musicals on the lot since Zanuck had taken over the studio, with hits such as *In Old Chicago, Alexander's Ragtime Band, Rose of Washington Square, Lillian Russell, Hello, Frisco, Hello*, and, of course, *The Gang's All Here*.

She had been agitating to do something besides musicals when Zanuck cast her in a 1945 noir titled *Fallen Angel*. It wasn't a great part— Faye plays a meek heiress—but what enraged Faye was Zanuck cutting some of her scenes in order to better feature Faye's costar Linda Darnell, in whom Zanuck had developed an interest. As Faye recounted it, the day the film was finished, she left the set without stopping at her dressing room. "I dropped the key at the gate," she said, "and told them to give it to Mister Zanuck. He knew what he could do with it, too!"

The studio put out a story that she had turned down the part of Aunt Cissie in *A Tree Grows in Brooklyn* as well as Sophie in *The Razor's Edge*, but Faye said that was untrue. "I would have loved to have done [Aunt Cissie] and I wasn't able to play Sophie because I was doing something else at the time. I think Mister Zanuck put that out about me turning down roles. *He* turned them down!"

Faye didn't make another movie for more than fifteen years, and when she did it was back at Fox, when Zanuck was otherwise engaged in Europe. The picture was a mediocre remake of *State Fair*, but the main selling point as far as Faye was concerned may have been that Zanuck was no longer running the place.

By the time Faye made *Fallen Angel*, Betty Grable was first among equals on the Fox lot. Off-screen, she was a lot like she was on-screen: unpretentious and hardworking, unless it was opening day for the race-tracks, in which case she would close down whatever picture she was working on and go off to watch the horses. Zanuck would never have allowed any other star to get away with this, but Grable was the mortgage lifter for the entire studio.

Grable had been working in the movies since she was a teenager and seems to have been installed at Fox as a means of keeping Alice Faye in line or, if things went south, replacing her. She was the right woman at the right studio at the right time. She had a great smile and projected an uncompli-cated version of the girl next door. Besides all that, there was a war on. It was no accident that Zanuck made a Grable film titled *Pin-Up Girl*. In 1946 and 1947, the Treasury Department would list Grable as America's highest salaried woman, at $300,000 a year. Grable would be the undisputed queen of the lot until the late 1940s, when simple charms displayed in simple films no longer meshed with an increasingly complicated time.

Beyond Zanuck's sensitivity—or insensitivity—to the talent on hand, his most important characteristic was the fact that he took responsibility for his own decisions. Milton Sperling promoted a noir script that every-one agreed would be a great change of pace for Grable. The film was pre-viewed under the title *Hot Spot*. The audience thought they were coming to see a Betty Grable musical, and the dark noir made them mutinous. The result was a disaster. Sperling figured it was going to be his turn to walk the plank, but Zanuck refused to let other executives put the blame on Sperling. "Whatever he did, I told him to do. It's my responsibility, not his. I okayed the script, I okayed the cast and the budget."

Zanuck took the picture back to the editing room and changed the title to the bloodcurdling *I Wake Up Screaming*, which definitively told the audience the picture wasn't a musical. It didn't make much money, but it didn't lose any, either. It was the first and last time Betty Grable worked in anything but a musical.

Zanuck's brilliance came into play on his serious prestige movies, as he carefully guided the writers through the dramatic shoals. The first script of *How Green Was My Valley* was written by Ernest Pascal, and it displeased Zanuck: "This is a revolutionary type of story, therefore, our treatment should not be revolutionary. Now it fumbles around and I get the impression that we are trying to do an English *Grapes of Wrath* and prove that the mine owners were very mean and that the laborers finally won out over them. All this might be fine if it were happening today, like *The Grapes of Wrath*, but this is years ago and who gives a damn? The smart thing to do is to try to keep all of the rest in the background and focus mainly on the human story as seen through Huw's eyes."

Philip Dunne's rewrite addressed Zanuck's concerns, but there was still a structural problem—a third act in which Huw becomes an adult and faces some of the same issues his parents had. "Now is the time for us to start talking in terms of drama and audience. I was bored to death by the repetition of the strike business and of starving babies, etc, etc. It all seems old hash to me." Zanuck decided to jettison Huw as an adult and keep everything in the past tense. John Ford directed the film with his usual fine eye for photographic beauty and emotional heartbeat. *How Green Was My Valley* beat out *Citizen Kane* as the Best Film of 1941. "When I think of what I got away with . . . and won the Academy Award with the picture, it is really astonishing," said Zanuck in retrospect. "Not only did we drop five or six characters, but we eliminated the most controversial element in the book, which was the labor and capital battle in connection with the strikes."

Zanuck never stayed still for long, because he couldn't afford to. Other than his time away for the war, 20th Century-Fox in the 1940s was a one-man show. "Every creative decision was either authorized, or okayed, or created by me," he asserted. "Every script! There was no individual, no executive between me and the back lot. I was The Executive. I decided whether we made something or didn't make it." For the initial draft of *Laura*, he objected to the dialogue—"very ordinary"—and instructed the writers to construct dialogue for Waldo Lydecker like that of Monty Wooley in *The Man Who Came to Dinner*—"sarcastic and brutally funny remarks."

He also put his finger on the script's primary problem: "Laura is a mess. She is neither interesting nor attractive, and I doubt if any first-rate actress would ever play her. As it is now she seems terribly naive—a complete sucker . . . unless you work hard on Laura she will continue to be a nonentity."

What he wanted for the picture was a roster of eccentrics similar to that of *The Maltese Falcon*. And he got what he wanted, except for Laura herself, who remained indistinct, more of a symbol of romance than an actual human being, although Gene Tierney's remarkable beauty diverted the audience from noticing and made it easy to understand her stunning impact on the other characters.

Although Fox was very successful, Zanuck was always looking to make it more so by luring appropriate talent to the lot. In 1942, Zanuck brought Ernst Lubitsch to Fox. The two men had known each other since they both did time at Warner Bros. in the 1920s. As with everybody else in Hollywood, Zanuck thought Lubitsch was an artist, and more or less gave him his head . . . except when it came to casting.

Lubitsch and Samson Raphaelson, his favorite writer, were very happy with their script for *Heaven Can Wait*, but Zanuck wasn't too sure. The story as well as the main character struck him as indolent and lacking in the sort of drive that he prized in his films. Henry Van Cleve was born wealthy, stayed wealthy, married well, and indulged himself with a variety of other women until he died. Where was the conflict?

Zanuck was curious about why Lubitsch wanted to make "such a pointless picture." Lubitsch replied that he wanted to introduce the audience to some characters, and if the audience found those characters likeable, he believed the picture would succeed.

Zanuck hadn't hired Lubitsch to turn him into someone else, so he let the picture go ahead. The script had been written with either Fredric March or Rex Harrison in mind for the lead, probably because their off-screen behavior was similar to that of Henry's. But Zanuck asked Lubitsch for a personal favor: test Don Ameche for the part of Henry. A few days later, Lubitsch invited Raphaelson to look at Ameche's test. "Isn't that the vorst luck in the world," said Lubitsch when the lights went up. "Vat are we going to do? The guy is good!"

In fact, Ameche gave a finely calibrated, graceful performance embodying both subtlety and charm. The picture succeeded both critically and commercially, although the director's time at the studio was compromised by a major heart attack he suffered shortly after the completion of *Heaven Can Wait*. He produced two pictures (*Dragonwyck*, *A Royal Scandal*), the latter of which he had planned to direct, but his doctors said it was a bad idea.

Lubitsch returned to directing in 1946 with *Cluny Brown*, a charmer that failed to break even. He undertook *That Lady in Ermine*, a return to musicals, as a favor to Zanuck, who realized that Betty Grable needed something new if her stardom was to sustain in the postwar era. But Lubitsch died of another heart attack shortly after the film began production, and the picture was finished—in more ways than one—by Otto Preminger. Produced for just under $2.5 million, it returned domestic rentals of $1.5 million.

A more comprehensively successful hire was Joseph L. Mankiewicz, who had been chafing as a producer at MGM, when what he really wanted to do was direct. Louis B. Mayer had a lot more respect for producers than he did directors, so Mankiewicz jumped ship. Neither he nor Zanuck ever regretted it. Mankiewicz began directing *Dragonwyck* under the supervision of Ernst Lubitsch, who was unhappy with the movie and took his name off the credits.

After that, Mankiewicz gained assurance with every picture. *The Ghost and Mrs. Muir* was a lovely, delicate fantasy romance between a widow and a ghost. It wasn't terribly successful commercially, but Zanuck stuck with Mankiewicz, and he responded by writing and directing three bona fide classics: *A Letter to Three Wives*, *No Way Out*, and *All About Eve*.

Zanuck and Mankiewicz had a successful partnership, allowing for occasional contention. At one point, Zanuck called him "an arrogant bastard." Writing about the script for *A Letter to Three Wives*, Zanuck opined that "if he gets a hit with this, he'll be unlivable." Things only got worse, and Zanuck was partly to blame. The original script was called "A Letter to Four Wives," but Zanuck found one of the couples dull and suggested cutting them out of the script. As *A Letter to Three Wives*, the picture won Oscars for Best Director and Best Screenplay, which did nothing to tamp down Mankiewicz's ego. *All About Eve* won the same Oscars a year later.

Zanuck was more involved with *No Way Out* than on the other Mankiewicz pictures, because it was a personal project for the producer involving race relations. (Zanuck was that vanished creature, a socially liberal Republican.) The plot involved a young Black intern (the twenty-two-year-old Sidney Poitier) who treats two white brothers who have been shot while attempting a holdup. One brother dies and the other brother, a racist played with venomous energy by Richard Widmark, believes that the doctor killed his brother and determines to take his revenge.

A number of directors wanted to make the script, including Otto Preminger, Jean Negulesco, and Robert Rossen. Zanuck decided to hand the picture to Mankiewicz. In the script, Poitier's character dies, and Zanuck thought that was a mistake. As he said in one of his script conferences, "If his death resulted in *something*, if something were accomplished either characterwise or otherwise, it would be different and I would accept it. Perhaps the reason I shrink from this is because it violates a cardinal principle, which I have always adhered to, and that, is, 'Never kill the leading man unless something is gained by it.'"

Zanuck realized that social problems in and of themselves aren't enough to seduce an audience into paying attention—what's needed are characters they care about and conflict to which they can relate. To that end, he wrote writers Lesser Samuels and Philip Yordan, "We must conscientiously avoid propaganda, but . . . the final result . . . should be a picture which is actually powerful propaganda against intolerance."

Zanuck was also determined that Poitier's character be more than a profile showcasing the actor's innate dignity. He wanted the picture to "go into Luther's home. I would like to see how real Negroes in a metropolitan city live. I would like to see them as human beings. Perhaps Luther has a mother, and a father. . . . We will go into Luther's home. We will see real Negroes and how they live, as human beings. He will have a real brother, a real sister, a real father—all human beings."

The picture just about broke even.

Not every hire worked out. Zanuck signed Preston Sturges to a particularly rich deal in December 1946, after Sturges's partnership with Howard Hughes hit the rocks. Sturges went on salary for a whopping $7,825 weekly and was treated with consideration and deference by Zanuck, even though he was clearly feeling pressure from his board of directors.

"I realize you have no desire to put me or the studio personally on the spot," he wrote Sturges, "but unless it is possible for you to do your screenplay on *The Symphony Story* in eight weeks after you finish the writing of *Bashful Bend* then I will really be over a barrel. I am not in the habit of urging authors to write fast, but in these precarious days when every dollar really counts, I have to give a monthly accounting of my activities to the executive committee of the Board of Directors."

Sturges responded with two commercial disasters: *The Symphony Story* would be retitled *Unfaithfully Yours*—an intermittently funny, gleefully misogynistic movie with Rex Harrison and Linda Darnell—and *The Beautiful Blonde from Bashful Bend*, made at Zanuck's request in an attempt to broaden Betty Grable's skill set. By the time Sturges completed the Grable script, Fox had paid him $234,750. The picture turned out to be abysmal in every possible way, which made two major directors who hit the rocks trying to move Betty Grable out of her niche. Together,

Unfaithfully Yours and *The Beautiful Blonde from Bashful Bend* cost more than $4 million and brought in about half that.

As with Lubitsch, Zanuck gave Sturges complete freedom; unlike Lubitsch, Sturges couldn't handle that freedom. That said, Zanuck always retained an affection for rogues and called Sturges "a most extraordinary and ingenious creature. The whole thing was like a party. He directed in a red fez. He would have a Doberman pinscher on set with him. Before he would start, he would stuff a handkerchief in his mouth to stop from laughing.

"He was brilliant in conversation, but he was drinking like mad. He had a restaurant and it was losing a bloody fortune, a boat company which was losing more and more. I got him at the end of his career."

After World War II, Zanuck developed a new approach to his business, based on a growing belief that the movie industry would have to change. "I recognize that there'll always be a market for Betty Grable, and Lana Turner and all that tit stuff. But [the audience] is coming back with new thoughts, new ideas, new hungers. It's up to us to satisfy them with our movies. They'll want to know more about our world, and this is where I think we at Fox have to plan to measure up to their new maturity. We've got to start making movies that entertain but at the same time match the new climate of the times. Vital, thinking men's blockbusters. Big-theme films."

None of the Fox films of the period got the attention that Zanuck lavished on his production of *Wilson*. He had come back from the war convinced that Woodrow Wilson's League of Nations would have spared civilization World War II. Wilson, he believed, was a political prophet who had birthed a successor in Wendell Willkie, the moderate Republican who ran against Franklin Roosevelt in 1940. Zanuck's own politics were erratic. He considered himself a liberal Republican, but became close to Franklin Roosevelt even though he was campaigning for Willkie. Years later, he would be impressed by Eugene McCarthy but vote for Richard Nixon. Perhaps he simply respected star quality wherever it landed.

In any case, Zanuck threw himself into *Wilson* and *One World*, an adaptation of Willkie's nonfiction bestseller of 1943. Two years after losing the presidency to Roosevelt, Wilkie had set off on a journey around the world that lasted forty-nine days. On an airplane called the *Gulliver*, he traveled to Africa, Europe, Asia, and Latin America. *One World*, his resulting book, sold millions of copies while making one central, optimistic point: that active American promotion and intervention would be needed in the postwar world in order to foster economic interdependence that would bring about political stability and cooperation with the Soviet Union. It was a can-do message that said that the world was either pro-American or pan-American, and it struck a nerve.

Zanuck paid $100,000 for the rights to *One World* in the spring of 1943, and for the next year and a half expended a great deal of time and no small amount of the studio's money in trying to make a movie out of the book.

Through the fall of 1944, Zanuck and screenwriter Lamar Trotti worked on *Wilson* and *One World* more or less simultaneously. Zanuck wanted a scene where the Willkie character tells a war widow that she should not be heroic and patriotic about the death of her husband. Rather, she should be angry. "In every picture I have seen lately," Zanuck wrote in a memo, "someone always tells the mother or the father to keep their chin up, they have made a noble sacrifice in giving up their son or sweetheart to the war. This is nonsense . . . when we lose our loved ones . . . we should be damned mad about it and ready to strangle the first jerk who gets up at the peace table and starts yammering about Isolationism or the preservation of the British Empire or anything that does not guarantee equality of opportunity for all."*

Zanuck worked himself up to a fine messianic lather about *Wilson* and *One World*. "I can tell you that unless these two pictures are successful from every standpoint, I'll never make another film without Betty Grable in the cast." It was all in vain. When it was released in August 1944, *Wilson* lost more than $2 million, probably because its title character was a slightly dull, stiff-backed Presbyterian—not an inaccurate representation. Besides that, a movie about avoiding war released while the nation was still enmeshed in a struggle for survival seemed mistimed. Zanuck convinced himself that his mistake was structural; he should have told the story through the eyes of Wilson's second wife, who ran the country after her husband suffered a stroke in office.

Zanuck's original plan for *One World* had been to create the character of a world traveler, analogous to Willkie, to fill the narrative with funny or interesting anecdotes from the book, and have famous radio broadcasters interview the traveler after each of the six legs of his world trip. Willkie himself suggested minimizing the documentary and maximizing the drama, but the drama was all theoretical. Zanuck brought on Dudley Nichols to work on the script, and what finally emerged was a rough docudrama. We meet Willkie in a small town in Indiana. He goes to church, where he picks up a smattering of conversations reflecting the garden-variety isolationism of small-town America. Willkie has dinner with a friend, who is confused about what's going on in China and Africa.

---

* During the war, Zanuck had made movies full of patriotic fervor, such as *The Purple Heart*, but some of his veiled anti-war feelings crept into *One World*, as well as his later production of *Twelve O'Clock High*, wherein Gregory Peck's General Savage is gradually rendered catatonic by the stresses of command.

All this inspires Willkie to vow to counter the misinformation. The script settles into a visual representation of Willkie's around-the-world trip to foster world cooperation.

Zanuck made overtures to MGM to lend him Spencer Tracy to play Willkie, but Tracy wasn't interested. Zanuck's first choice for director was Sam Wood, but he was booked up for the foreseeable future. Zanuck thought about Lewis Milestone, but when he ran the project past Elia Kazan, the director told him the material was "dated." Kazan recommended that the film begin with the death of a son of Willkie's friend back home in Indiana, to set up an emotional quest for world peace on the part of Willkie.

The script was completed in January 1944, and, despite Zanuck's best efforts, that's where it stayed—a script that didn't want to be made. The world was beginning to separate into three worlds, not one. Wendell Willkie died unexpectedly of a heart attack in October 1944, and Zanuck spent the rest of the year trying to get the picture off the ground. He gave the script to John Ford in January 1945, but Ford passed in favor of *My Darling Clementine*, which showed great good sense.

Franklin Roosevelt's death in April 1945 was the final blow, as a film extolling one of Roosevelt's opponents would have been unseemly. Much to the delight of Fox stockholders, *One World* was never made, but the project indicated Zanuck's sincere idealism and concern for the greater good.

———————

Darryl Zanuck understood that if a story worked well once, it would work well again. And again. And again. It had to be disguised, the deck had to be shuffled, but a good story is a good story. A Tyrone Power movie called

Love is News, about an heiress who falls in love with a reporter who gives her a hard time, was ripped directly from Frank Capra's *It Happened One Night*. Zanuck later converted the story into *Sweet Rosie O'Grady*, a Betty Grable musical, and then did another version sans music with a more mature Tyrone Power in 1949, who must have been appalled to remake his own movie. *Folies Bergere*, a Maurice Chevalier musical from 1935, was remade as *That Night in Rio*, then still later as a Danny Kaye vehicle.

Producers get old. Stories don't.

CHAPTER SEVEN

NO WAY OUT

AFTER WORLD WAR II, THE MOVIE BUSINESS BEGAN A long financial decline. The deflation sped up when television arrived at the end of the decade, but the signs were visible before that. For one thing, it was getting harder and harder to make B pictures that could make any money, simply because costs kept rising and grosses didn't— quite the contrary. Monogram Pictures rebranded itself as Allied Artists and upgraded the product, while PRC was reconstituted as Eagle-Lion, but it was still a struggle.

As far as Zanuck was concerned, B pictures existed to make money, period. In 1945, he began to give serious thought to closing Sol Wurtzel's operation on Western Avenue. Wurtzel offered to undertake the production duties for the Bs himself, and Zanuck was happy to oblige. Wurtzel formed his own production company and between 1945 and 1950 produced eighteen features that Fox released that remain obscure even by the standards of B movies. Among the titles: *Roses Are Red*, *Second Chance*, and *Half Past Midnight*. As a group, they were markedly inferior to the films Wurtzel had been making under the Fox umbrella, simply because he cast the new films with nonentities as a money-saving gambit. Actors such as Lloyd Nolan and Cesar Romero spent a lot of time in Wurtzel's older B movies, and generally elevated the result because of their energy and style. They could front a B movie and leave the audience feeling entertained. No actors in Wurtzel's last series of Bs were as much fun. As profit-making ventures, they didn't make any money. Sol Wurtzel retired in 1950 and died in 1958. John Ford delivered the eulogy at his funeral.

Between 1946 and 1953, the American movie industry lost nearly 50 percent of its audience (by a count of the total attendees). That's not attrition, that's bleeding out. What was happening was simple—TV production basically replaced B pictures (a huge amount of early series television was produced, directed, and written by B movie veterans) while the generation that fought in World War II was focused on careers and children rather than Hollywood. In the 1950s, studios that were mired in their traditional way of doing things—we're looking at you, MGM—slashed their rosters of contract talent in a desperate attempt to lower overhead, while United Artists gradually rose to the head of the creative pack, at least partly because their business model didn't involve a physical studio or any contract talent whatever.

Zanuck's idealistic films like *Wilson* and his attempt to make *One World* were swept away by the outright wish-fulfillment of Disney's *Song of the South*—a huge hit in 1946—or by the fraught ambivalence of *The Best Years of Our Lives*, William Wyler's masterpiece of the same year that hit a nerve with the public. Then there was the proliferation of noir, which is actually more of a style than a genre. For all the importance that has retrospectively been attached to noir, it never amounted to more than about 16 percent of Hollywood's output, and was not particularly strong commercially. On the other hand, in hindsight it's clear that noir not only reflected but defined the emotional anxieties of the period.

Zanuck knew things had to change and fast. In the middle of 1946, *Diamond Horseshoe*, a lavish Grable picture, returned domestic rentals of $3.1 million. Zanuck figured that it would either break even or return a very minor profit because of its high cost of $2.5 million. This, he knew, was a state of affairs that was untenable, because the movie industry was not going to be coasting at high tide forever. What he wanted, he told his producers and directors, was more care in preproduction.

Take *Margie*, a lovely Henry King picture in Technicolor about a teenager in the 1920s that proved to be the studio's second-biggest grosser of 1946, returning $4 million in domestic rentals against a cost of $1.6 million. Result: major profits. As Zanuck asserted in a memo, "The picture contained 15 sets and the picture is the only picture this year that has come in under the budget. If you examine what made this possible, even with a director who takes the care that Henry King takes, you will realize that it was made possible by the original design of the production."

But *Margie* proved an outlier. Costs continued to rise, grosses started to decline. In May 1947, Zanuck bombarded his directors with a memo demanding economy *now*. He requested that directors be on the set by 8:30 a.m. and that the first shot of the day be completed by 9:30 a.m.—this at a time when the average first shot wasn't in the can until 10:38 a.m. "This in itself would account for a minimum of one full week on an average picture."

The problem was that the industry had grown used to the fat and happy days of World War II, when more or less everything made money. Production had been efficient and costs had been less. But in the years after the war, labor costs were rapidly increasing, as was everything else. As Zanuck pointed out, in 1947 Fox productions were averaging six set-ups a day; five years before, they had been averaging $9\frac{1}{4}$ setups per day.

He wanted directors to plan their shots in advance so as to cut down on the time spent consulting with the director of photography, thereby allowing more time for shooting. He also thought there were too many superfluous angles being shot. "Even if only one superfluous angle per day is shot, this could easily add six to nine days to a schedule." He didn't want directors to leave the set early to look at dailies. Rather, they should wait till the shooting day was over at six p.m.

Zanuck figured that if everybody cooperated, they might be able to reduce a conventional shooting schedule by as much as two weeks per picture. Besides that, he offered opinions on the product of all the other studios—what was right with them, more often the negative example of what was wrong with them.

"*The Treasure of the Sierra Madre* was a box-office failure in spite of receiving high critical approval and the reason it failed was because it turned out to be one long, detailed character study. It lacked pace, excitement, and the sweep of action. I think the same story told in hard-hitting, realistic terms with accent on honest and legitimate melodrama would have found a different reception from the public. Let us not fall into this pit."

In 1944, the producer Louis de Rochemont came to see Zanuck with the idea of making a feature in the vein of the popular *March of Time* shorts. They used a voice-of-God narrator and nonprofessional performers in a documentary style. Zanuck thought that format was fine for twenty minutes but wouldn't sustain drama for ninety minutes or longer. What he and de Rochemont came up with was the idea of a hybrid—factual technique, factual dramatization, shot on locations, but with actors. As Zanuck put it, this was a blending of "fact and drama."

"It is not enough just to tell an interesting story. Half the battle depends on *how* you tell the story. As a matter of fact, the most important half depends on how you tell the story."

The first of these pictures was *The House on 92nd Street*, and the format proved popular through movies such as *Call Northside 777*, *Boomerang*, and *13 Rue Madeleine*. Even without the narrator, the use of real locations grounded films such as *Kiss of Death*—tough movies for a tough time. The story for *Kiss of Death* struck a particular spark; Zanuck told a conference that "if we do not get Ben Hecht then we must get someone as good for the dialogue. This is the kind of script that can be written in six weeks at the outside, and Hecht would probably do it in three."

The neorealist format worked splendidly until it was coopted by television in series such as *Dragnet*, and the novelty wore off. The influence of the de Rochemont films filtered into other Fox films that dealt with social problems. There was *Gentleman's Agreement*, about anti-Semitism, starring Gregory Peck, Dorothy McGuire, and—on hand to lend the picture some desperately needed verisimilitude—John Garfield.

Zanuck handed that project to Elia Kazan, who had come to Fox in the midst of a brilliant Broadway career to direct *A Tree Grows in Brooklyn* and promptly endeared himself to everyone by admitting that he knew nothing about how to make a movie. "I know how to direct people, but I don't know what to do with the camera," he said.

Zanuck gave him Louis Lighton, a wise, kindly producer who went back to the silent days, and Arthur Miller as cameraman. Miller had shot *How Green Was My Valley* for John Ford. Kazan watched and learned and *A Tree Grows in Brooklyn* emerged as an exquisite tone poem worthy of its source material. Kazan's opinion was that "Darryl . . . was the best executive I've ever known. . . . The important thing for all of us who worked at Fox during those years was that the man heading our studio didn't back off when he was challenged."

"I sort of liked [Zanuck] personally," Kazan said. "He was always straightforward when I was working with him. He didn't go behind my back. He [was] a dominant, aggressive man but not a dishonest one. He was essentially a fair guy when he was not challenged in a competitive way. He often explained to me that you have to make popular or program pictures in order to afford the others, the pictures he had to nurse, shepherd and look after. He was a tough little guy with a narrow, intense vision."

Kazan said that Zanuck reduced central dramatic conflicts to one of several basic questions: *"Will he fuck her or won't he? Will he catch her or won't he?* That's what he said we should always keep uppermost in mind when we were making any film."

All these pictures were made for a reasonable cost, and controversy was embedded in their DNA. The result was that they were all profitable to one degree or another, a difficult proposition in and of itself in a time when revenues were suffering a consistent decline.

Screenwriter Moss Hart clashed with Kazan on *Gentleman's Agreement* and complained that Kazan was cutting scenes without consulting him. Zanuck sent Hart a memo that reveals his anxieties: "I would rather get it good *now* than to have to chop it up and try to trim after the picture is finished. These things are to be expected, particularly in a film where you have eighty percent talk and twenty percent action. Rest assured that to the best of our joint ability we will eliminate nothing that is essential or significant to either the story or the theme, but I am sure you agree that by all means we must not make a dull picture even though it be significant and important."

It's hard to figure out what Zanuck meant by "twenty percent action," as the only event that could be considered action consists of a few seconds when John Garfield decks a bigot. *Gentleman's Agreement* was entirely too genteel, and in later years Kazan seemed slightly embarrassed by it, but it won the Oscar for Best Picture, an early example of the movie industry's bent for self-congratulation.

Zanuck followed it up with *The Snake Pit*, about the treatment of the mentally ill, and *Panic in the Streets*, a Kazan production about the spread of a pandemic. *Pinky*, about a Black girl who passes for white, began as a John Ford picture, but after he bailed Zanuck pressed Kazan into taking over.

All of these pictures were hits, some of considerable size. *Pinky* was the highest grossing Fox film of 1949, with domestic rentals exceeding $4 million. None of them transcend their period, but that's often the case with movies that capture a specific moment of social unrest. (See *Easy Rider*.) These movies, along with *Call Northside 777*, directed by Henry Hathaway; *The Snake Pit*, directed by Anatole Litvak; *No Way Out*, directed by Joseph L. Mankiewicz; and Kazan's *Panic in the Streets*, can be seen as a strong, belated return to the films Zanuck had been making at Warners in the early 1930s. They weren't as fleet in their storytelling as the Warner pictures had been, but they still focused on telling the truth about social issues that would prove more intractable than Zanuck—or anybody else—imagined.

Sooner or later, every long-lived studio executive experiences a runaway production. Zanuck's was *Forever Amber*. The studio had paid $200,000 to Kathleen Winsor for the rights to her novel, which had sold 20 million copies worldwide. In the title role, Zanuck cast Peggy Cummins, a twenty-year-old English ingénue who had appeared in only three films. She arrived in Hollywood in October of 1945 and was scheduled to play Betty Cream, a spoiled society girl in Ernst Lubitsch's *Cluny Brown*. But Zanuck tested her for *Amber* and in December he announced that Cummins would play the part, while John Stahl, who was coming off the huge hit of *Leave Her to Heaven*—nearly $6 million in domestic rentals—would direct. Zanuck asked Philip Dunne to rewrite the script, and production got under way in June 1946.

On August 4, Zanuck pulled the plug, having already spent one million dollars. Philip Dunne said that John Stahl's direction was "hopelessly old-fashioned" and that Peggy Cummins was "not up to it." Vincent Price, who had been playing Lord Aimsbury, said that had she not "looked so young, Miss Cummins would have been perfect."

Zanuck had no choice but to double down, bringing in Ring Lardner Jr. to rewrite the script, and replacing Stahl with Otto Preminger, who Zanuck obviously regarded as the directorial equivalent of a relief pitcher—Preminger had previously replaced Rouben Mamoulian on *Laura* and would replace Lubitsch on *That Lady in Ermine*.

Preminger wanted to borrow Lana Turner from MGM to play Amber, but Zanuck insisted on Linda Darnell, who was already under contract and would cost the production much less than Turner. The new version of *Forever Amber* finally got under way on September 4, 1946. Richard Greene replaced Vincent Price, while John Russell replaced Glenn Langan, who had been playing Black Jack. The accrued costs for both versions of the film amounted to a staggering $6.3 million. When the film opened in October of 1947, it featured some beautiful Technicolor photography by Leon Shamroy, a fine score by David Raksin, and just enough of the novel so that the audience didn't feel cheated.

Forever Amber amassed domestic rentals of $6 million, making a profit highly doubtful. The fault would have to be placed at Zanuck's feet, if only because he let more than a month of shooting go by before making the decision to cancel the first version of the picture. Most of the blame fell on Cummins, who would retrieve part of her reputation with her raw, sexual performance in Joseph Lewis's *Gun Crazy*, although that was a B movie that took years to amass a reputation.

These were difficult years for Zanuck in that his "controversial" pictures did reasonably well, but the bread-and-butter pictures he had specialized in were no longer sure things at the box office. Besides that, there was the House Committee on Un-American Activities, whose 1947 hearings questioned the loyalties of actors, writers, and directors, some of whom worked at 20th Century-Fox.

Zanuck's attitude toward the blacklist was sublimated fury, if only because someone was basically telling him who he could and could not hire. The director Jules Dassin was among the people about to be blacklisted, and Spyros Skouras, the new chairman of 20th Century-Fox, wanted him off the lot. Zanuck showed up at Dassin's house one night, which took Dassin by complete surprise. "Coming to my house was like visiting the tenements, because I lived on the wrong side of town. He said, 'Get out. Get out fast. Here's a book. You're going to London. Get a screenplay as fast as you can and start shooting the most expensive scenes. Then they [the New York office] might let you finish it.' That was *Night and the City*. . . . I really respected the guy."

Dassin also saw a side of Zanuck that was usually concealed, when he told Dassin to write in a part for Gene Tierney because she had just had a disastrous love affair and was suicidal. "I know her," said Zanuck. "She'll go to work and it'll save her."

"This, from Zanuck," remembered Dassin, "the guy who is known for being so . . . tough, so heartless. We wrote in a part for her. Darryl sent me a one-word telegram. 'Thanks.' That was the unknown Zanuck."

In later years, Dassin would refer to Zanuck as "a mensch."

———

Zanuck worked more or less as a successful football coach, supportive of people who responded best to support, demanding with people who needed a fire under them. When Lewis Milestone was making *The Halls of Montezuma*, Zanuck wrote him a memo telling him he was pleased by the rushes, but cautioned Milestone not to get too creative. The memo is essentially a lesson in tough love: "I believe you can contribute business and ideas to a finished script and that you can give much in the way of characterization. I think it is *fatal* for you when you try to do anything in addition.

"You have a perfect knack for picking the wrong story, and I think that more than anything else this has contributed to the 'bad luck' you have had in the past four or five years. . . . On *Arch of Triumph*, where you had practically complete authority as both producer and director, you made one of the worst pictures I have ever seen in my life—and there was no need for it, although I would never have picked the story for myself.

"Personally, more than anything else I would love to be a portrait painter, but long ago I came to the realization that if one man has *one* talent, he should be grateful and satisfied."

Nothing was too small to concern him. Take *The Gunfighter*, the classic Henry King western with Gregory Peck. Zanuck had been out of the country when it was shot, and when he came back to town and saw the large moustache that King and Peck had chosen for Peck's character, his heart sank. He told Henry King, "I would give $25,000 of my own money to get that moustache off Peck."

IIis forebodings were fulfilled. When the film was released, Zanuck wrote producer Nunnally Johnson that it would do about 70 percent or 75 percent of the business of *Yellow Sky*, a previous Fox western with Peck that Zanuck regarded as inferior to *The Gunfighter*. *The Gunfighter* was a pet project, if only because Zanuck felt it had the potential to be a classic western in the vein of *Stagecoach*. "To my mind *Stagecoach* was the best of them all," he wrote Nunnally Johnson, the producer of *The Gunfighter*. "*The Ox-Bow Incident* was great from an artistic standpoint, but the lynching theme rendered it unpopular."

The Gunfighter was indeed excellent, but not on the level of *Stagecoach*. It even made money, but not much, and Zanuck blamed the film's severe aesthetic. "It violates so many true Western traditions that it goes over the heads of the type of people who patronize Westerns and there are not enough of the others to give us the top business we anticipated."

But the focus of Zanuck's ire remained Peck's moustache. He quoted the remarks overheard by an usher at Radio City Music Hall: "'If they wanted an ugly man, why didn't they take an ugly actor? Why waste Peck?' This comment occurred hundreds of times, particularly from women and young girls."

Zanuck liked westerns because the genre emphasized action, but different times demand different approaches, so he took a flyer at science fiction with *The Day the Earth Stood Still*. Initial casting ideas for the part of the extraterrestrial Klaatu ran to Claude Rains, but Zanuck saw Michael Rennie on stage in London and recommended him to director Robert Wise.

Zanuck zoned in on what he felt was the script's biggest problem—it opened on Klaatu's spaceship. "When you open a picture on something that does not 'exist,'" he wrote, "you have great trouble in capturing your audience." He suggested opening the film "as realistically as you possibly can," suggesting a variation on the Orson Welles radio broadcast of *The War of the Worlds*—use radio voices that bring the startling news of the spaceship's arrival. Zanuck also suggested the idea for the repeated phrase "Klaatu Barada Nikto"—the only way that Klaatu can control his giant robot Gort.

Buttressed by a thrilling, innovative Bernard Herrmann score, *The Day the Earth Stood Still* cost less than $1 million and grossed twice its cost. It was a small success, but science fiction was not a genre that really interested Zanuck.

In the early 1950s, Fox struck gold with Marilyn Monroe, one of the primary stars of the decade. It was a partnership stunted by the mingled backgrounds of the people involved. Zanuck's relationship with Monroe was complicated by her past personal relationship with Fox chairman Joe Schenck and, quite possibly, Zanuck himself. As far as Zanuck was concerned, Monroe was a none-too-bright starlet who had unaccountably become a movie star through a fluke of the camera. He simply could not bring himself to fully respect her as either an actress or a woman. From Monroe's point of view, her past history with Zanuck and Schenck only made her more conscious of their lack of respect toward her, producing a toxic combination of insecurity and anger.

Zanuck was also annoyed by her lack of professionalism and her affectations. When Zanuck slotted Monroe in *Don't Bother to Knock*, a decent movie directed by Roy Ward Baker, she made what would become her standard request to have her drama coach Natasha Lytess on the set. Zanuck responded with a subtly scathing memo in which he termed her request "completely impractical and impossible. . . . The reason we engage a director and entrust him to direct a picture is because we feel that he has demonstrated his ability to function in that capacity. Whether the final performances comes out right or wrong there cannot be more than one responsible individual and that individual is the director. . . . You cannot be coached on the sidelines or the result will be a disaster for you."

He went on to say that Monroe's part in John Huston's *The Asphalt Jungle* was "a comparatively simple part in which you were very effective, but it did not particularly call for any acting" compared with the part in *Don't Bother to Knock*.

"I am sure you realize how ludicrous it would be if every actor or actress felt that they needed special coaching from the sidelines. The result would be bedlam, and whatever creative ideas the director might possess would be lost or totally diffused."

It didn't work. Monroe couldn't work without a personal crutch. Lytess worked as her on-set drama coach through *The Seven Year Itch*, after which Monroe replaced her with Paula Strasberg, the wife of Actors Studio head Lee Strasberg.

For all of Zanuck's heavy lifting, throughout the early 1950s the box office continued a slow drift downward. Something had to change. Zanuck sent out a memo stating that "this is a tough business today and we have had entirely too many casualties. We must have the guts to examine each story and each project with a cold and realistic eye." He considered a series of radical proposals, including asking contract directors to make one picture a year for free, making only stories regarded as surefire, and once again urging directors to shoot less footage to save on production schedules.

He backed off the idea of asking directors to work for free, and none of the other ideas would save enough money to effect serious change. The problem, as Zanuck realized, was that "producing companies no longer could depend on the movie-going habit. More powerful attractions were necessary to lure a public whose leisure time and inflation-shrunken dollar were being savagely competed for by television, [paperback books], magazines, sports, hobby industries and a variety of other spare time and money distractions."

Something else was needed, and that something was the size of the screen. In September 1952, *This Is Cinerama* debuted and caused a sensation over what was essentially a series of disconnected short subjects along the lines of MGM's legendarily inane one-reel travelogues. Cinerama was the classic example of the *how* being more important than the *what*. Zanuck always believed that any industry problems could be solved by good pictures, but the success of *This Is Cinerama* proved them wrong. Cinerama involved three 35mm projectors, each of which required a projectionist, and a fourth technician to handle the soundtrack, which was on separate reels of 35mm film. With each projector's image shown at twenty-six frames per second side by side onto a screen curved at a 165-degree angle, the Cinerama screen gave an impression of immersive involvement, especially if you were seated in the sweet spot—main floor, in the center.

But the size of the screen, the necessary customizing of each theater that showed the process, the three projection booths, and attendant high labor costs meant that the system was extremely expensive to install and run. Grosses were huge, but profits were modest. In fact, Earl Sponable, who had been Fox's head of research and development since 1926, had looked at Cinerama in 1950 and wrote in a memo that "the process has many technical limitations and is of no interest to 20th Century-Fox in its present form."

And so the industry began a search for an equivalent to Cinerama with one projector, thus avoiding the obvious joins between the three 35mm panels. Earl Sponable and Herbert Bragg, Sponable's assistant, began an emergency canvassing of alternatives to Cinerama in late October 1952, more or less at the same time that Mike Todd was beginning the research process for what became Todd-AO. Sponable and Bragg looked at the system that would eventually be adopted by Paramount under the name VistaVision, but then Bragg remembered the work of Henri Chretien from a quarter century earlier.

Chretien's invention amounted to a lens that fitted onto a conventional 35mm camera and optically squeezed a horizontally wider angle onto standard 35mm film. The image was roughly two times wider than it was high. Reversing the optics and installing the result on a 35mm projector reversed the squeeze. The result was an entirely different image than audiences had been used to, without any of the problems that dogged Cinerama.

The next year in the lives of the technical and creative men and women of 20th Century-Fox would be a desperate gamble against an imperfect system and insane deadlines, which forced a series of desperate improvisations. As one historian noted, "Directors hand-waved their way past the creative limitations set upon them by the lenses. Producers biked lenses back and forth between [sets] when there weren't enough to go around. Engineers glued damaged lens assemblies back together in the middle of the night. Bodyguards were hired to protect the lenses and private investigators were engaged to get information on the competition."

Of course, the movie industry has been a series of desperate improvisations for more than a hundred years, so it was business as usual, albeit with more at stake.

Chretien was something of a self-taught mathematical genius and a leading figure of the French optical science industry. He got the idea for widescreen presentations while watching Abel Gance's *Napoleon* in 1926. For the film's triptych sequences, Gance used a jerry-rigged system involving three 35mm cameras mounted one on top of the other. The misalliance in height between the three cameras was noticeable on screen, but the technical issues were swept aside by the sheer splendor of Gance's heroic shooting and cutting.

Chretien realized that one camera with an anamorphic lens would give the same effect with fewer complications. Chretien made a few lenses to demonstrate what he was talking about, but the coming of sound torpedoed the development of Chretien's invention, just as it had subverted William Fox's Grandeur.

By November 13, 1952, Fox had located Chretien in Nice, who told them that he still had several of the lenses he had made in the 1920s. On December 1, 12, and 13, Sponable engaged in negotiations with Chretien, writing his assistant, "He is a pleasant old fellow about 75—beard and all."

Sponable realized that the lenses looked interesting, but the optics were quite slow, absorbing a great deal of light and requiring wide aperture settings if they were to work. He finally procured an option on December 18. A day after that, some test footage that Fox had made with Chretien's lenses attached to a Movietone newsreel camera were screened for Spyros Skouras in Paris. That test was also shown to Zanuck a few weeks later. On January 26, Sponable and Skouras traveled to Nice and cut their deal with the inventor on February 10. According to Zanuck, they got Chretien's signature on the contract one day before Jack Warner's representative contacted the inventor.

By January 1953, the tests had convinced Zanuck that the anamorphic lens would revolutionize movies. "AM ABSOLUTELY CONVINCED THAT OUR BIG SCREEN FRENCH SYSTEM WILL HAVE AN ENORMOUS EFFECT ON AUDIENCES EVERYWHERE AND THAT IT IS A MAJOR DEVELOPMENT FOR THE INDUSTRY," Zanuck cabled Skouras. "I THINK ITS MAIN VALUE LIES, HOWEVER, IN THE PRODUCTION OF LARGE SCALE SPECTACLES AND BIG OUTDOOR FILMS SUCH AS THE ROBE, TWELVE MILE REEF, THE STORY OF DEMETRIUS, HELL AND HIGH WATER, PRINCE VALIANT, KING OF THE KHYBER RIFLES, SIR WALTER RALEIGH AND RIVER OF NO RETURN. IN TIME WE MAY FIND A WAY TO USE IT EFFECTIVELY FOR INTIMATE DRAMAS AND COMEDIES BUT AT THE PRESENT

TIME SMALL, INTIMATE STORIES OR A PERSONAL DRAMA LIKE MY COUSIN RACHEL WOULD MEAN NOTHING IN THIS SYSTEM....

"IT IS MY OPINION THAT WE HAVE APPROXIMATELY NINETY PERCENT OF THE AUDIENCE VALUE OF CINERAMA, BUT THE LOSS OF TEN PERCENT IS MADE UP MANY TIMES BY THE CLEAR FOCUS OF OUR PICTURE AND OF COURSE BY THE PRACTICAL CONSIDERATIONS SUCH AS USING OUR OWN CAMERA AND PRO-JECTION MACHINES AND ONE NEGATIVE....

"PERSONALLY I BELIEVE THAT OUR SYSTEM WILL PUT EVERY OTHER SYSTEM OUT OF BUSINESS AND OUR MAIN DIFFI-CULTY NOW LIES IN GETTING SUFFICIENT LENSES."

On January 29, it was decided that the new screen system would be called "CinemaScope." It wasn't an original term—the name had been copyrighted by Don Fedderson for a kinescope process used by KLAC-TV. Fedderson sold his copyright to Fox for $50,000, and later became the successful TV producer of *My Three Sons*, among other shows.

By February, the studio was about to start production on *The Robe* and *How to Marry a Millionaire*, the first two CinemaScope productions. Zanuck knew exactly what he wanted from both pictures—safe, proven entertainment. "I do not want stories that will be helped *by* Cinema-Scope," he told story editor David Brown. "I want stories that will *help* CinemaScope."

Fox began production on *The Robe* on February 24, 1953. In the interim between the purchase and the beginning of the first production, the Fox engineers made some changes in Chretien's design. Because of Fox's determination to approximate Cinerama as much as possible, the engineers widened Chretien's ratio of 2:1 to 2.66:1. Fox also innovated with four-track stereo sound on CinemaScope prints—two magnetic tracks on either side of both sets of sprocket holes.

What made all this a truly spectacular gamble was that Chretien's European patents had expired in 1951, and his invention had never been patented in America at all. In short, Chretien's invention was in the public domain, but the fact that his system was more or less road-ready gave it a huge advantage over any newly devised systems that still faced months, if not years, of testing.

That said, there were problems with Chretien's lenses, as well as the first batch manufactured to duplicate them. For one thing, Chretien's lenses were designed as an attachment to conventional camera lenses, not a replacement for them. This meant that there were two lenses that needed to be precisely focused, not one. In practice, focusing with the early CinemaScope lenses was extremely difficult at the best of times, and the fact that the compression ratios on Fox's adaptation were slightly different than Chretien's lenses made things even more difficult.

There was also a distinct tendency toward the lenses creating a perceptible curve to any vertical lines. The lenses thus had a tendency toward slightly broadening faces and giving actors heavier jowls than they actually had, a phenomenon that became known as the Cinema-Scope mumps. The great Technicolor cameraman Jack Cardiff remembered that this meant that you couldn't get much closer to an actor than seven feet. The problem wouldn't be solved until the second generation of CinemaScope lenses, which came online in early 1954 and were manufactured by Bausch & Lomb.

Fox began production on the first three CinemaScope films—*The Robe, How to Marry a Millionaire*, and *Beneath the Twelve Mile Reef*—with precisely three lenses, one per picture. "We have no protection lenses," Zanuck wrote Skouras in a telegram on March 5. The situation wouldn't be eased for months. By November, Bausch & Lomb had delivered 250 more lenses, but there would still be shortfalls; as late as March

1954, Fox was bicycling 40mm and 50mm CinemaScope lenses between *The Egyptian* and *Broken Lance.*

Fox's investment was in the neighborhood of $10 million. Herbert Bragg, Earl Sponable's assistant, remembered that Fox paid $2.25 million to Bausch & Lomb for the crash manufacture of CinemaScope lenses.

While all this was going on, Fox began negotiations with other studios, informing them that renting CinemaScope lenses would cost them $25,000 per picture. With no viable alternatives in-house, MGM, Columbia, and Disney committed themselves to the process, but Paramount stuck with VistaVision, which, in truth, produced the sharpest, most pleasing image of all the widescreen processes, but was hampered by its lack of stereophonic sound.

Besides the inherent problems with the Chretien lenses, the process needed huge amounts of illumination, so lighting sets in the early days of CinemaScope took 30 percent to 40 percent more time than it had before. Freddie Young, the great English cameraman (*Lawrence of Arabia, Doctor Zhivago*), said, "I was in Hollywood while they were shooting *The Robe.* I was on the set with the cameraman, Leon Shamroy, and because you had longer focal lenses, and therefore less depth of focus than normal, they wanted more light so that you could stop down and get more depth. They had three rails [of lights], one above the other, all the way around the top of the set, full of 5K's and 10K's, pouring light onto the sets."

Zanuck was not merely ramrodding the conversion of 20th Century-Fox from one era to another, he was also acting as the primary cheerleader for that conversion. In March, he was looking at comparative rushes from the conventional 35mm version of *The Robe*, shot for theaters that were waiting to invest in widescreen, and the CinemaScope version. He told Jack Warner that "the superiority of CinemaScope is almost unbelievable. From the standpoint of 'audience participation' alone it is like looking at the first talkie and trying to compare the sound with what we have in pictures today."

Zanuck was trying to persuade Warner to license CinemaScope and deemphasize 3-D, on which Warner had placed his bets. "I think you will clean up with [*House of Wax*] . . . but you and I know that this industry cannot exist if we have to depend on trick effects and stunts such as throwing objects at the audience."

By mid-March, Zanuck informed his studio that once a few small-screen pictures already in production were finished, "Twentieth Century-Fox will concentrate exclusively on subjects suitable for CinemaScope" and would abandon preparations and screenplays on any film that could not be used to take advantage of the new format for at least the next eighteen months. "For the time being intimate comedies or small scale, domestic stories should be put aside and no further monies expended on their development. . . . If CinemaScope does nothing else it will force us back into the movie picture business—I mean moving pictures that *move*."

Among the pictures that Zanuck jettisoned in favor of his all-CinemaScope program was Elia Kazan's *On the Waterfront*, which Zanuck (understandably) could not see as a color and widescreen production. Columbia picked up the project, shot it in small-screen black and white, and emerged with a classic.

Throughout this process, Zanuck was pretending to a confidence that, in the still of the night, he didn't really have. In retrospect, he would say that "this was the biggest goddamned gamble in screen history. [Producer of *The Robe*] Frank Ross was petrified as he visualized all his chances of participation [profits] going down the drain in excessive costs. In fact, his participation brought him a fortune."

As for Warners, first they stalled, then they panicked. On March 5, 1953, the studio announced that it would shut down all operations for three months and wait for a shakeout in all the competing technologies. At the same time they made huge cuts in their staff list. Among the people let go were Michael Curtiz, the company's ace director since he joined the company twenty-six years earlier. A few months later, Warners shut down their animation department.

After unsuccessfully attempting to duplicate Chretien's lenses with other suppliers, Jack Warner pushed all his chips to the center of the table and bet on 3-D. As Zanuck had sensed, *House of Wax* was a hit, which led Jack Warner to announce that the studio would put twenty-two 3-D movies into production, essentially converting all production to that format. Among the pictures were *Hondo*, *The Command*, and *Dial M for Murder*. They dropped plans for "WarnerSuperScope," an anamorphic process that, curiously enough, had exactly the same specifications as CinemaScope. The only difference was that Warners had contracted with Zeiss to make the lenses instead of Bausch & Lomb.

Ultimately, Jack Warner's flailing indecision forced him to give up any rational chance for a competing, exclusive-to-Warners widescreen system. In 1954, Warners shot *A Star Is Born* in CinemaScope and, soon after that, *Rebel Without a Cause* and *East of Eden*.

It is doubtful that Zanuck's wildest fantasies could have encompassed the size of the hit constituted by *The Robe*. A few weeks before the film opened, Zanuck watched the completed picture for the first time and wrote Philip Dunne that it was "one of the great pictures of all time." Posterity wouldn't agree—stripped of its technology, *The Robe* was little more than an obvious, uncredited remake of DeMille's *The Sign of the Cross*—but it was an immediate smash hit. It premiered at the Roxy Theater on September 16, 1953, and grossed $364,428 in its first week—a world box office record for seven days. By the time its theatrical run was complete, it had earned domestic rentals of $17.5 million.

How to Marry a Millionaire, the second CinemaScope picture, made $8 million in rentals, far more than the $5.3 million earned by *Gentlemen Prefer Blondes,* which also starred Marilyn Monroe but was in standard format. *Beneath the Twelve Mile Reef,* an underwater picture shot on location in Florida that starred Robert Wagner, brought in $5.7 million. The three CinemaScope pictures Fox released in 1953 jacked up their net profits by 13 percent. In 1954, profits for the first thirty-nine weeks of the year rose 400 percent. Fox announced that 13,500 theaters in the United States and Canada and another 7,000 theaters overseas bought the CinemaScope lenses and installed the wide, curved screen.

The most immediate result of the CinemaScope process was that the 1:33 format that had been the norm since 1900 was rendered obsolete. In the same way that sound sequences in part-talkies negatively emphasized the lack of dialogue in silent films, so CinemaScope negatively emphasized the boxy dimensions of the conventional screen ratio. The new screen size would no longer be a square, but a rectangle, whether wide or extra-wide. Films using widescreen technology accounted for less than 10 percent of movies in 1953; by 1959 that figure had risen to 40 percent.

Creatively, CinemaScope brought with it problems that went beyond soft spots and bulging faces. For one thing, that vast expanse had to be filled somehow. Zanuck told his directors to try and spread actors across the frame, which had the unintended consequence of some of the early CinemaScope films repeating the stultifying horizontal blocking of early talkies. The rate of cuts also slowed down, with many scenes played out in medium shots in order to continually emphasize the width of the screen. The lack of cutting became noticeable, and for all the visual splendor CinemaScope provided, some of the films also needed the charge that brisk editing can provide. Besides all that, the problems with focus tended to make directors opt for the easy alternative of keeping the actors immobile; in practice, tracking shots forward or backward were rare.

It followed that many directors didn't think CinemaScope was any sort of great leap forward. Delmer Daves, the director of *Demetrius and the Gladiators*, the sequel to *The Robe*, remembered a meeting with Zanuck that left him shaken, not stirred. "Was this the end of the close shot, or the two shot? What could you do about all of that out-of-focus space when you're on someone two feet away from the camera? Was all the intimacy of filmmaking going to be lost? Darryl didn't have any answers."

Fritz Lang famously grouched that the format "was perfect for snakes and funerals." Howard Hawks said that "if the CinemaScope size had been any good, painters would have used it more—they've been at it a lot longer than we have. . . . We have spent a lifetime learning how to compel the public to concentrate on [a] single thing. Now we have something that works in exactly the opposite way, and I don't like it very much."

John Ford let it be known that he didn't care for CinemaScope, and Zanuck took Ford's indifference—or hostility—as a personal affront. He took it upon himself to sell the new system to his favorite director. "You are a long-shot master," Zanuck wrote Ford. "In some strange way you have always amazed me by what you can do with what might be just an ordinary long shot. If any medium was ever devised especially for you, it is CinemaScope." Zanuck offered to host a private screening for Ford of several of their unreleased pictures. "You have always been progressive and I believe I can convince you."

Ford tried CinemaScope with *The Long Gray Line* and *Mister Roberts*, but he was too much a master of classical composition to be enthusiastic about the dimensions of the process. With the exception of his sequence

in Cinerama's *How the West Was Won* and his 70mm *Cheyenne Autumn,*
Ford stuck with the modified 1.66 ratio until the end of his career.

The process even spawned some good intramural jokes. In Charlie
Chaplin's otherwise moribund *A King in New York,* King Shahdov attends
a widescreen picture and the audience's heads move in a perpetual
extreme swivel like the crowd at a tennis match.

By the mid-fifties, the box office charge administered by Cinema-
Scope was beginning to flag, if only because a bigger picture was not
necessarily a better picture. Fox devised a new wrinkle they called CinemaScope 55, with a 55mm negative that could produce prints in that
size as well as 35mm. Both *Carousel* and *The King and I* were shot in
CinemaScope 55, but neither of the pictures were exhibited in that system because Zanuck came to believe that the audience couldn't differentiate between conventional CinemaScope and CinemaScope 55. At that
point, the studio blinked and bought a piece of Todd-AO, a 70mm process
that was used for all of Fox's big-budget spectaculars, from *South Pacific*
through *Cleopatra* and *The Sound of Music.*

After all the frantic hurly-burly, CinemaScope proved to have a limited life span. By 1960, it was being supplanted by Panavision, whose
lenses were sharper and easier to work with. The last Fox picture in CinemaScope was *In Like Flint* in 1967, after which Fox switched over to
Panavision, as had the rest of the industry.

Injecting a huge dose of fresh thinking is not often accomplished by
men in their fifties, who have often settled into a comfortable groove,
but Zanuck's decision to go all-in on CinemaScope was his penultimate
hurrah. The business was changing in ways Zanuck didn't like, if only
because it was getting much harder to control the changes.

In 1951, Zanuck signed a contract with Samuel Fuller, whose film *The Steel Helmet* Zanuck had admired. Fuller was a man in the style of Wellman and Zanuck himself—modestly sized, but with a personality that could fill the Rose Bowl. Besides that, Fuller smoked cigars that were at least as large as Zanuck's. The deal was for Fuller to write and direct six pictures for Fox, one a year, which left him free to do another independent picture of his own choosing every year.

For his part, Zanuck was the man for Fuller because, as he remembered, "he was the only mogul who didn't talk about money. . . . More than any other studio head, Darryl loved stories. That made me love the guy from the first moment I met him. He'd get excited hearing about the yarn for your next picture. . . . Darryl would even act out scenes with me. He'd even get on the floor when there was a body in the script. If he said, 'OK, let's do it,' your movie was in production."

Fuller and Zanuck had only one disagreement, about a script that Fuller was determined to make about the nineteenth-century newspaper business, called *Park Row*. Zanuck proposed a title change to *In Old New York*, which Fuller refused. Zanuck also didn't want to use Gene Evans as the hero. "Look, Sam, your script is terrific. But your hero is in love with a linotype machine. The audience won't get it. We need stars. We need color. We need CinemaScope. Here's what we do. We cast Greg Peck as your crusading editor. Then we get Susan Hayward as the love interest. Or maybe Ava Gardner. Dan Dailey can play the guy who jumps off the Brooklyn Bridge. Mitzi Gaynor can be the barmaid. We write some songs and make it as a musical!"

Fuller was horrified, but Zanuck wouldn't budge. "With unknown actors in a black and white picture, your period piece is a loser, Sam."

Fuller made his movie independently with $250,000 of his own money, all of which disappeared down the drain, despite the fact that the film had a strong dramatic pulse and remarkable filmmaking brio. Fuller didn't take the rejection personally, going on to make a series of excellent pictures for Fox, including *Pick Up on South Street, Hell and High Water, House of Bamboo, China Gate*, and *Forty Guns*. He turned down Zanuck's offers to direct *The Desert Fox* and even *The Longest Day*.

Television had been bedeviling the movie industry for a number of years, so it made good sense for the studios to coopt some of TV's more obvious talents. Directors such as John Frankenheimer and Sidney Lumet were snapped up for far more money than the networks could pay. Herbert Swope Jr. had been directing *Robert Montgomery Presents* on television. The reviews of Swope's shows were excellent, his relationship with Montgomery indifferent. "He was terribly chic all the time and gave the show superficial supervision," remembered Swope. "He was very full of himself."

When Swope got an offer to come to Hollywood and produce pictures for 20th Century-Fox for $1,500 a week—twice what he was making in television—he didn't have to think about it. Swope talked about the move with his uncle Girard, the father of the photographer John Swope. "Tell me about your contract, Herbert," asked Swope.

"It's a splendid contract," said Swope. "A seven-year contract with yearly options."

"Congratulations, Herbert. You have a one-year contract."

Zanuck was out of town when Swope arrived at Fox. Swope noticed that nobody sat in Zanuck's chair in the executive dining room. Publicity head Harry Brand sat at the opposite end of the table, while Dick Powell and Jerry Wald sat in other chairs.

When Zanuck returned, he came into the executive dining room smoking a cigar and swinging his sawed-off polo mallet. He sat down, looked around the table, didn't nod to anybody. He then put a napkin under his lip and wiped his upper teeth. "You know," said Zanuck, "this is an amazing thing. Here we are gathered together, and we all know each other except this man here. Swope has joined us. Can any of you think of a worse time to join the movie industry than now?"

Swope noticed that Zanuck's preference for his isolated projection and editing quarters had a tactical component. "It kept him away from people and that fact helped him maintain control. When I made my second picture, I read a script that was one of the bunch that Charles Feldman had sold to Darryl in bulk. Like an idiot, I sent Darryl a note saying it would make a hell of a movie, except the title was poor.

"I came back from lunch to find my note back on my desk. Written on the bottom of it was this: 'My Dear Swope, let us retain the title.'"

When it came to scripts, Swope found Zanuck "very much on top of his game. He was strict and to the point. He was tremendous on script and could even rewrite. And a hell of a good croquet player."

Ah, croquet. Zanuck remained serious about the game, so much so that if you were a good player, you would get an invitation to play even if you made lousy pictures. Swope became part of Zanuck's weekend croquet circle, along with George Sanders—"a large intelligence and a terrible snob"—Howard and William Hawks, and, until he got sick, Humphrey Bogart. "The best player was Louis Jourdan. We'd line up and start. At Louis's turn, he'd pick up a cigarette with two fingers, inhale, drop the cigarette on the ground, clean out every wicket, come back to the first wicket, pick up the smoldering remnant of the cigarette and take another puff. On the croquet court, Louis was a machine."

Swope remembered that Sam Goldwyn was a strong competitor but not a strong player, and always ready to argue over whether or not he had hit or missed a stake. "Did Sam cheat? Yes, he cheated. Zanuck never cheated. He was all muscle and strength."

Croquet was an extension of life at the studio—success mattered, particularly if you were unsure of yourself, of your status. Swope produced a batch of pictures—*Hilda Crane, The True Story of Jesse James, The Bravados*—and then took over Fox's TV operation.

Buddy Adler arrived at Fox to produce movies at about the same time as Swope, so it was old home week—the two had known each other in New York. Swope was surprised by the status that Adler had, because in his previous incarnation Adler had been "a man about town at the El Morocco Club. Compared to Zanuck, Adler was very casual, very loose."

Change was in the air at 20th Century-Fox, and it involved a lot more than new hires. Philip Dunne saw a gradual alteration in Zanuck. "[Zanuck] started telling me how much money Frank Ross had made and kept on *The Robe*. He'd kept it because he got a capital gain on the whole thing because he'd developed the project and sold it. Zanuck figured out that on this one picture Frank had made and kept as much money as Zanuck had made and kept in ten years. Made and kept is the thing. He said, 'I'm in the wrong business.' I always had the feeling that he resented this very much, and was beginning to feel trapped. I also think he was tired. . . . He had to burn himself out sometime. Creatively, he had to burn out."

Zanuck was now fully primed for his designated bout of middle-aged crazy. The parade of transient girls in and out of his office at four p.m. had diminished after World War II, but for the first time anonymous women were replaced by a single obsession. Her name was Bella Wegier, but Zanuck changed her name to Bella Darvi, a combination of his and his wife's names.

They met in June 1951 on the Champs-Élysées. At that time, Bella Wegier was the companion of the actor Alex d'Arcy. She was a thirty-three-year-old Polish Jew who had been in a concentration camp during the war. She married in 1950, but that broke up quickly. She was passionate about gambling, which meant that she was always broke. The two couples had dinner that evening, and the Zanucks thought she was charming. The next day Wegier sent flowers to Mrs. Zanuck as a thank-you.

Zanuck and Wegier began their affair while they were still in Paris. The day after they consummated their attraction, she told him she had been banned from casinos because of her indebtedness and was on the verge of selling her wardrobe to raise money. She needed two thousand dollars. No problem—Wegier was free and clear by the next day.

In November 1952, she arrived in Hollywood and moved into the Zanucks' beach house at Santa Monica. Richard Zanuck was off at Stanford, while Darrylin was living with her husband, Robert Jacks, in Malibu. Bella's roommate was Zanuck's daughter Susan. The affair with Zanuck picked up where it had been left in Paris. Word got around—word always gets around. All this occasioned much gossip around town. Virginia Zanuck was universally liked and respected, but nobody could figure out the situation. Was she simply oblivious? Or was this some sort of ménage à trois?

The publicity machine began churning out stories about an exciting new actress who had been rechristened Bella Darvi. "She's got zip, zoom and zowie and in *parles vous*, she's *ravisante, chi chi*, and *tres elegante*. In any language that's hot stuff."

Zanuck was besotted and ordered up a screen test. To no one's surprise, he thought she photographed magnificently. He tossed her into two Fox pictures: *Hell and High Water* and *The Racers.* Her reviews weren't very good, but the pictures were pretty ordinary. Zanuck decided to double down and feature her in one of his personal productions, his big picture for 1954: *The Egyptian*, which was going to cost just a hair under $4 million.

The only problem was the fact that Darvi remained a compulsive gambler. "Gambling was absolutely a mania with her," said Zanuck. "She would win $150,000 one night and the next day she would have to pawn her jewelry, and then be back gambling again. I've seen her strip her rings and jewelry off and throw them on the table to call a bet." Psychologically speaking, movie producers are gamblers—they have to be—but even Zanuck was alarmed by Darvi's mania, which didn't mean he was able to pull himself away.

When Richard Zanuck returned from Stanford, he was as confused as everyone else. "I was really rocked. I didn't think it was possible. His taste left a lot to be desired. For a guy who could have had anyone, he went straight to the gutter."

Philip Dunne believed that Zanuck was essentially Victorian, pointing out the emphasis he placed on courage, self-reliance, and honor in his movies. "And we mustn't forget that it was the Victorians who strictly limited women to three categories: virgins, faithful wives and whores." Zanuck had signed Marlon Brando to play the title character in *The Egyptian*, but after a read-through of the script with Darvi, Brando walked off the picture, breaching his contract. Brando had to make *Desiree* as a make-good, but at least he was working with professional actresses: Jean Simmons and Merle Oberon. Zanuck cast around for a replacement for Brando and came up with Edmund Purdom, a dignified but bland MGM contractee.

Philip Dunne watched dumbfounded as the Zanuck who had always been in total command, who had erected an impregnable wall between his private life and his professional duties, suddenly became a passive supplicant to his mistress. "This mildly talented woman was granted powers he had always withheld from any of his other associates, male or female," wrote Dunne.

Zanuck asked Dunne to rewrite a scene of Darvi's in *The Egyptian* and then accompanied the writer to the set to get Darvi's approval. Later that day, Dunne was having lunch with Nunnally Johnson and asked him what on earth was happening. "Well," said Johnson in his Georgia drawl, "Bella made Darryl take her to bed, and until then Darryl thought it was somethin' you did on a desk."

Darvi's performance in *The Egyptian* is reminiscent of Hedy Lamarr at her most glacial—simultaneously beautiful and uninteresting, and with one expression: an attempt at frozen imperiousness. Darvi undoubtedly had talents, but acting wasn't one of them.

The Egyptian seems to have broken even, but it was the last hurrah for Bella Darvi. The story that went around Hollywood is that Zanuck's daughter Susan found out about her father's affair when she heard the two of them making love down the hall from Susan's room. Whatever happened, Virginia finally threw Darvi out of the house. Darvi left for France, and eventually Zanuck did, too. "I was still infatuated or sex crazy or whatever you call it," he said. "That was the beginning of the end of our marriage. . . . And it was all my fault."

Zanuck eventually got clear of her—Darvi returned to life in and around the Monte Carlo casino and committed suicide in 1971—but the pattern he had established with Darvi would be repeated for most of the rest of his life. He would take on a girl—usually a sultry brunette—feature her in some unsuccessful films, while playing the off-screen role of sexual supplicant.

In retrospect, it can be seen that the affair with Darvi was the beginning of Darryl Zanuck's move toward the door. "My separation and break-up from Mrs. Zanuck came at the same time as my divorce or break-up with Hollywood. Both turned together. Both came to head together. My mood was to escape, to get away from the scene, the social scene, the studio scene and everything connected with it. I felt I didn't give a goddamn. I felt I never would be able to create anything again."

Aside from burning out after thirty years of seventy- and eighty-hour workweeks, the problem was that the movie business was altering in ways Zanuck loathed. Besides the diminishing audience, Zanuck believed that he was spending too much of his time as "a negotiator, an executive, a peacemaker" instead of a moviemaker. He regularly inveighed against the Breen office, the enforcement arm of the Production Code. He would proclaim that they reflexively castrated any script that was in the least controversial, and he began to openly favor the comparative freedom of European filmmaking.

Late one night he was having a drink with Philip Dunne and he began venting. "In a very short time, the business will be completely dominated by the stars and their agents," he proclaimed. "Last week in this office a goddamn agent started to tell me how a script should be rewritten. I kicked the bastard out, but next week he, or another like him, will be back. We made the stars, but they've forgotten that. Now they think that they're entitled to run the business. Faces, that's all they are, just faces, but in today's market it's only faces that count, not brains. I'll tell you one thing: they'll never run my business, because I won't be here."

The studio he had built and energized, the studio that was unthinkable without his presence, was about to find out what life was like without a creative production head.

In March 1956, Darryl Zanuck announced that he was stepping down as production head at 20th Century-Fox in order to function as an independent producer releasing through Fox, with headquarters in Paris. Virginia Zanuck found out about all this in the newspapers. She was pointedly not invited to relocate with her husband.

Under the terms of his deal with Fox, Zanuck was to receive $150,000 a year as a consultant's fee, and the studio would fully finance the films he chose to produce. Zanuck would get 50 percent of the profits after the studio broke even on its investment. Zanuck left the studio in good shape. The films Fox released in 1956 included a roster of critical and commercial hits: *The King and I, Anastasia, Love Me Tender, The Man in the Gray Flannel Suit, Bus Stop,* and *Carousel.*

Zanuck told Hedda Hopper why he was leaving. "I just got . . . fed up with being an executive and no longer being a producer. That's what the job became. Actors are now directing, writing and producing. Actors have taken over Hollywood completely with their agents. They want approval of everything—script, stars, still pictures. The producer hasn't got a chance to exercise any authority!

"Now, I've got great affection for Duke Wayne, but what right has he to write, direct and produce a motion picture? What right has Kirk Douglas got? What right has Widmark got?. . . . What the hell, I'm not going to work for them!"

He was just getting warmed up. He deeply resented actors cutting themselves in creatively and financially on pictures when they didn't assume any financial risk. Basically, he thought the students were running the college. Most of the founding generation of moguls shared Zanuck's beliefs, but when push came to shove, Jack Warner and the rest of them had a less pugnacious attitude. They adapted and pretended to like it, but Zanuck could not play the game. Besides that, Jack Warner would never have walked away from the studio that bore his name. It wasn't a job; it was his identity.

This interview would come back to bite Zanuck . . . hard. When he needed John Wayne for a part in *The Longest Day,* Wayne charged him a whopping $250,000 for two weeks' work when almost all of the other actors in the film were working for 10 percent to 20 percent of that. Zanuck paid the money.

Before he left for Europe and independent production, Zanuck designated Buddy Adler as his successor. Adler had produced *From Here to Eternity* at Columbia and *Soldier of Fortune, The Left Hand of God*, and *Bus Stop* at Fox. They were all strong commercial pictures, but in hindsight Jerry Wald would have been a better choice. Adler looked the part—he was handsome, with white hair—but most of the veterans at Fox thought he was an empty suit. Certainly, Adler's script notes don't inspire much respect—he was always making tiresome criticisms about irrelevant details of a character's backstory, and was incapable of the total command that Zanuck brought to character and construction.

Most of Adler's time as production chief at Fox was spent cutting budgets. He forbade location work, allowed only one printed take per shot, and put an emphasis on reusing old sets rather than building new ones. Adler personally produced *South Pacific*, which Fox distributed for its general release, but it was Jerry Wald who produced most of the big hits of the Adler era: *Peyton Place*; *The Best of Everything*; *The Long, Hot Summer*.

Wald began as a writer at Warners and worked his way up to producing *Mildred Pierce* and *Johnny Belinda*. He then went over to RKO, which didn't last long—Howard Hughes was in the process of defenestrating the studio. Wald landed at Columbia, where he made *The Eddy Duchin Story*, then went to Fox with a contract that specified eighteen pictures over five years and a hefty percentage of the profits. Clearly, he had to hit the ground running, and he did.

Wald's specialty was taking potentially exploitive material and giving it a surprisingly refined, meaningfully dramatic treatment. Of course, if Wald had been running the company, it's entirely possible that the roster of his hits would have been mangled by other, less expert hands. Not all of Wald's Fox pictures were hits, or even good—*The Sound and the Fury* was a lamentable botch of Faulkner—but he was far and away the closest to Zanuck's particular combination of ambition and savvy.

Tactically, Adler made one huge blunder. Not only did he allow CinemaScope to be used for black-and-white pictures, he contracted with low-end producer Robert Lippert's Regal Pictures to turn out cheap B pictures using CinemaScope, which Lippert redubbed RegalScope. Lippert released twenty RegalScope films in 1957 alone—a fatal cheapening of what had been the premium Fox brand only four years earlier.

Among the pictures Adler backed, George Stevens's *The Diary of Anne Frank* verged on a runaway production. *Anne Frank* took place in an attic, cost nearly $4 million, and radically underperformed commercially. Fox promptly canceled Stevens's planned *The Greatest Story Ever Told*, which was even more expensive and eventually lost even more money for United Artists.

Because Adler didn't supervise anywhere near as closely as Zanuck, producers and directors were basically left to rise or fall based on their own strengths . . . and weaknesses. "The big asset that Zanuck had that really made the thing go was his unquenchable enthusiasm for what he was doing," said Philip Dunne. "He loved it and he was in love with the story. Good or bad, he made himself love it. You went out from there thinking, 'We're going to have the greatest [film] the world has ever seen.' Every time. Good or bad. This was invaluable. You run into the other kind, the frightened producer like Adler, who had no love for it, who was mistrustful, suspicious and frightened all the time. You walked out and you said, 'My God, what am I doing? Why are we doing this picture?'"

Zanuck had left the pipeline well stocked with projects, so the studio made money in 1957 and 1958, but by 1960 the studio posted a loss of almost $3 million, which was disturbing because 1960 was, by and large, a good year at the box office. Adler died of cancer in 1960, and in 1961 the loss increased by a multiple of seven.

The leadership of the studio fell to Chairman of the Board Spyros Skouras, who, for no good reason other than loyalty, named Robert Goldstein to succeed Adler. Goldstein didn't last long, at which point Skouras turned to his fellow Greek Peter Levathes, who had been the studio's head of TV production. It was the combination of Skouras and Levathes who put into production Greek-centered pictures such as *The 300 Spartans* and *It Happened in Athens,* which didn't appeal to anybody outside of Greece, and very few people within Greece.

Zanuck was not pleased by all this, but he was in no position to alter Skouras's decision. "I have had very little association with Peter Levathes," wrote Zanuck in June 1962. "I am sure that he is an excellent executive, and that he has showmanship instinct, but he is completely devoid of any sort of production experience. . . . He has to start every conference with . . . 'I realize I am not a producer . . . nevertheless I feel . . .' Your top people listen politely . . . and do as they see fit."

The nadir was 1961. Although Fox made *The Hustler,* one of the great pictures of the decade, and *The Comancheros,* an entertaining John Wayne western that was Michael Curtiz's last picture, codirected without credit by Wayne, the rest of the year was a total washout: *Wild in the Country*; *Snow White and the Three Stooges*; *Francis of Assisi*; *Sanctuary*; *Return to Peyton Place*; *Marines, Let's Go*; *Voyage to the Bottom of the Sea*; *All Hands on Deck*; *The Fiercest Heart*; *Pirates of Tortuga*; *The Wizard of Bagdad* . . . no need to go on. The losses for the year totaled $22.5 million.

1962 would be even worse. *Tender Is the Night, Hemingway's Adventures of Young Man, Satan Never Sleeps,* and a third version of *State*

Fair cost $15.5 million in total. They returned worldwide rentals of $10 million. Levathes walked the plank, and the top choices to replace him included Otto Preminger, Mike Frankovich, and James Aubrey, a CBS executive who was known as The Smiling Cobra.

"Utterly idiotic recommendations," snarled Darryl Zanuck from Paris. "I frankly wanted to vomit." Now confident of the withering incompetence of the regime at Fox, Zanuck began to plan his return from Elba. In a memo he let the dogs loose: "If and when Spyros decided that he wanted to step out of the presidency, I would present the following concrete recommendations based on the industry as it exists today. Whether or not I become the President is actually immaterial. I own with my family about 280,000 shares of stock, and the voting control of it all. I have a personal interest in the survival of the Corporation as well as a certain amount of pride in what was once described as 'the best operating studio in the industry.' I also have selfish interests.

"I would close down the studio and only complete the films that are either already in production or committed for. . . . I would sell the studio to the Fox Realty Company or a third party. . . . I firmly do not believe that our world grosses will suffer radically even if we do not start another picture in the next six to eight months."

He went on to admit that his record as an independent producer had been, uh, *spotty*, but "I believe that I have now profited by my error of judgement, and I am no longer confronted with private or personal problems which obsessed me prior to commencing *The Longest Day*. I will continue to make mistakes in this highly speculative business, but the 'know-how' I have acquired as a result of my failures and the lessons I have learned have been of enormous value."

Zanuck might have been driven to act by a heartfelt "Shane, come back!" letter written by Philip Dunne: "I have so much to say now that

I don't really know how to begin. So perhaps I won't begin at all, but merely tell you that you are sorely missed by all the people with any pretensions to integrity and professionalism who are still to be found at 20th Century-Fox. That includes . . . Charles Brackett, Jerry Wald, Mark Robson, Walter Lang and all the rest of us who shared the stimulus of your leadership in the great days of what was once a great studio. . . .

"I can no longer bear to enter the mortuary that used to be the commissary, so I bring my lunch every day and eat with the grips and electricians on the set. . . . There is one thing that should be said, and that is if the studio is to be saved, someone has to move—and move fast. I was never much of a company man, as you know, but now I see the studio dying before my eyes. . . . I almost wish the liquidators would take over and give it a quick and painless death, rather than see it eaten out from the inside by the rats, termites, lice and nameless creeping things that now infest the place. If I sound like some Cato mourning the great days of the Roman Republic, that is exactly how I feel."

Dunne's nostalgia was understandable, but the fact was that Zanuck had not been covering himself with glory since becoming an independent producer. His roster of pictures included *The Sun Also Rises, Island in the Sun, The Roots of Heaven*, and *Crack in the Mirror. Island in the Sun* made money and created a minor sensation because for the first time in a movie, a Black man kissed a white woman. Because the man was Harry Belafonte, it made Joan Fontaine seem merely a woman of good taste rather than a civil rights crusader.

The Sun Also Rises was shot in Mexico instead of Spain, where the Hemingway novel is set, because Mexico was cheaper. The cast was premium—Tyrone Power, Ava Gardner, Errol Flynn—but fatally overage for a story of disillusioned expatriate veterans after World War I. It broke even, but *The Roots of Heaven* and *Crack in the Mirror* were dead losers.

Aside from Zanuck's choices in material, there were problems with his decisions about the making of these pictures. *The Roots of Heaven* was shot in Cameroon, in temperatures of up to 130 degrees F. Almost everyone got dysentery, and malaria also swept through the company. All this contributed to a budget overrun of 33 percent. Errol Flynn attributed his own good health during the shoot to the fact that he refused to drink anything but Smirnoff vodka.

The underlying problem was that Zanuck, for the first time in his life, was not paying full attention to his movies. The novelist and screenwriter Peter Viertel, who wrote the script for *The Sun Also Rises*, understood what was happening: "An American businessman who made a fortune and suddenly women come into his life. They show him how to live. It's *Dodsworth*. He wanted to sit in cafes. He wanted to savor life. He fell in love with France, a very sensual, attractive country. He wanted to change everything about himself. In that way he's as interesting as Gauguin. You could write a *Moon and Sixpence* about Darryl. You could also write a *Blue Angel*."

Richard Zanuck also saw what was happening, but without the cultural references. "He wasn't thinking as clearly as he did. I mean, he still had the same enthusiasm for the pictures. But his main thrust really was the belief in the girls, really. 'Cause behind every picture, you'll see, there's a girl that he was going with. . . . He thought he could make anybody a star. And he thought that he could make any good subject into a successful picture. It didn't work out that way. So it was just a bad period. . . . Until *The Longest Day*, there wasn't anything that showed the real brilliance of the old DFZ. . . . It was because the motivations were wrong for making the pictures."

In fact, each of Zanuck's independent productions featured one of his mistresses. Bella Darvi had given way to Juliette Greco, who would eventually give way to Irina Demick. They were all beautiful, in the aristocratic, look-but-don't-touch tradition that tantalized Zanuck, but audiences weren't interested.

What was interesting was the sexual dynamic Zanuck exhibited with each of his mistresses. The sexually aggressive lord of the studio was nowhere to be found. Rather, he was an aging boy-toy who tried to curry the favor of a young woman by carrying her small dogs and making her a movie star. It never worked. "It was a one-sided affair," John Huston would remember about Zanuck's infatuation with Juliette Greco. "She was openly rude to him and spoke slightingly of him behind his back."

Richard Zanuck didn't quite know what to make of his father's latest iteration. "In some peculiar way," he remembered, "we had reversed roles. I became the father and he was the son. We had some very frank and strange discussions. They were quite unique in that I would be telling him—as he had told me years before—'For God's sake, can't you go out with the same girl twice?' . . . 'You're staying out too late and not getting enough sleep. Don't make a fool of yourself in public.' Sometimes he would abide by what I said because I was living a rational life at that time. I was a married man with my own children."

Fred Hift, who worked as a publicist for Fox out of the Paris office, said that Juliette Greco talked about her exploits with Zanuck. Greco reported that Zanuck would put a string of gorgeous pearls around her neck, then ask her to take all of her clothes off, leaving only the pearls. "When someone asked her why [she would do that], she answered, 'Well, they were nice pearls.'"

Zanuck soldiered on. His new obsession was not a woman—Juliette Greco eventually walked out on him—but a project: *The Longest Day*, Cornelius Ryan's epic history of D-Day. This, Zanuck believed, would be his ticket back to the top of the heap. It would be expensive, and

Spyros Skouras was shuddering over the cost—$8 million—but Zanuck was determined to forge ahead, even when people close to him tried to warn him away. Richard Zanuck, for one, thought it was a bad idea.

"What scared me was that we were getting into an eight or an eight and a half million dollar picture, which at that time was really fantastic. I thought, 'Jesus, this is liable to be really the end of the line.' I asked him, 'Who cares about World War II?' Most of the theatergoing public wasn't even born at that time. He was setting out to duplicate the entire invasion without using any stock or library footage. It was awesome."

Zanuck had two primary decisions to make. One involved shooting the picture in black and white or color, the other the nature of the casting. He opted for black and white for authenticity, and he opted for stars in order to help audiences keep track of the dozens of characters in the film, as well as for box office insurance. With those decisions made, he amassed an international cast of stars and a variety of directors.

Production began in the summer of 1961 and was completed, within the budget, in six months, although not without difficulty. Zanuck decided to shoot the landing at Omaha Beach in November, which meant that Robert Mitchum and Henry Fonda had to jump into a frigid Atlantic and react as if it was June. Zanuck also went through a roster of directors before finally settling on Ken Annakin to direct much of the picture. Annakin was originally signed to direct only the sections of the picture that dealt with the British, but those scenes came off so well, Zanuck assigned him to reshoot the Free French sections as well.

Zanuck hovered ceaselessly by the camera, always searching for ways to make a scene just a little better. Finally, he made an executive decision. "You know, I've always envied directors," he told Annakin. "I know I'm not a director, but I would really like to feel that this was my picture. Would you help me take over?"

For weeks, working with American stars such as Robert Mitchum, John Wayne, and Robert Wagner, Zanuck directed the picture. "I suppose I had enough experience with him not to be jealous of him in any way," said Annakin, "and I thought, Why the hell shouldn't I let him do it, if it makes him feel closer to the film? I had got to like Zanuck sufficiently by that time, and it was fun. After all, he had demonstrated at every moment during the production of the film that he was the master of it, and neither writers nor directors had been allowed to interfere with the way he wanted it. And somehow I got the feeling that no matter what might happen to him in the future . . . this would be regarded as his swan song, his greatest contribution to the cinema, and that if he never made another movie and departed now, he would be doing it in a blaze of glory."

In fact, the scenes Zanuck directed are among the best in the picture. "This is a cinch," he told his son. "All my life I've been baffled by this. It's the easiest thing in the world." Although he didn't take any directorial credit, Zanuck estimated the proportion of his footage in the finished picture was as high as 60 percent, and Richard Zanuck agreed that it was more than half.

So things were fine in Paris. But in Rome, the world was breaking apart. A picture called *Cleopatra* was turning into one of the great catastrophes in movie history.

CHAPTER EIGHT

THE RAZOR'S EDGE

O N SEPTEMBER 28, 1960, ROUBEN MAMOULIAN BEGAN shooting *Cleopatra* at Pinewood Studios in England, with a cast including Elizabeth Taylor in the title role, Peter Finch as Caesar, and Stephen Boyd as Marc Antony. Production crawled along, hampered by Taylor's chronic breathing problems that were exacerbated by the cold, damp English climate. On January 19, 1961, Mamoulian quit and Fox chairman Spyros Skouras accepted his resignation.

The day before, Skouras had a meeting with Joseph L. Mankiewicz and his agent, Charles Feldman. Skouras was currently paying Mankiewicz $8,000 a week to write an adaptation of Lawrence Durrell's *Justine*, but he begged Mankiewicz to put it aside and take over *Cleopatra*.

In and of itself, this was a strange, almost incomprehensible choice on Skouras's part. For all of Mankiewicz's skill with dialogue and actors, there was nothing in his résumé to suggest that he possessed the visual skills to energize a spectacle of ancient Rome. His most recent pictures consisted of a catastrophic adaptation of Graham Greene's *The Quiet American* that starred, for no discernible reason, Audie Murphy, and a wildly overwrought, albeit entertaining, version of Tennessee Williams's *Suddenly, Last Summer*.

For Feldman, the offer was a no-brainer. "Hold your nose for 15 weeks and get it over with," he told his client. After the lawyers were through with their haggling, Fox agreed to pay Mankiewicz $1.47 million to buy him out of Figaro, his production company, and an equal amount to NBC, his partners. Then there was his salary and expenses. In other words, hiring Mankiewicz cost Fox more than $3 million before he shot a foot of film.

With the deal complete, Mankiewicz flew to London on February 1 and looked at Mamoulian's footage—all ten minutes of it. He termed it "catastrophic and unusable." Fox paid off Peter Finch, and Skouras told Mankiewicz he wanted to start shooting on March 15 with a new script.

And so Joe Mankiewicz set to work while Elizabeth Taylor drew her salary: $125,000 a week for the first sixteen weeks, $3,000 a week for expenses, plus 10 percent of the eventual gross. For overtime, she got an extra $50,000 a week.

By March 3, Taylor had contracted pneumonia, which necessitated an emergency tracheotomy. Skouras decided to move the production back to Hollywood. After the sets were dismantled, shipped, and began to undergo reconstruction, Skouras changed his mind and decided to shoot exteriors in Rome during September and October, then shoot the interiors back in Hollywood. On June 30 he changed his mind again and decided that the entire picture would be shot in Rome. While all this was going on, Ranald McDougall came on to help Mankiewicz with the script.

Then came the matter of casting. Mankiewicz wanted Laurence Olivier for Caesar and Richard Burton for Antony. Olivier wisely passed, so Caesar went to Rex Harrison. Skouras wanted to retain Stephen Boyd, because he was under contract, but he eventually gave Mankiewicz what he wanted, which cost $250,000 in salary for Burton, and an extra $50,000 to buy him out of his contract for *Camelot*.

In Rome, Fox spent $6 million building outdoor sets for the Roman Forum and Alexandria Palace, which were actually larger than their historical antecedents.

Production began all over again on September 25, 1961, with an incomplete script that Mankiewicz continued to write at night after directing all day. Mankiewicz took injections of speed after lunch to get through till dinnertime, another shot afterward so he could get some writing done. Sleep became a problem because of what Mankiewicz termed "too much amphetamine and coffee."

Between the self-imposed pressure and a continuing flow of panic from Skouras and his minions, Mankiewicz began to fold. At one point, he threatened to quit. Things, he believed, had never been worse.

And then Elizabeth Taylor and Richard Burton began their affair.

On January 26, 1962, Taylor told Mankiewicz that she had fallen in love with Burton. Worse, she had told her husband, Eddie Fisher, all about the affair. At that point, Mankiewicz began months of playing shrink to the stars while simultaneously trying to whip an unmanageable beast of a movie for which he was completely unsuited into some sort of dramatic shape.

On February 17, Burton told Taylor he wasn't going to leave his wife, which led to Taylor swallowing what she said were fourteen sleeping pills. She was taken to the hospital, but Mankiewicz was unconcerned. "If she can count them, she'll be fine," he said. As news of the affair leaked out, the world media went certifiably insane.

On May 28, 1962, Mankiewicz called "Cut" on what he thought was the end of the main shooting of *Cleopatra*. At this point, Fox had spent more than $30 million, which is why they decided to forgo shooting the battle of Pharsalia, which was supposed to begin the picture. Rex Harrison was so upset that he offered to pay for the shoot himself.

Back in Hollywood, Fox had been trying to make a modestly budgeted romantic comedy with Marilyn Monroe and Dean Martin called *Something's Got to Give*, one of the more prophetic titles in movie history. Monroe looked luminous, but could not bring herself to show up with any regularity. Finally, Fox canceled the movie and wrote off a $2 million loss. Shortly afterward, Monroe died from an overdose of sleeping pills.

The board of directors fired Spyros Skouras, after which the studio also canceled the battle of Philippi. Among the names floated to take over the studio were Otto Preminger and Mike Frankovich. Over in Paris, Darryl

Zanuck clutched his chest at either possibility. "Preminger," Zanuck said, "was likely to go bankrupt running a kid's softball team. And Mike Frankovich . . . couldn't count up to fifteen unless you lent him one of your hands."

In the latter part of June, an alarmed Darryl Zanuck hurled himself into the abyss if for no other reason than to protect his stock holdings in the company. Zanuck's 280,000 shares of the company included 100,000 owned by Virginia, with another 137,000 shares owned by his children. The Zanuck family stood to lose an immense amount of money if the studio couldn't be stabilized. At least one member of the Fox board of directors, John Loeb by name, was openly agitating for liquidation.

Zanuck proclaimed that the board of directors had no business interfering in a picture made for a company that was showing $35 million in operating losses. The board relented and Mankiewicz returned to Italy to direct the battle of Philippi and a cheap version of the battle of Pharsalia for the second half of the film.

The board and stockholders alike suddenly wanted Zanuck to ride to the rescue and rend order out of this turbulent, chaotic sea of mismanagement and atrocious decision making. The losses were staggering. In 1962, Fox lost $39.8 million after taxes. The mounting debts forced the studio to begin divesting. First to go was its entire land holding in Westwood, sold to the Alcoa Aluminum Company. The price for the 334-acre lot was $43 million, with Alcoa promptly leasing back 75 acres to Fox as its core holding. The remainder of the land formed the foundation for the shopping and office complex known as Century City.

While all this was going on, Zanuck was finishing *The Longest Day*. The final cost was $7.75 million. Zanuck planned to release *The Longest Day* as a reserved seat roadshow picture, but the board of directors wanted a fast influx of cash and planned to release it in a saturation booking. To forestall the throwing away of his dream project, Zanuck announced his candidacy for the chairman of the board. *The Longest Day* was released as Zanuck wished and returned $17.5 million domestically.

On July 25, 1962, Zanuck was elected chairman. Afterward, he asked his son Richard to make a list of people who could function as the next production chief. He had no intention of re-upping for his old job, he told Richard. In fact, he had no intention of going back to Los Angeles; he was going to live in either Paris or New York.

Richard returned to his father's suite a few hours later and handed him a piece of paper with one name on it: Richard Zanuck. "There isn't anybody better for the job than me," he told his father. "Nobody knows the studio better than I do, nobody knows the personnel better than I do, and nobody knows you better than I do."

"You are absolutely right," replied Zanuck. And just like that, Richard ascended to the job his father had always expected him to have.

Nepotism was involved, but not on a lunatic level. Richard had graduated from Stanford, worked as a laborer at Fox, then in the editing rooms, then in advertising. He had broken in as a producer on *Compulsion*, a solid, modestly budgeted courtroom drama of 1959 based on the Leopold and Loeb murder case. Richard had also worked with his father on the elder Zanuck's independent productions.

On August 31, Darryl Zanuck wrote Joseph Mankiewicz that he wanted to see a first cut of *Cleopatra* no later than the first week of October. Mankiewicz had settled on *Cleopatra* being two separate films of about three hours apiece. Zanuck said that plan was a nonstarter—it would be one film of four hours, give or take. After seeing Mankiewicz's rough cut, Zanuck essentially took over the editing, relegating Mankiewicz to dubbing sessions with the principals. After the dubbing was finished, Zanuck fired him.

After many dueling press conferences centering on Mankiewicz's outrage and Zanuck's need to cut his losses—literally—the two men cooled down sufficiently to work together on reshoots in February 1963. On March 4, Mankiewicz finally finished shooting *Cleopatra*.

Holding fast to his eminently sensible belief that a movie that was dull at six hours would be less dull at four, Zanuck cut the picture to 243 minutes. Publicly, Fox said that *Cleopatra* cost $44 million, but their books actually carried the cost at $42 million. In its first release, *Cleopatra* returned $26 million in domestic rentals. Eventually, it turned a profit.

Despite Mankiewicz's belief in what he and his cast had accomplished, the film has never gathered many adherents. For one of the few times in her career, Taylor is clearly disengaged and walking through the part. In any case, Burton does enough acting for both of them with a performance that consists entirely of vocal calisthenics. Only Rex Harrison's Caesar summons the proper tone of imperial asperity, but he's murdered halfway through the movie.

Cleopatra destroyed Joseph Mankiewicz's self-confidence and emotional equilibrium, while giving Darryl Zanuck control of his studio once again. The problem was that, in the still of the night, Zanuck wasn't completely sure he wanted it.

In a letter he wrote to Jack Warner in January 1962, Zanuck had confessed his true feelings: "When I last talked to you, I said that I was ready to go back to Hollywood. I still am ready, but I am beginning to weave and wobble. . . .

"I am not bitter, but I just have reached the age and the point where I cannot spend my days with people I would not like to have dinner with at night."

20th Century-Fox was his once again. There was one question that was on everybody's mind, including Zanuck's: What was he going to do with it?

CHAPTER NINE

WHAT A WAY TO GO!

WHEN RICHARD ZANUCK ARRIVED BACK AT THE studio on Pico, there were only about fifty people at work. "Everybody else had been canned," he remembered. "We just sat around looking at each other. We closed down the commissary to save money and everyone—secretaries, producers, carpenters—ate lunch in a little electrician's shed. It's an awful thing to say, but things were so tight, we were trying to figure out ways to get another janitor off the payroll."

Among the people who had been canned was Charles Brackett, who had come to the studio ten years earlier and produced a long roster of hits that included *The King and I*, *Titanic*, and *Journey to the Center of the Earth*. Brackett's former partner Billy Wilder was outraged at the high-handed treatment handed out to his friend, and wired Richard Zanuck, "No self-respecting picture-maker would ever want to work for Fox. The sooner the bulldozers raze the studio the better it will be for the industry." Soon, the only thing shooting on the Fox lot was the TV show *Dobie Gillis*.

Eventually, the commissary was reopened, which was a good thing, as it was one of the most beautiful buildings in Old Hollywood, with a huge mural of the Fox studio and stars circa 1938. Prominently featured in the mural was the face of Darryl Zanuck, whose eyes seemed to follow you around the room.

The actual Darryl Zanuck remained in New York, and he and his son communicated via phone calls and memos. The relationship was oddly formal; the son referred to the father as "DZ," while the father referred to the son as "Dick Zanuck."

In some ways the elder Zanuck was the same man he had always been. Command agreed with him. As he told one writer, making movies went like this: "Sweat or go crazy. Get off or get on. Cancel or rewrite. The critical moment! Once you're embarked, you're embarked. You can embellish with a cast, with photography, location work. But when you get to it, the script is half of it. And before the script, the subject matter. You can bluff, but your bluff will catch up with you. You can have all the campaigns you want, but when you get right down to it, it's do they want it? And if they don't want it, they don't care who says it's good."

In other words, the success or failure of a given movie is usually decided by the story. It's what gives movie producers the shakes or a taste for substances that reduce anxiety.

In other ways, time had not been kind to Darryl Zanuck. Years of self-indulgence and the success of *The Longest Day* had nudged a man who was never given to modesty toward something approaching egomania. Fred Hift, a former reporter for *Variety*, had begun working for Zanuck as a publicist on *The Longest Day*, and after that he became Fox's European advertising and publicity director. Hift remembered, "I can't pretend . . . that I was particularly fond of Darryl Zanuck. Not that he ever behaved badly with me. On the contrary, within his limits, he was generous and at times, when he was in his raconteur mood, he could be fun. . . .

"The trouble was that the mythical Zanuck—the show-off genius who knew how to manipulate people and get the best out of them, the powerful and often ruthless woman-chasing czar in whose presence strong men quavered and females swooned—was pretty close to the real Zanuck.

"The Zanuck I knew was an opinionated, spoiled, often very cruel man who showed kindness only to his girlfriends; he had very little sense of real loyalty except to those whose talents and technical abilities he admired (and needed), and he seemed to have real problems relating to people as human beings."

Hift went on to enumerate events during the planning of publicity for *The Longest Day*. The place was Zanuck's cabana at the Eden Roc. The temperature was in the high 80s. Zanuck was in swimming trunks and drinking a cold beer while the publicity minions were in suit and tie and dying from the heat. "Zanuck, with a big pitcher of ice-water next to him, never thought of offering anyone a cold drink. It would never have occurred to him that we might be uncomfortable. We were there to serve him, and that's as far as it went."

The indifference to basic human needs vanished when the subject of one of Zanuck's girlfriends came up. Hift recalled that Zanuck once cut short a helicopter ride to Sainte-Mère-Église because one of his girl-friends complained that the hotel, counter to his instructions, had put a call through and woken her up at nine a.m. Zanuck rushed back to the hotel and demanded that the entire reception staff be fired.

Hift was unnerved by Zanuck's love of arbitrary danger—during one helicopter ride, Zanuck kept urging the pilot to fly lower and lower until the man flatly refused to descend another foot. "I never really under-stood Darryl Zanuck," said Hift. "He was rarely interested in anything except matters concerning moviemaking. The human element didn't seem to exist for him. He never went to the theater and he hardly ever read a book (except in synopsized form). His sense of humor, when he showed it, was often cruel and hurtful. The only thing he respected was technical proficiency. He loved gossip. And he knew very well that the power he exuded also generated fear. In fact, he encouraged it."

Hift was able to recall only one instance where Zanuck delighted him. During the production of *The Longest Day*, John Wayne asked Hift's sec-retary about her nationality. She said she was "half and half—half French, half American." Wayne was in his super-patriot mode that day and replied, "There is no such thing. You're either 100 percent American or nothing."

Hift's secretary told Zanuck about the exchange, and the five-foot, six-inch producer confronted the six-four actor. Zanuck was actively offended by Wayne's boorish remark. In front of the French crew, Zanuck braced Wayne. "Tell them what you told Hift's secretary," he said to Wayne. "I'm sure they'd like to know."

Wayne wouldn't repeat his remark, whereupon Zanuck said, "Well, if you won't tell them, I will. I think they deserve to know how you feel." After Zanuck told the crew about Wayne's remark, they refused to speak to the actor for the rest of his time on the film. "It was as if he wasn't on the set," remembered Hift. "It was one of the few occasions when I felt proud of Darryl F. Zanuck."

With Zanuck *fils* and *père* back in full control, they embarked on a policy of two lavish roadshow films every year, to be sold as reserved-seat attractions, anchoring an overall slate of twenty-four pictures. The first of the roadshow pictures was *The Sound of Music*, which quickly became the biggest hit in studio history with rentals in excess of $83 million. The new policy seemed to be emphatically confirmed.

Darryl Zanuck's initial casting choice for the part of Maria was Doris Day, who might have been a little elderly, but he acceded to Richard's choice of Julie Andrews after Richard screened footage from *Mary Poppins*, which was still shooting when they were casting *The Sound of Music*.

20th Century-Fox was back in a big way, and the studio embarked on an ambitious program of both production and infrastructure. Richard Zanuck instituted a New Talent School, hoping to develop a roster of potential stars at a modest cost of about $175 a week apiece. Among the follow-ups to *The Sound of Music* was *Those Magnificent Men in Their Flying Machines*, a sort of make-good on Zanuck's part to Ken Annakin for his yeoman work on *The Longest Day*. *Those Magnificent Men* turned out to be a solid commercial hit, with profits of more than $10 million.

Richard felt confirmed in his choices. "We're going all out for the big, family-type show that I suppose you could call pure entertainment," he told a reporter. "I'm very much aware that what we do here is seen by millions of people around the world. My first responsibility is to the company I work for, but I also have a responsibility as a person and as a filmmaker to put on things of which I can be proud. I don't intend to jeopardize that responsibility."

Remember this statement.

Other (supposed) roadshow blockbusters from Fox over the next few years included *The Blue Max*; *The Bible*; *Doctor Dolittle*; *Star!*; *The Sand Pebbles*; *Patton*; *Hello, Dolly!*; and *Tora! Tora! Tora! Patton* was a success, *The Blue Max* made some money, and *The Bible* broke even, as did *The Sand Pebbles*.

Eyes awash in fantasies of huge profits from *The Sound of Music*, other studios also went all in on musical spectaculars. Warners spent $15 million on *Camelot* and $6 million on *Finian's Rainbow*, while Paramount sank more than $50 million into *Half a Sixpence*, *Paint Your Wagon*, *On a Clear Day You Can See Forever*, and *Darling Lili*. MGM did a musical version of *Goodbye, Mr. Chips* as well as *The Great Waltz*. Universal made *Thoroughly Modern Millie* and *Sweet Charity*. Columbia made *Lost Horizon* with a score by Burt Bacharach. United Artists went with *Chitty Chitty Bang Bang*, *A Funny Thing Happened on the Way to the Forum*, *Fiddler on the Roof*, and *Man of La Mancha*. Disney made *The Happiest Millionaire* with Fred MacMurray and Greer Garson—just the cast that audiences in the mid-sixties were hungry to see.

Unfortunately, *The Sound of Music* was the last hurrah for a certain kind of Hollywood musical. The vast majority of the musicals that followed in its wake were financial as well as critical catastrophes. The Fox representative who attended preview screenings of *Doctor Dolittle* reported that even children were walking out, and Richard Zanuck always referred to *Star!* as "our Edsel," which was unfair to the Edsel.

Perhaps the problem was an excess of exclamation points and a lack of good movies.

John Gregory Dunne caught up with Darryl Zanuck in his office on West 56th Street in New York. Zanuck was just about to leave for the premiere of *Doctor Dolittle*, which was the first flop out of the roadshow box. Zanuck's office featured a Van Gogh and a Picasso, both copies—the building was now a glorified warehouse and no one wanted to risk authentic Impressionist paintings in such a lax, unsecured environment.

Zanuck was dressed in gray, with the only dab of color the rosette of the Legion of Honor he wore in his buttonhole. The cigar was always lit, and the conversation always amounted to a more or less free-flowing disquisition on the glory of Darryl F. Zanuck.

Doctor Dolittle had been a difficult shoot. The studio's first choice for the title character had been Rex Harrison, but after agreeing to make the picture, Harrison backed out. Fox then hired Christopher Plummer, after which Harrison changed his mind, which meant that the studio paid Plummer his full salary of $300,000 to go away. The production spent $1 million simply to train, house, and feed the menagerie of animals the picture required. Eventually, the movie went $6 million over the already generous $12 million budget.

"We've got $50 million tied up in these three musicals, *Dolittle*, *Star!*, and *Hello, Dolly!*, and quite frankly, if we hadn't made such an enormous success with *The Sound of Music*, I'd be petrified," said Zanuck.

"I was put under tremendous criticism when I sent Dick out to head up the studio. What could I do? He was the only one I could trust. What was crippling this company was the disloyalty, the fighting between the money people in the East and the picture people in the West. We don't have that anymore.

"I'm the only studio president who's been a producer, a director, a writer and an editor. Who knows the goddamn business. Well, when I took over I cleaned house. I knew things were bad, but not that bad. I paid off millions in contracts and threw out every goddamn script we had in preparation. They were all lousy.

"And then I sent Dick out there. I let him alone. . . . And then I thought if I went out there myself, I'd be cutting the ground out from under his feet. People would say, 'Hell, the old man is here, Dick's just an office boy.' So I let him alone. He calls me, he talks me into some things, and I talk him out of some things, I'm a picture maker and we've done all right."

The conversation turned to the future. Zanuck spoke highly of a possible picture about Malcolm X. "A picture like this can make a social contribution. Like *The Snake Pit*. After I made that, eleven states changed their laws about insane asylums. And *How Green Was My Valley*. It was laid in England, but it was the first picture to attack unfair unionism."

As John Gregory Dunne noted, "There [was] not so much paternal pride in Darryl Zanuck's voice as there [was] pride in his own executive acumen. He had picked a man to go to Los Angeles, the man had done the job he was asked to do, and the man incidentally was his own son."

Over the next several years, the roadshow losses were partially made up by some modestly budgeted films that became big hits, such as *Valley of the Dolls*, *The Planet of the Apes*—which also threw off profitable sequels—*M*A*S*H*, and *Butch Cassidy and the Sundance Kid*. The problem with hits like *Butch Cassidy* was that a lot of the profits reverted to the pockets of the talent who had made the movie, a fact which undoubtedly enraged Darryl Zanuck.

The fault was not so much in the execution, but in the entire concept of what audiences were looking for. Nowhere to run, nowhere to hide.

In fact, *The Sound of Music* was a fluke throwback to gentler times and led Hollywood to throw money at supposedly presold properties whose audience was either dead or disinclined to see throwback musicals.

The profits from *The Sound of Music* were further dispersed by nominal pictures such as *How to Steal a Million*, a pleasant but unremarkable comedy that cost a pricey $6.5 million because of its pedigree: stars Audrey Hepburn and Peter O'Toole, script by Harry Kurnitz, direction by William Wyler. It lost money.

The wheels began to come off in the first half of 1969, when the losses came to $13.1 million, which was amortized by selling South African theater holdings for $11 million. The studio wrote off $15 million on *Star!* and another $11 million on *Doctor Dolittle*. The studio stopped paying dividends and was spending $2 million a year in interest on its $24 million version of *Hello, Dolly!*, which couldn't be released until the Broadway show closed.

Besides *Star!*, the roster of stiffs included *Justine*, *Staircase*, *The Chairman*, and *Hard Contract*. Even allowing for *Butch Cassidy and the Sundance Kid*, it was a terrible year. A particularly egregious flop was *Che!*, a botched biography of the Cuban guerrilla Che Guevara that starred Omar Sharif as Guevara and Jack Palance as Fidel Castro. The film was fairly pricey at $5.1 million, got withering reviews, and did little business. Darryl Zanuck refused to admit that he might have been the wrong man to make that picture.

"I was proud of the movie. It was absolutely authentic in every goddamn detail. . . . One day, when bombings and wanton disregard of life and respect for law and order have become unfashionable, we're going to reissue *Che!* Seen again by an enlightened majority, it may be recognized for what it was—an accurate portrait of a brilliant but misguided rebel." To this day, *Che!* is so obscure that it's never really been parodied as brutally as it deserves.

In later years, Richard Zanuck gave the impression that he was being pummeled by his father's decline. "The last 15 years of his life he became very paranoid. It was scary. Some of the board members [came] to me and said, 'You should play a bigger role. As a matter of fact, you should be president of the company.' But I didn't want to be president of the company; I was already head of production. Some of the franker ones said to me, 'Your father is losing it.' A couple of them even said, 'You've got to hide him.' He was making a fool of himself with the girls and obviously drinking on top of it."

1969's results looked good compared with those of 1970, when the studio lost $77.4 million. Things got so bad that in July 1970 Richard Zanuck canceled all of Fox's political donations. "I know this is going to be very difficult in the cases of [Governor] Ronald Reagan and [US Senator] George Murphy," he wrote his executive assistant, "since you and I are both on their campaign fund-raising committees and I know they will expect similar contributions from the company as in the past. Both men, as we all know, have been very good to Twentieth Century."*

Economies became drastic. All wrap parties had to be paid for by the producer or director, not charged to the studio. Likewise, since night screenings in New York were pricey, they were canceled unless they were at the request of Darryl Zanuck. Richard suggested selling the Fox TV station in Minneapolis, even though it was profitable, because he thought it would decline in value "with the ultimate increase in cassette viewing." Cassettes wouldn't become ubiquitous for ten more years, but would not negatively impact the value of TV stations.

---

* Murphy had given a speech on the floor of the US Senate supporting the assistance of the Defense Department in making *Tora! Tora! Tora!*

Discussions began about auctioning off Fox's collection of props, which filled a three-story warehouse that covered most of a city block. Not surprisingly, Darryl Zanuck was against it: "WE SHOULD HOLD OFF ON ANY SALE OF PROPS AT THIS TIME," he telegraphed Richard. "I KNOW WE COULD USE THE MONEY BUT THE LONGER WE WAIT THE MORE WE CAN GET FOR THEM STOP HOWEVER MY BASIC REASON IS THAT IT WILL BE PICKED UP BY THE PRESS AND IT WILL GIVE THE OPINION THAT WE ARE REALLY SCRAPING THE BOTTOM OF THE BARREL."

There was undoubtedly an element of nostalgia in Darryl Zanuck's unwillingness to part with pieces of his studio, and perhaps even an element of self-preservation—once you started selling pieces of a studio, the economies might extend to jettisoning a certain elderly chairman.

But the Fox props fell prey to corporate desperation in February 1971 when two thousand of them were auctioned off for $364,480 net to the studio. Paul Newman's bicycle from *Butch Cassidy and the Sundance Kid* went for $3,000; Julie Andrews's gros point roses carpetbag from *The Sound of Music* brought $650.

It can safely be assumed that they have since appreciated in value.

The studio tried to counter the fire-sale atmosphere by pointing to the Best Picture win of *Patton*, and to the fact that two of their pictures—*The Panic in Needle Park* and *Walkabout*—were invited to the Cannes Film Festival. It didn't seem to help.

Richard prepared a list of studio personnel to be let go as soon as possible, including Elmo Williams, the producer of *Tora! Tora! Tora!*, and Frank McCarthy, the producer of *Patton*. Richard ended up firing ten executives, at a savings of more than $500,000 for the year. That same month, Fox failed to renegotiate a $25 million financing arrangement with Equitable Life Assurance, which meant they defaulted on a $25 million loan from Metropolitan Life Insurance.

The studio cut its output for the next year to twelve to sixteen films, which implied a corresponding number of staff cuts. In August, Darryl Zanuck announced that Fox's cash flow was just fine, and there would be no problem maintaining operations and perhaps even paying down some of Fox's bank debt. Somehow, they anted up $6.3 million on July 30, following payments of $7.5 million in the first part of the year.

Stan Hough, the studio's production manager, remembered that there was tension between the Zanucks over *Tora! Tora! Tora!*. Darryl wanted to make it, seeing it as a logical extension of *The Longest Day*, while Richard thought it was a bad idea. Richard looked at it logically— *The Longest Day* was about a daring, successful Allied operation that made victory inevitable, whereas *Tora! Tora! Tora!* was about the raid on Pearl Harbor, an equally successful Japanese operation that destroyed America's Pacific fleet. And there was something else: *The Longest Day* featured twenty-five honest-to-God movie stars, from John Wayne, Henry Fonda, and Robert Mitchum to Sean Connery. *Tora! Tora! Tora!* featured a cast of competent but uninspiring character actors, probably so all the money could be spent on the attack sequence.

Fox enlisted Akira Kurosawa, indisputably one of cinema's great masters, to direct the Japanese sequences, but Kurosawa shot for three weeks and produced no usable footage. A neuropsychologist examined him and wrote to Zanuck that Kurosawa was "suffering from disturbance of sleep, agitated with feelings of anxiety and in manic excitement. . . . It is necessary for him to have rest and medical treatment for more than two months." Richard Zanuck had to travel to Japan to tell Kurosawa the studio was replacing him, which he termed "one of the worst things I ever had to do." Kurosawa went on to make *Dodeskaden*, which failed commercially, and he attempted suicide in December 1971. He remained unemployed until a few years later, when Mosfilm offered him financing to make *Dersu Uzala*. The success of that film propelled him to the late glories of *Ran* and *Kagemusha*.

Tora! Tora! Tora! brought the disagreements between Richard and Darryl into the open. "Dick and Darryl weren't getting along at all," said Elmo Williams, the producer. "Dick being head of production, that meant I was reporting to him. Darryl, on the other hand, was taking a very personal interest in the film and on several occasions said, 'Now, look, you report directly to me. Don't report to Dick.' This made a very difficult situation."

The best case for *Tora! Tora! Tora!* was an eventual breakeven.

On May 30, 1970, Darryl Zanuck peremptorily ordered his son to pull in his horns: "IN ADDITION TO PREVIOUS ECONOMIES AND ELIMINATIONS OF PERSONNEL AT THE STUDIO YOU WILL EFFECTIVE AS OF TODAY DISPENSE WITH THE SERVICES OF ALL STUDIO EMPLOYEES THAT ARE NOT ACTIVELY ENGAGED IN FINALIZING THE EDITING, SCORING AND RERECORDING OF OUR COMPLETED FILMS STOP YOU WILL FOLLOW THE SAME TERMINATION PROCEDURES WITH ALL PRODUCERS, WRITERS OR DIRECTORS WHO ARE NOT NOW ACTIVELY ENGAGED IN FUTURE PRODUCTIONS THAT HAVE BEEN APPROVED BY THE BOARD OF DIRECTORS AND ME STOP YOU ARE NOT TO DISPENSE WITH THE SERVICES OF ANY EMPLOYEE WHO HAS A CONTRACT BUT YOU ARE TO REFER ALL THESE TO ME FOR CONSIDERATION AND DISPOSITION STOP IF YOU ARE NEGOTIATING FOR ANY FUTURE PROJECTS THAT HAVE NOT BEEN APPROVED BY ME YOU WILL SUBMIT SAME TO ME FOR MY APPROVAL BEFORE CONCLUDING NEGOTIATIONS STOP."

It was at this point that Richard Zanuck declared his independence. On June 2, 1970, he sent his reply: "I AM SHOCKED BY THE CONTENT AND THE METHOD YOU HAVE CHOSEN TO CONVEY YOUR MESSAGE DATED MAY 30 1970. IT IS INCONCEIVABLE THAT IN ANY WELL ORDERED AND PROPERLY MANAGED CORPORATION THE CHAIRMAN AND CHIEF EXECUTIVE OFFICE WOULD ISSUE AN ORDER OF THIS MAGNITUDE WITHOUT FIRST CONSULTING THE PRESIDENT OF THE CORPORATION AS WELL AS ITS TWO EXECUTIVE VICE PRESIDENTS. IN REGARD TO ECONOMIES YOU ARE WELL AWARE THAT THE STUDIO HAS REDUCED ITS EXPENDITURES AND PERSONNEL TO A FAR GREATER EXTENT THAN ANY OTHER DIVISION OF THE COMPANY. THESE ECONOMIES HAVE BEEN ATTAINED OVER A LONG PERIOD OF TIME AND FURTHER DRASTIC CUTTING IS UNDERWAY. . . . FURTHERMORE I AM SURPRISED TO HAVE RECEIVED THIS UNILATERAL COMMUNICATION FROM YOU SINCE OVER THE PAST WEEKEND YOU HAVE REFUSED TO ACCEPT TELEPHONE CALLS NOT ONLY FROM ME BUT FROM THE EXECUTIVE VICE PRESIDENT OF CREATIVE OPERATIONS WHO WAS TRYING TO REACH YOU FROM LONDON. ON EACH OCCASION THAT I WAS ABLE TO GET THROUGH TO YOUR ROOM AT THE PLAZA HOTEL YOU OR ONE OF YOU ASSOCIATES HUNG UP ON ME. THIS UNNATURAL BEHAVIOR RESULTED IN THE LOSS TO THIS CORPORATION OF A MOTION PICTURE PROJECT WHICH BOTH THE EXECUTIVE VICE PRESIDENT IN CHARGE OF CREATIVE OPERATIONS AND MYSELF REGARDED AS A HIGHLY PROFITABLE VENTURE. . . .

"AS CHIEF EXECUTIVE OFFICER YOU HAVE THE AUTHORITY TO ISSUE ANY ORDER. HOWEVER AS PRESIDENT OF THIS CORPORATION AND AS A DIRECTOR IT IS MY DUTY TO INFORM YOU

THAT TO CARRY OUT YOUR ORDER IN THE MANNER YOU STIPU-LATE WOULD IN MY OPINION RESULT IN A LOSS OF PRODUCTIV-ITY INJURIOUS TO THE CORPORATION. . . .

"YOUR LACK OF FAMILIARITY WITH THIS STUDIO ORGA-NIZATION IS UNDOUBTEDLY THE RESULT OF YOUR FAILURE TO BE PRESENT AT THIS PLANT FOR MORE THAN THIRTY DAYS DURING THE LAST EIGHT YEARS. . . . THEREFORE BECAUSE OF MY RESPONSIBILITY AS PRESIDENT I MUST DEFER ANY SUCH ACTION AS YOU HAVE ORDERED PENDING PROPER CONSULTA-TION WITH ME. IF THS SUGGESTION IS NOT ACCEPTABLE TO YOU THEN I WILL BE COMPELLED TO DISCUSS THIS MATTER AS WELL AS THE LONG TERM FUTURE OF THIS CORPORATION AND MY ROLE AS PRESIDENT OF IT WITH THE MEMBERS OF OUR BOARD OF DIRECTORS."

In the long history of fraught father-son relations, this exchange has to be considered primary. The conflict was built into the professional relationship—if Richard Zanuck was going to be the studio head, he had to be able to make his own decisions, but Darryl Zanuck reserved the right to peremptorily countermand his son. The elder Zanuck had little choice but to either accept his son's proposition or banish him from the company. Since Zanuck's primary identity was as the founder of 20th Century-Fox, a position which had always taken precedence over his paternal duties, what followed was predictable.

Part of the problem was Darryl Zanuck's developing grudge about and scapegoating of David Brown, who was the executive vice president of creative affairs Richard Zanuck had referred to. Brown was a genial, rather professorial man who had served as story editor at Fox in the 1950s, and Darryl Zanuck had developed a paranoid fixation that his son's loyalty to Brown exceeded his loyalty to DFZ.

"He came to hate me," said Brown. "I was Dick's Svengali. That whole thing. I became the enemy. And I had been fond of D.Z. We were both, Dick and I, fond of him. But by this time in his life he was only good for two or three hours a day."

In Darryl Zanuck's mind, his son's refusal to acquiesce to his peremptory demands was not merely disloyal, it was a betrayal. And so the final showdown began to take shape.

Since the string of blockbusters that Richard Zanuck had put into the works had mostly bombed, he overcorrected and lurched to making exploitation pictures on the cheap. Richard hit first on sex, then on sex squared in the form of Russ Meyer. Sex came calling in the form of *Myra Breckinridge*, Gore Vidal's best-selling novel about a transsexual movie star, while Meyer had grossed $6 million with a soft-core film titled *Vixen* that had cost $72,000.

Meyer was a lusty, funny man without pretensions, but with obsessions. "I like women who enter into sex like it was a soccer match," he said. Richard commissioned Meyer to make *Beyond the Valley of the Dolls*, with a script by the *Chicago Sun-Times* movie critic Roger Ebert. The film cost a reasonable $2 million and returned nearly $7 million in domestic rentals, but the studio's profit was lessened when they had to pay Jacqueline Susann $1.4 million to settle a lawsuit over an unauthorized sequel to her novel. In addition, *Beyond the Valley of the Dolls* came at a cost, that of loss of prestige. Beyond that, it also infuriated Darryl Zanuck, who thought the film was an abysmal exercise in filth.

Richard Zanuck, who had made statements only a few years before attesting to his high-minded principles ("I . . . have a responsibility as a

person and as a filmmaker to put on things of which I can be proud . . .")
was now engaged in flagrant low-end exploitation.

Meyer went on to make his second picture for Fox, *The Seven Minutes*, based on a bestseller by Irving Wallace—a fast flop. *Myra Breckinridge* cost more than $5 million—Fox paid Mae West $350,000 to make an ill-advised comeback—and lost a lot of money and even more in prestige. A scene involving Raquel Welch, a dildo, and a muscle boy strapped to a medical table occasioned stampedes of walkouts.

The reviews for all these pictures were dire. The prevailing attitude on the part of both critics and the public was simple: "What the hell are they thinking?" That same year, Richard took the high road with *The Only Game in Town*, a bittersweet love story with Elizabeth Taylor and Warren Beatty, miscast as her lover after Frank Sinatra ducked out. The director was George Stevens, who had directed Taylor in earlier triumphs such as *A Place in the Sun* and *Giant*. Taylor was making $1.125 million, Beatty was making $750,000, and the picture was made entirely in Paris, despite the fact that the story took place in Las Vegas, because Taylor wanted to be close to her husband. Richard Burton was shooting *Staircase* for Fox with Rex Harrison, in which they played a bickering gay couple.

Stevens directed the picture for sober realism, but Taylor had gained too much weight to play a showgirl, which only accentuated the age disparity between her and Beatty. Both pictures were complete failures critically and commercially—*The Only Game in Town* lost $7.5 million. George Stevens never directed another film. As for *Staircase*, that only lost $5.2 million, while *Justine* lost $6.6 million.

While Fox was crumbling, Darryl Zanuck was largely focused on the career of one Genevieve Gilles. They had met at Maxim's when she was nineteen and he was sixty-three. She was a fashion model and, yes, beautiful. As was his pattern, Zanuck spoiled her. There was a large diamond that cost $150,000. Then there was an emerald with a matching bracelet, and a pair of earrings made of gold coins minted in Iran. After that came furs—five minks, two foxes, a sable, an ocelot. Her favorite designer was Yves St. Laurent, so that designer had a sudden windfall. To break up the monotony she also wore Valentino. When they went to Monte Carlo, where Zanuck liked to gamble, he would give her the bulk of his winnings.

Zanuck's relationship caused problems in his relationship with his son. "I had a very large loathing for this girl," Richard Zanuck told Stephen Silverman. "I had weathered, rather pleasantly in most cases, many of my father's other girls, so it wasn't that there was any rivalry or jealousy between son and girlfriend. It was just that this particular one was really bad news and caused, him, myself, and the company a lot of trouble. When she knew that she had a real enemy in me, she did a lot of unfair and unfortunate pillow talk, which didn't help my father's and my relationship."

Richard went on to explain that he wasn't suddenly possessed by the spirit of Goody Two-shoes, but the fact that the studio was faltering while Zanuck was once again planning a glorified vanity production with his girlfriend was a considerable political problem. "What happened fundamentally was that there was a fear among his closest associates in New York that if something weren't done, there would be severe criticism by the board and the stockholders."

In 1970, Garry Marshall and Jerry Belson wrote and produced a picture called *The Grasshopper* starring Jacqueline Bisset and Jim Brown. It was about a young girl who leaves Canada and comes to LA, where, after a long series of bad choices, she becomes a prostitute—a burned-out case at twenty-one.

The Grasshopper opened in May, and a few weeks after it quickly closed, Marshall and Belson got a call from someone who said he was Andre Hakim, calling for Darryl Zanuck. Belson was not in the mood for jokes, so he hung up. A few minutes later the phone rang again. This time it was Jerry Paris, who had directed *The Grasshopper*. Andre Hakim had called him right after Belson hung up. He told Paris that Darryl Zanuck had seen *The Grasshopper*, loved it, and wanted Marshall, Belson, and Paris to make a movie for him. There were first-class plane reservations and rooms at the Plaza for all three of them.

They eventually arrived at the Plaza and were told by Hakim—one of Zanuck's sons-in-law—that they were free until ten p.m., when Mr. Zanuck would meet them in his seven-room penthouse suite. That night, they were ushered into the sanctum sanctorum. They saw a little man wearing a bathrobe and smoking a large cigar. He was shouting into a telephone. The general gist of the diatribe was that Howard Hughes was a goddamn liar and it was time to sell the shares.

Zanuck hung up and welcomed his prospective filmmakers. There was a gold crest on his bathrobe, on his slippers, and on the handker-chief that hung out of the pocket of the robe. He shuffled a little bit as he walked, but his handshake was, remembered Belson, "a bone crusher."

Zanuck explained that he was looking for a vehicle for Genevieve Gilles, and he had been impressed by *The Grasshopper*. He wanted them to write and direct a vehicle for his star and pitch him some ideas the next evening.

So far, so bad. Zanuck was outlining everything he wanted in a confi-dent, brisk manner, but he would occasionally come to a dead stop and . . . zone out. It was as if a radio signal suddenly disappeared. When this happened, Andre Hakim would either nudge Zanuck or prompt him with a key phrase, at which point Zanuck would pick up the thread and return to his oration.

At one point, Zanuck returned to his bedroom and emerged with a photo of Gilles. She was wearing a nightgown, her lips were puckered, and she had signed the photo with a lipstick kiss. He closed the meeting by telling the three men he was sure they were going to give him a hit, and after that he had another project in mind for them. It was an Elliot Gould movie called *Move,* and all the movie needed was rewrite and a director. The partners glanced at each other. *Move* was playing in Manhattan while Marshall, Belson, and Paris were talking to Darryl Zanuck.

The next morning, Marshall, Belson, and Paris watched all the extant film on Genevieve Gilles. The first one was a short subject called *The World of Fashion* that had dozens of costume changes for Gilles and constituted a lavish screen test. The men agreed that she was indeed beautiful. That was followed by *Hello-Goodbye,* a film she had just made for 20th Century-Fox. Ronald Neame had been hired to direct, and he believed that a partial reason for his employment was that "I was no threat. I was then already an elderly gentleman. Of course, I don't think Darryl was much older. In any event, he was very protective of her. He had detectives surrounding her."

Ronald Neame had been shooting for two weeks when he quit because of Zanuck's interference. Neame demanded that he be paid in full. Zanuck agreed, but made Neame promise not to discuss his involvement with the picture for a period of three years. If he broke the agreement, he'd have to forfeit his salary.

Jean Negulesco, Neame's replacement, insisted that Neame had been shooting for three and a half months and about twenty minutes had been shot. Negulesco thought the footage was excellent, but . . . only about twenty minutes. Negulesco had made pictures such as *Johnny Belinda* and *The Best of Everything* and was quite a reputable director, but it was clear that this was a salvage job, pure and simple.

Hello-Goodbye cost nearly $5 million. Zanuck paid Negulesco twice his salary, so much money he was able to buy an apartment in Paris with the excess. The plot involved a beautiful girl torn between a poor young auto mechanic (Michael Crawford) and a rich man with a lot of expensive cars (Curt Jurgens). "It's a perfect feature introduction for her," said Zanuck, "and she doesn't have to be Sarah Bernhardt to play it."

The first word of the film was "Hello," the last was "Goodbye." It was a hopeless vanity production.

When the screening of *Hello-Goodbye* ended, Marshall, Belson, and Paris again looked at each other and realized their fantasy of a sinecure at 20th Century-Fox had just gone up in smoke. They would have to turn down the job. That night they returned to the penthouse suite at the Plaza, where Miss Gilles was in attendance to pass judgment on their nonexistent idea. They were stalling, and Belson was sweating. Finally, he burst out with an impromptu pitch. "We do a movie about an International Beauty Contest—Miss World or something. The finals are in Paris and Genevieve is Miss France. While the girls are rehearsing in their bathing suits, some kidnappers show up. They grab five beauties and take them to a remote location."

Seized by an equal measure of desperation and greed, Belson continued talking. Gilles would organize a resistance wherein the girls would stop their bitching and backbiting and escape. "Miss Canada lulls a guard to sleep by playing her accordion. Miss USA tap dances to drown out the sound of a hacksaw—stuff like that!" They all escape in time for Genevieve to win the Miss World contest. "Robert Shaw would be great as the boss of the kidnappers!" said Belson as he wrapped up.

Zanuck leapt up. "I love it! It's damn good! I want to buy it!"

A few days later, a check for $10,000 arrived at Marshall and Belson's office. Jerry Paris was in favor of cashing the check and going ahead with the beauty contest story, but Marshall and Belson had too much pride. The story was idiotic, and the executive producer was obviously in the early stage of dementia. Of course, good movies have been made under worse circumstances. After more bickering, they sent the check back. They never heard from Darryl Zanuck again.

Hello-Goodbye was released later that year and lost $3 million. Compared with the losses on pictures like *Hello, Dolly!*, which lost $13.7 million, it was the proverbial drop in the bucket. The difference was that any studio in Hollywood would have made *Hello, Dolly!* Nobody but Darryl Zanuck in mental decline would have made *Hello-Goodbye*.

Neither Genevieve Gilles nor Jean Negulesco ever made another film. The reality was that Darryl Zanuck was failing. "He was showing some very early signs of senility," said Richard. "He became paranoid, partly, I think, because he felt his power with women and in life generally emanated from that position at the studio. He felt that any removal of that power would de-ball him. Not only in the business world, but in his social life. He was scared things would crumble for him if he was moved aside."

The long radio silence that Belson, Paris, and Marshall had observed became a common occurrence. Darryl Zanuck would be conversing, suddenly fall silent for as long as five minutes, then pick up the conversation again. "Everyone around him just behaved as if nothing was wrong," said one executive.

The accumulated losses mixed with the obviousness of Zanuck's impairment finally forced a stockholders revolt, and that led to the usual amount of internecine warfare. Business consultants were called in to examine the Zanucks' track record and gave out with the remarkable observation that 20th Century-Fox had subsisted on "non-recurring phenomena"—that if you took *The Sound of Music*, *M*A*S*H*, and *Butch Cassidy and the Sundance Kid* out of the equation, the years that the Zanucks had run the studio in tandem were a disaster. "If it had not been for *Sound of Music* and sale of old features to TV, the corporation would have gone bankrupt on features produced during period 1963-1970," wrote one financial analyst.

To be specific, of the 120 films that the Zanucks had made since retaking control of the studio, eighty-four had lost money, nine were better than breakeven, twenty-three produced "adequate" profit, and three were smashes relative to cost: *The Sound of Music*, *Zorba the Greek*, and *M*A*S*H*.

To which David Brown retorted, "Idiots, this is a business of non-recurring phenomena. Make ten films, and if two work, then you have glory and profit."*

Darryl Zanuck attempted to put an end to the brawl by signing off on the board's decision to fire Richard Zanuck, whose contract was terminated in December 1970, four years before it was due to expire. He was told to be out of his office by noon. "He fed his son to the sharks," is the way David Brown put it.

For Richard, it was a devastating betrayal. "It was like an execution," he said. "I felt terribly let down that my own father could do this to me," Richard Zanuck remembered. "He was very cold ass at that meeting, very cold ass. Jesus Christ, it was brutal. And my father, talking, just sitting there, he showed absolutely not any ray of compassion for me.... It was an execution.

---

* Brown was right. To a great extent, the contemporary movie studio's dependence on a production philosophy based on preexisting intellectual property—i.e., superheroes in spandex tights—is an attempt by MBAs to ward off the hard fact that the movie industry has *always* subsisted on "non-recurring phenomena."

"Nobody was looking at me. It was like I had the plague or something. And the loss of the company, my position. Everyone makes the mistake of assuming that their positions will go on forever, and it only came to me afterward that . . . nothing was permanent. Fox studios, which I had been controlling for so long, for nine years, a semi-demi king there, was suddenly no longer mine. It came at such a great loss that I no longer controlled it. And it made it no less agonizing that the man who had taken it away from me, who had replaced me, was my own father."

At bottom, Darryl Zanuck sacrificed his child for a temporary assertion of his failing power. But Richard understood that "if I had lost, so had he." Once the tumbrils start rolling, nobody's head is safe. "At any moment they choose, they can dismiss you too," Richard told his father. "Without more than a flicker of a glance at me, he shrugged his shoulders and casually said, 'It will never happen,' and went on to other business."

Richard Zanuck returned to the studio in Westwood. His car was parked at the curb in his designated parking space. "I couldn't get into the car because the painter was down on his knees in front of the thing painting my name out. I couldn't open the door without asking him to stand up so I could drive off. . . . It gave me an extraordinary feeling. From being a king, or a crown prince, suddenly I was made to feel like a criminal. The guard was watching me as if I was about to steal an ashtray."

Elmo Williams, who had produced *Tora! Tora! Tora!*, was named head of production.

William Fox would have understood the situation perfectly. "I do not know whether foxes ever run in packs, but I have read about wolves," he told Upton Sinclair, "and have learned that a wolf is not attacked so long as he is well and strong, and is running at the head of the pack. It is only when something happens to him, so that he stumbles and falls, that the other wolves fall upon him."

As it had been with William Fox, so it was with Darryl Zanuck. In the spring of 1971, just a few months after he had separated his son from the job he had been born into, Darryl F. Zanuck was given the title of chairman emeritus and removed from control of 20th Century-Fox. Virginia Zanuck threw her share of the company against her estranged husband, saying he was "destroying" the dynasty he had spent decades building. What all this meant was that for the first time since 1923, Darryl F. Zanuck was out of the movie business.

Darryl Zanuck could have taken some comfort in the fact that nobody who ever ran a major studio had done it better. But like most men of great achievement, Zanuck lived completely in the present and future, not the past. What he had done was unimportant; what he would do was now nonexistent.

In February 1972, the old man had surgery for cancer of the jaw. Zanuck was concerned about being disfigured, so the operation was performed from inside his mouth, which necessitated removing several teeth and part of his tongue, not to mention muscles and lymph nodes from his neck, and a portion of his jaw. While Zanuck was in the hospital, his suite at the Plaza was burglarized and six paintings were cut from their frames. Three of them were fakes that had been painted for *How to Steal a Million*, but three were originals. There was no forced entry, so the burglary had to be considered an inside job.

Richard Zanuck was unsure about what to do when his father was hospitalized. He was processing his bitterness over being fired, but he was also afraid of being rejected yet again. Finally, he picked up the phone and called. "Dad, I hear you've been ill. Would you like me to come and see you?"

"Of course," said Darryl Zanuck.

"Shortly after that," said Richard, "every time I would go to New York on . . . business, I would go and see him, and we became close again."

The strange thing was that Darryl gave no sign that he was aware of any estrangement. He seemed oblivious to the fact that he had seriously hurt his son.

"I decided he didn't feel he had wronged me at all, and therefore had no guilt about it. He had simply felt he was losing control [at the studio] and that, for him, was unthinkable. In the movie business, he didn't care who got hurt, even his own son, so long as he didn't get hurt himself."

After the surgery, Zanuck couldn't eat solid food for a month, and was understandably depressed. It was around this time that his memory issues got worse—he would get lost on his daily walk in Central Park. This was not what Genevieve Gilles had signed up for, and she began to spend more time away from Zanuck. In April, she was in Paris while he was still marooned at the Plaza, and he sent her a cable: "DEAR GENEVIEVE, HAVE TELEPHONED FOUR TIMES TODAY AT EXACT HOUR YOU SUGGESTED AND HAVE BEEN UNABLE TO REACH YOU. I STILL LIVE AT THE PLAZA HOTEL, PLAZA 9-3000, SUITE 1125. WILL AWAIT YOUR CALL." He signed it, "LOVE, LISA AND TINA"—his Yorkies.

A November deposition made Zanuck's deteriorating condition a matter of public knowledge. He couldn't give the address of Fox's offices in New York, didn't remember when he had begun working for the company or the number of shares he owned.

Once again Zanuck had to be hospitalized, and his three children came to visit. He was in no condition to be left alone, not now, not ever, so they had to move him. The question was: Where? Richard suggested a spa in Switzerland, but Darrylin insisted on taking him back to Ric-Su-Dar in Palm Springs. Richard pointed out that their parents had had almost no contact for seventeen years, but agreed to call his mother anyway. To his surprise, she gave him a flat order: "Bring my husband home." When the children talked to their father, he calmly agreed to return to Palm Springs and his wife.

On April 7, 1973, Zanuck flew back to California. Virginia Fox Zanuck, who had not seen him in seventeen years, was there to meet him. Zanuck ran to meet her, took her hand, and obediently followed her to the limousine. He was in bad shape, weighing about ninety-eight pounds, mostly incontinent, and had developed an aversion to bathing, which meant his scalp was crusty and his ears were caked with wax.

He seemed glad to be in familiar surroundings. He needed help getting dressed, watched TV for hours, went swimming in the pool, and was happy to lavish attention on his two Yorkies. He paid little attention to anything going on around him.

"Darryl Zanuck took too long to die," one old friend remarked. It was an opinion echoed by his son in a roundabout way. "It was a very sour period," said Richard Zanuck. "He never fully recovered from the blow of being eased into oblivion by the company he founded. There was a rapid deterioration, physically and mentally."

In his last years, Darryl Zanuck eerily replicated the last, aimless years of his peers Louis B. Mayer and Jack Warner. Once separated from their studios, these men around whose belief systems and whims a major American industry had been formulated, lived the aimless, diminished lives of elderly men with no reason to get up in the morning. The movies had been the vehicle through which they imposed their vision on the world, as well as how they defined themselves. Once that was gone, so was their life force.

When Philip Dunne wrote his memoir, he sent Zanuck the chapters that concerned him. Virginia reported back that she had read the chapters to her husband, and he "remembered almost everything," although he thought Dunne had been "much too kind to his old boss." She told

Dunne that Zanuck was doing "somewhat better" and was enjoying "the big event of his day: going with his nurse to Hamburger Hamlet for a chocolate malted."

Darryl Zanuck's last interview seems to have taken place in 1975. The reporter found him "mellow, mild, at times different, halting and forgetful."

"I get up about 8:30 and take a quick shower," Zanuck said. "Then I head for the main house and breakfast with Virginia. Usually it's fruit and hot cakes. I glance at the morning paper. The world right now doesn't seem to be in very good shape to me. Then I rest for an hour and walk the dogs. . . . In the afternoon I start watching TV for a few hours. Every now and then they show an old movie of mine, and it brings back memories. . . .

"Every time they show something like Eddie Robinson or Marilyn Monroe or Betty Grable or Ty Power or Dick Widmark—the so-called Golden Age of Hollywood—it conjures up memories. I don't want to sound immodest. People have accused me of being a lot of things. But a lot of that Golden Age of Hollywood—it was of my making."

Zanuck's grandson Andre Hakim Jr. moved into the Palm Springs house in 1975, with the job of keeping an eye on the old man. He wasn't to be left alone, because Virginia was afraid that Genevieve Gilles would somehow invade the house and spirit him away. This didn't make much sense—it had been more than two years since anyone named Zanuck had heard from Gilles—but Virginia wasn't taking any chances.

His grandson found Zanuck fretful, constantly asking the time, worried about his dogs, prone to wandering off. Hakim was startled to notice that his grandfather talked to him as if Andre Jr. was actually Andre Sr. Another visitor to the estate reported that Zanuck was docile, but needed help getting dressed and often refused to bathe.

As his mental faculties declined further, Darryl Zanuck increasingly passed the time by watching cartoons on television. On October 29, 1979, he had a heart attack, then a stroke followed by pneumonia. With characteristic will, he struggled on for nearly two months until his death on December 22, 1979, at the age of seventy-seven.

The obit in *Variety* succinctly stated the case for the defense: "In some ways, his career matched in dramatic and romantic interest, and surpassed in adventure, many of the films he had made. Achievements ranged from being the only three-time winner of the coveted Irving G. Thalberg Memorial Award to, at times, near oblivion in the industry he helped foster."

Orson Welles spoke at the funeral. Seated in the family pew, Richard Zanuck cried through the ceremony for the man who had given him life, then given him a career, then tried to destroy that career. Welles paid tribute to the man who had frequently bailed him out with loans or acting roles. Zanuck, Welles said, did not live by the traditional maxim of the movie business: You're only as good as your last picture. With Zanuck, "you were as good as he decided you were, as a human being . . . if he took you on, you stayed.

"If I did something really outrageous, if I committed some abominable crime . . . that if all the police in the world were after me, there was one man, and only one man I could come to, and that was Darryl. He would not have made me a speech about the good of the industry, the good of the studio, he would not have been mealy-mouthed, he would simply have hid me under the bed. Very simply, he was a friend. I don't mean just my friend. I think that friendship was something he was very good at. That's why it's just so very hard to say goodbye to him."

Darryl Zanuck's estate was worth about $4.5 million, and he left the bulk of it to his children. Nothing was left to his wife, although it was clear that he had taken care of all her financial needs before his death.

Slightly more than six months after Zanuck's death, his daughter Susan was found dead in squalid conditions in her house in Palm

Springs. She had been living on $3,000 a month disbursed from a trust fund established by her father, but at the time of her death there was less than $50,000 in her estate. The autopsy determined that Susan had died of arrhythmia brought on by a fatty liver, caused by years of heavy drinking. She was forty-six years old. Susan's son Dino died in 1981 at the age of twenty-two from an overdose of cocaine and morphine. He was flat broke, having blown his inheritance on drugs. Virginia Zanuck died in 1982 and left an estate of between $10 million and $12 million.

The settling of the Darryl Zanuck estate took years, largely because he had made three different wills in the space of three years. The 1969 will had left Genevieve Gilles 50 percent of his tax-exempt securities, or approximately $500,000. The rest of the estate went to his ten grandchildren. A 1971 will included his youngest grandchild, who had been left out of the 1969 will, and reduced Gilles's portion of the tax-exempts to 45 percent. Richard Zanuck was dropped completely from the will, but Gilles was given an equivalence in the estate with Zanuck's two daughters. One final insult: the daughters' money was to be doled out as income from their trust funds, but Gilles would get her money in a lump sum. A 1973 will left Genevieve about half of his estate, approximately $2 million.

The probate battle went on for the better part of a decade. In 1989, the estate's value was down to $3.1 million, and Richard, Darrylin, and Susan's children were due about $600,000 each—loose change for Richard, who was quite wealthy by that time, but a considerable windfall for the others.

By the time taxes, lawyer's fees, and bequests had been paid out, the residue of the estate went to Darrylin. She also inherited the three houses that Zanuck and Virginia had owned. Darrylin became the unofficial representative of her late father, donating nearly $700,000 to the University of Nebraska for scholarships, which doled out $5,000 grants to worthy students until the year 2000. *Variety* noted a central irony: "The scholarships will sustain people in the very environment [Zanuck] went to great lengths to avoid." Darrylin tried writing a memoir that would put right the various incorrect—read "scandalous"—things that had been written about her father, but it didn't sell. Darrylin Zanuck died in 2015 at the age of eighty-four.

As for Richard Zanuck, in 1972 he formed Zanuck/Brown Productions with his friend David Brown. One of their first productions at Universal was *The Sting*, which was followed by *The Sugarland Express*. The latter film didn't do well, but Zanuck and Brown were impressed by the director, Steven Spielberg. They hired him for their next picture, called *Jaws*.

Jaws out-grossed *The Sound of Music*. More important, it completely changed the equation of success in Hollywood, changed the way movies were marketed and released. It made saturation booking safe for films of quality as well as exploitation. Richard went on to produce a distinguished roster of films, including *Cocoon*, *The Verdict*, and *Driving Miss Daisy*, which won the Best Picture Oscar in 1989. Richard Zanuck said that with just a couple of films he had made more money than his father had made during all the years he had run 20th Century-Fox.

"I've always thought that at a certain point, Dick became the father and Darryl in a strange way became the impetuous son," said David Brown. "Darryl had the capacity to make every picture, even the most modest, minor little thing, into the Second Coming. And Dick would have the difficult job of bringing him back to earth.... I always detected in the relationship between DFZ and Richard something resembling sibling rivalry, between a young man and man who never wanted to grow old."

In later years, when Richard Zanuck spoke of his father, the tone was of great respect without any perceptible trace of love. Richard saw his father as a man who was relentlessly honest and straightforward in business, took responsibility for his decisions, and freely admitted when he was wrong. His word was always good. This same man was married for fifty-five years, abandoned his wife when it suited him, lived openly with a series of mistresses, and cut his son loose when his own career was threatened.

Richard Zanuck would say of his father that he had no real friends, referred to him as a man "who was kind of tough to get close to." He could have been speaking of Jack Warner or Louis B. Mayer. Despite the lack of any filial affection, he knew his father was something remarkable: an authentic force of nature and a great producer of motion pictures.

"For a little guy coming out of Wahoo, Nebraska," Richard said, "he did all right in a very tough town."

CHAPTER TEN

THE TURNING POINT

IN THE EARLY 1970S, 20TH CENTURY-FOX WAS LIKE A PARTY without a host. Darryl Zanuck had been responsible for the company's formation as well as its creative identity. There was a vacuum waiting to be filled.

The new president was named Gordon Stulberg. Since Zanuck's production philosophy of a few blockbusters every year to anchor the program had proven a net failure, the new regime went in the other direction. Big budgets were hard to find; the budget ceiling was set at $2.5 million, and many films were made for less: *The Culpepper Cattle Company, The Heartbreak Kid, When the Legends Die.* It was not a roster of pictures calculated to stir the heart. Or, for that matter, the box office.

The only big hits the studio had in the early 1970s were *The French Connection* and *The Poseidon Adventure*, but the latter's success was muted by the fact that the studio had only put up half of the $5.5 million budget, which meant they only got half of the profits. Nevertheless, those two hits were enough to keep the doors open. In the main, however, the pictures were underwhelming, and so were the financials. Fox paid no dividends from 1970 to 1972, and in 1973 the stock price dropped to $5 a share, down from $41.75 in 1969, just before the studio's problems became overwhelming.

If the history of movies proves anything, it is that the movie business is one of cycles. Fox was due for a revival. The lessons of *The Poseidon Adventure* were repeated on *The Towering Inferno*, which was co-financed by Fox and Warners. Cost: $14 million. Rentals: nearly $100 million. And, to be honest, some of the lower budget pictures paid off: *Dirty Mary and Crazy Larry* and *Harry and Tonto* made money, while negative pick-ups such as *The Three Musketeers* and its sequel proved quite profitable. On the other hand, *At Long Last Love* and *Lucky Lady* were wipeouts. *The Rocky Horror Picture Show* looked to be more of the same, until it caught on at midnight screenings and stealthily returned $50 million to the studio.

Stulberg was replaced by Dennis Stanfill in December 1975. Stanfill was not a movie guy, he was a money guy. He had worked at Lehman Brothers, then went to the Times-Mirror company as treasurer. In fact, Stanfill had no particular passion for the movie business. "The industry got too much money too easily" was how Stanfill characterized the period before he went to Fox. "The movies became pets of the conglomerates. And then there was *Sound of Music,* which Dick Zanuck and everybody else agrees was the most expensive movie Hollywood ever made because it led everybody into those expensive carbon copies. And if there is anything that seems clear, it's that carbon copies don't work."

Stanfill had a hunch about the future. "Fox has probably thought too specifically in terms of the word 'movies' for too long. We have to define what it is we do more broadly as audio-visual entertainment."

Stanfill closed the New York office, cut overhead, and sold off the 2,600-acre Fox Malibu Ranch, where hundreds of pictures had been made, including *How Green Was My Valley*. In the wake of *At Long Last Love* and *Lucky Lady,* something more seemed to be required, so Alan Ladd Jr. was named head of worldwide production in January 1976.

Ladd had known all about Hollywood since birth, and had worked his way up the ladder—first as an agent, then producing in partnership with Jay Kanter and Elliott Kastner. He had been working as Fox's vice president for creative affairs since 1973 and had recently been responsible for bringing Mel Brooks's *Young Frankenstein* to the studio. Columbia thought the project reeked of inside baseball and bailed when the prospective budget hit $1.8 million. The same things that had scared Columbia off enticed Ladd, who was tickled by a loving satire of the horror pictures of Ladd's childhood. He raised the budget to $2.8 million and had the satisfaction of seeing the picture return domestic rentals of $39 million. It was a preview of coming attractions.

Ladd's first project was a horror picture called *The Omen*, which was nothing special in broad outline, but which Ladd classed up by casting Gregory Peck and Lee Remick, thereby making it acceptable to older audiences. After that came Mel Brooks's *Silent Movie*. The two pictures returned $90 million on a combined cost of less than $7 million. People began to pay attention to Alan Ladd Jr.

To paraphrase Al Jolson, they hadn't seen anything yet.

Even mediocre pictures did well. Ladd picked up *Silver Streak* after Paramount let their option lapse, and cast Gene Wilder and Richard Pryor. It returned close to $50 million in rentals. Ladd stuck with Paul Mazursky, who responded with several penetrating character studies. *Next Stop, Greenwich Village* didn't make much money, and many studios would have jettisoned Mazursky at that point, but Ladd stuck with him, and Mazursky came through with *An Unmarried Woman*, which hit the zeitgeist squarely. Arthur Laurents wrote an original script called *The Turning Point* that became a considerable hit directed by Herbert Ross, and Fred Zinnemann was turned loose on *Julia*, Lillian Hellman's historically bogus, self-regarding memoir that Zinnemann cast perfectly (Jane Fonda as Hellman, Jason Robards Jr. as Dashiell Hammett, Vanessa Redgrave as Julia) and mounted beautifully.

All these pictures captured that sweet spot combining commercial and critical success, and none of them had the telltale down-market, drive-in smell of the pictures made by the previous administration.

And then came *Star Wars*.

Books and every mode of media devoted to *Star Wars* have saturated the public in the more than forty years since its release. Suffice it to say that Universal refused to spend $8.5 million for George Lucas's follow-up to *American Graffiti*, despite that film's success. *Star Wars* struck them as far too insular for a mass market subject and a large budget, especially given Lucas's intention to cast the three main roles with unknowns. But as far as Ladd was concerned, *Star Wars* was an affectionate equivalent of *Young Frankenstein*, and had even larger potential. The picture ended up costing $10 million, which did not please the studio, but all complaints ceased when the film was released and became a cultural phenomenon that shows no signs of abating as it nears a half-century in age.

Fox's stock had been hovering around $6 a share a year before the film's debut, but rose to $27 after the film was released. By 1980, *Star Wars* had brought in just under $200 million in domestic rentals, obliterating the record established only a few years before by *Jaws*.

Ladd couldn't put a foot wrong. *The Other Side of Midnight*, a bad Sidney Sheldon potboiler, made money, and *The Fury*, a lurid guilty pleasure from Brian de Palma, did better than its mainly lousy reviews indicated. Ladd brought in Robert Altman in the hope that he would be a complement to Paul Mazursky in making pictures that wouldn't cost much but would appeal to upscale audiences. Altman was given his head on a series of modestly budgeted pictures (*Three Women, A Wedding, A Perfect Couple, Quintet*) that, in the main, earned just about what they deserved.

The hits kept on coming in both genre pictures and unclassifiable character studies. *Norma Rae* was followed by *The Rose*, and *Breaking Away* found an audience. *Alien*, an impeccably engineered monster movie set on a spaceship, scared audiences all over the world.

With the exception of *Star Wars*, few of these pictures were aimed at teenagers. These were movies about adult concerns, made by adults for adults. If there was a theme to Ladd's tenure at 20th Century-Fox, it was intelligent movies for intelligent audiences. With pictures like Ladd was making, the bar is set high—execution was everything, and execution can't be faked. For years Ladd expertly matched the right director with the right script, the right actors with the right director.

Not even Darryl Zanuck had ever had four consecutive years like Alan Ladd Jr. By the middle of 1979, his contract was expiring and negotiations with Fox chairman Dennis Stanfill were not proceeding smoothly. In July, Ladd announced that he and his team would be leaving Fox and moving over to Warner Bros. The new operation would be called The Ladd Company.

For years, Ladd had been firmly tied into the zeitgeist, which is a tough position to maintain. Who knows what people will want to see eighteen months to two years in the future? And just as quickly as Ladd had been successful, he was unsuccessful.

The Ladd Company had some hits—*Body Heat*, *Chariots of Fire*, and the archetypal lowbrow comedy *Police Academy*, which spawned a bunch of sequels. But the flops far outnumbered the successes. Among others: *Outland*, *Looker*, *Tragedy of a Ridiculous Man*, *Blade Runner*, *Five Days One Summer*, *Lovesick*, *Twice Upon a Time*, *Star 80*, *Mike's Murder*, *Purple Hearts*. Most of these were modestly budgeted, but some, such as *Five Days One Summer*, lost their entire large investment. The films that ultimately pulled the plug were *The Right Stuff*, a film that nearly doubled its budget and failed commercially, and *Once Upon a Time in America*, Sergio Leone's four-hour epic of American gangsters that, in both its original version and the two-and-a-half hour version that the Ladd Company recut into chronological order for American audiences, was a commercial failure. The Ladd Company went out of business.

Fox after Ladd had its own problems. The year after Ladd left, Fox's only big hit was *The Empire Strikes Back*, Lucas's sequel to *Star Wars*. But Lucas owned the *Stars Wars* films outright, and Fox's payout was limited to its distribution fee. Still, *The Empire Strikes Back* brought in about $60 million to Fox just for distributing. The problem was that the studio was now flush with cash at a time when its owners were looking to cash out.

In 1981, Marvin Davis, a Denver oil executive, bought the studio with a partner for $722 million. In 1984, Davis bought out his partner for an additional $116 million. These were years in which the brio of the Ladd era was replaced by something coarser and more commonplace. Fox's biggest picture of 1979 was Bob Fosse's *All That Jazz*, which took $20 million in domestic rentals, followed by a Robert Redford vehicle called *Brubaker*. Both pictures had been in the pipeline when Ladd was running the studio. By 1981, the creative decline was obvious—the company's top grossers were *Cannonball Run*; *Fort Apache, the Bronx*; and Jerry Lewis's *Hardly Working*.

Drift had set in. The company did well with *Porky's*, an independently financed pick-up, but when it came to in-house productions, things got grim fast. *Author! Author!*, *Kiss Me Goodbye*, *I Ought to Be in Pictures*, *Making Love*, *Monsignor*, *Six Pack*—whether upscale or down-market, a nonstop string of losers. The only exception was Sidney Lumet's *The Verdict*, with Paul Newman—a picture Alan Ladd Jr. would have been happy to make, which, not coincidentally, was produced by Richard Zanuck and David Brown.

Sherry Lansing, the first woman to be production head of a Hollywood studio, was named production head at Fox in 1980, but resigned two years later. She had a far more successful run at Paramount, where she ran production for twelve years. Lansing was replaced by Joe Wizan, an agent turned producer, who greenlit *Rhinestone* with Sylvester Stallone and Dolly Parton—not a pairing to make people forget Tracy and Hepburn. Only *Romancing the Stone* and *Bachelor Party* alleviated the pain. Lawrence Gordon took over production in August 1984 and issued *Turk 182* and *The Man with One Red Shoe*. *Cocoon* brightened things, but only temporarily.

Finally, Marvin Davis bailed. He sold 50 percent of the company to Rupert Murdoch for $250 million, which helped paper over the fact that in 1984 Fox had lost $89 million. Six months later, Murdoch paid $325 million for the other 50 percent of the company. It was discovered that Davis had liquidated most of the studio's non-film assets in order to pay off the loans he had used to buy the studio. For the fiscal year ending August 25, 1984, in addition to the loss of $89 million, long-term debt had tripled to $392 million.

Things began to turn around: *Jewel of the Nile*, *Aliens*, and a remake that turned out to be a classic: David Cronenberg's *The Fly*. More important, Murdoch began to leverage the Fox name for newly created properties that extended his media footprint: Fox Broadcasting, Fox News, Fox Sports, et cetera, spreading the name of the company's founder into areas that even a wildly entrepreneurial man like William Fox would never have dreamt of.

The de-evolution that had horrified Darryl Zanuck when he had seen it coming in the mid-fifties was now in full bloom. In Zanuck's day, nobody at 20th Century-Fox had power unless it was delegated by Zanuck—all authority, and nearly all production decisions, flowed down from the office painted Zanuck green. If New York didn't want to make a picture— *How Green Was My Valley* is a prime example—Zanuck would simply reduce the budget so New York couldn't complain overmuch and shoot the movie anyway. In the case of *How Green Was My Valley*, Zanuck replaced William Wyler with John Ford, thereby converting the picture from a potential fourteen-week shoot to an eight-week shoot.

But by the 1980s, a production head at a studio was actually more of a management job than a creative job, as power had increasingly devolved to independent producers and agents who had relationships with even more powerful stars. In truth, many of those producers worked through Fox rather than for Fox: Joel Silver, whose action pictures (*Die Hard*, *Predator*, and many sequels both official and unofficial) would define the form for the next twenty years; Jon Landau, whose partnership with James Cameron would bring Fox *The Abyss*, *True Lies*, *Titanic*, and *Avatar*; and eventually Marvel, which constituted the most successful twenty-first century movie brand, albeit one that made only one (insanely repetitive) kind of picture. This meant that Kevin Feige was perhaps the only modern studio head successfully performing the creative functions that had once been limited to men named Mayer and Zanuck. The difference, of course, is that neither of them would have tolerated their job being focused on seducing a currently hot producer or star so that they could earn more money than the studio head.

Traditionally, Zanuck hadn't been particularly interested in sequels, and considered them mostly the province of Sol Wurtzel's B movie unit. For sequels, you had to go to MGM, with their long-running Tarzan, Thin Man, Dr. Kildare, Maisie, and Andy Hardy series. But financial pressure now mandated sequels for any huge success even if it was absurd, as with Bruce Willis's John McLane, who kept being embroiled in exhaustingly violent marathons long after he would have been retired. (Cumulatively, the *Die Hard* films made you appreciate the farsighted wisdom of recasting James Bond before the star becomes eligible for AARP membership.)

Even a movie like *Alien*—a fresh spin on a very basic premise with unattributed echoes of H. P. Lovecraft's obsession with a lost civilization's grotesque creatures exuding disgusting but picturesque body fluids—became a series. *Alien* was brought to a beautifully quiet and satisfying conclusion by Ridley Scott, but its huge success mandated a series of sequels, of which only James Cameron's wham-bam thriller *Aliens* managed to avoid creative embarrassment.

When it came to Cameron, most people in Hollywood thought his passion for yet another version of *Titanic* was pointless. The Germans had made a version; 20th Century-Fox had made a surprisingly emotional, successful version in 1953 with Clifton Webb, Barbara Stanwyck, and Robert Wagner; and the British had made *A Night to Remember* only a few years after that.

Cameron's pitch was simple, if not original: "Romeo and Juliet on the Titanic." There were many people in Hollywood who foresaw trouble, but after *The Terminator, T2,* and *True Lies*, everybody wanted to be in business with Cameron, so Fox and Paramount agreed to co-finance and split distribution rights. They knew it was going to be expensive, but nobody expected it to cost $200 million.

Similarly, nobody expected it to be the most successful movie in history, but that $200 million brought back billions. It was a movie that had everything—heady, first-time passion between Leonardo DiCaprio and Kate Winslet for the teenagers, a spectacular re-creation of the luxurious ship for adults, the tragic spectacle of tortuous death for the there-but-for-the-grace-of-God crowd, and a vulnerable performance by Gloria Stuart as the elderly Rose.

Cameron had been thinking of Lillian Gish as he wrote the part, but Gish had died in 1993. No matter. In casting the eighty-seven-year-old Stuart, who had starred at Universal in the early 1930s but had been professionally inactive for decades, he got a Lillian Gish performance—tremulous, but transparently open to the world, her memories enabling a jaw-dropping final reunion of the dead lovers right out of *Wuthering Heights* . . . or *The Ghost and Mrs. Muir*.

Cameron's gamble paid off. *Titanic* was the first film to earn more than $1 billion in receipts, ending up with just under $2 billion in returns, finally exceeding that number with a 3-D reissue. It was nominated for fourteen Academy Awards, tying the record set by *All About Eve* in 1950, and won eleven, including Best Picture and Best Director.

This unlikely experience was repeated with Cameron's *Avatar*, also made for Fox. Cameron will never be a critic's darling, but he knows what he's doing—a very basic story that scans in any language or culture, amplified by state-of-the-art special effects, all ramrodded by one of the most prodigiously gifted directors of action and spectacle in the history of the movies. Unfortunately, Cameron's expertise does not extend to dialogue, and the audience has to endure characterizations of villains more thunderously evil than anything since the heyday of Noah Beery Sr. It's a trade-off audiences have been willing to make since Cecil B. DeMille.

Through years good and bad alike, Rupert Murdoch never really got acclimated to Hollywood. By profession as well as inclination he was a tabloid journalist, and the natural outgrowth of that was his creation of Fox News. The pace of filmmaking, which could take years to move from planning to a completed movie, struck him as unnecessarily sluggish. Besides that, in the twenty-first century the audience was continually splintering into smaller shards because of the proliferation of dozens of cable and pay services, streaming, et cetera. By 2018, Murdoch was over eighty years old, and while he maintained his loyalty to newsprint (*The*

Wall Street Journal, The New York Post, etc.), 20th Century-Fox increasingly struck him as expendable.

The problem for motion picture production in the twenty-first century was one of scale. Disney had spent a combined $15.4 billion to buy Pixar, Marvel Entertainment, and Lucasfilm, and quickly exploited their new properties at the box office, on toy shelves, and at theme parks. The purchases proved a huge success—in 2018, Disney had 26 percent of the domestic market. Fox's share was 9 percent. If Fox was going to compete with behemoths like Disney, not to mention Warners, Murdoch would have to invest billions, with no guarantee of eventual success.

He was disinclined.

As for Disney, they were in a continually expansionist mode. Disney Plus was well along in the planning stages, but Disney had a library shortfall. The Disney studio under Walt and Roy had made an animated feature every two or three years, and perhaps three or four live-action features a year. There wasn't the huge library that a streaming service demands. The purchase of a legacy movie studio with a thousand movies and ten thousand TV episodes would help solve that problem, as well as give Disney a huge roster of remake possibilities.

In December 2017, it was announced that Murdoch had agreed to sell most of the company he had renamed 21st Century-Fox to the Walt Disney Co. for $52.4 billion. "This clearly will . . . give us more content, give us more producing capabilities for [our] services," said Disney chairman Robert Iger.

The announcement set off the usual amount of jockeying from late starters who hadn't been aware Fox was for sale. Comcast upped the ante and bid $65 billion for the same assets, a 19 percent bump over Disney's offer. For Comcast, a company facing pressure in its video business because of cord-cutting on the part of consumers in favor of Netflix, it made sense.

There would be more jockeying, but Disney wanted the deal more, and had more money. The deal finally closed in March 2019, when Murdoch sold his company to Disney for $71.3 billion, half in cash, half in stock. Included in the sale were the FX cable network, Fox Searchlight, Sky TV, Star India, Fox's one-third interest in Hulu, and the National Geographic properties. Murdoch held on to Fox News, Fox Sports 1, the Fox broadcast network, and its TV stations.

It was, said the *Wall Street Journal*, "a race for scale in Hollywood, where having a hit movie or TV show is no longer enough. Studios today need a deep stable of characters and franchises to sell streaming subscriptions, movie tickets, toys and theme-park admissions."

This purchase marked more than an ignoble ending for a movie studio. In the twenty-first century, the idea of movies as "non-recurring phenomena" has been more or less done away with as studios seek to concentrate on intellectual property, so as to ensure that every successful movie is as much like its predecessors as possible.

The result is that movie studios have much less of an individual identity than they used to—in Darryl Zanuck's day you could tell whether a movie had been made by MGM or Paramount or Warner Bros. just by looking at a minute or two of footage. The style of photography, the actors, the sound of the musical score—all were indications of a studio's individual footprint.

In the twenty-first century, studios don't really have personalities. A Marvel movie looks like a Marvel movie no matter which studio releases it. So it was that in January 2020, Disney announced that 20th Century-Fox would henceforth be known as 20th Century Pictures. The reasoning was obscure; some said that it was to distance Disney from Rupert Murdoch's remaining Fox properties. Others thought that the reason might simply have been an assertion of ownership—Disney could change the name of the company, so they did.

What it meant in practice was that for the first time in more than a century, the name of William Fox would be missing from movie screens the world over. Even though the new name privileged the company that Darryl Zanuck had founded over that of William Fox's, it was not something that Zanuck would have done, for all of his ego and will to power.

Before Disney changed the name, there was one last movie that encapsulated the 20th Century-Fox brand. *Ford v Ferrari* came out late in 2019. It was about Formula One racing, a subject filmmakers like, audiences not so much. But director James Mangold emphasized the personal story of a three-way relationship between Henry Ford II, race car designer Carroll Shelby, and Ken Miles (a driver and mechanic)—men who formed a Ford team that won Le Mans for four consecutive years.

Beneath the hardware, it was a character study of Shelby and Miles, two obsessives who create through teamwork and a shared gift for improvisation something neither of them could have accomplished alone. They bond through the classic movie reality of a fistfight that exhausts them both, but makes each of them realize the other man deserves respect rather than hostility.

The film combined good writing, committed acting, and propulsive attention to narrative, using but never abusing special effects.

It was a movie that earned respect from car people and movie people alike. Even as the company that made it was transitioning to another, speculative identity, *Ford v Ferrari* summoned the classical virtues of the filmmakers who had made 20th Century-Fox a name to conjure with: quality writing, sensitive direction, technical excellence. And never forgetting that a movie needs to move. It was a movie that Darryl Zanuck—or Alan Ladd Jr.—would have made in a heartbeat, a movie that embodied and ennobled the best of the pictures that 20th Century-Fox had made, no matter the era.

Tell the story . . .

⇒ **Acknowledgments** ⇐

MY CONVERSATIONS WITH THE LATE EVIE JOHNSON GAVE me an invaluable vantage point on Hollywood from the point of view of the wives. Evie was a scamp, an Auntie Mame who had survived it all. I miss her. I have also accessed my interviews with Jean Renoir from 1974, and with Herbert Bayard Swope Jr. from 2002. My friend Robert Wagner gave me many insights into the construction and operation of the Fox studio and how Darryl Zanuck ran it, while several interviews with Richard Zanuck helped me understand his father, his father's son, and, by extension, their respective eras of moviemaking. Richard's business partner David Brown also discussed Darryl Zanuck with me. My interviews with Paul Wurtzel gave me insight into his father's tortured relationship with William Fox and his far more businesslike relationship with Darryl Zanuck. The late Jim Rogers talked with love and honesty about his father Will Rogers and his family, while David Shepard gave me chapter and verse regarding Murnau and *City Girl*. Russ Meyer told me all about his misadventures at Fox, and my friend Bruce Goldstein explained the careers of his friends Harold and Fayard Nicholas.

My gratitude to Alan Rode for his loan of transcripts of Darryl Zanuck's story conferences, and to Will Coates for his typically superb research. My wife, Lynn, sat with me for months watching Fox pictures she hadn't seen and developed a liking for Victor Mature, which shows she has good taste.

At Running Press, gratitude goes to Cindy Sipala, who agreed with me that 20th Century-Fox was a good idea for a book. Mort Janklow has been my agent for more years than he probably cares to remember, and he and his associates Judythe Cohen and Michael Steger are all the backup any writer needs. And of course there are my friends at Turner Classic Movies: Charlie Tabesh and Scott McGee.

See you at the movies . . .

SCOTT EYMAN

☰ Bibliography ☰

Allvine, Glendon. *The Greatest Fox of Them All*. New York: Lyle Stuart, 1969.

Basinger, Jeanine. *The Movie Musical!* New York: Knopf, 2019.

Behlmer, Rudy. *Memo from Darryl F. Zanuck: The Golden Years at 20th Century Fox*. New York: Grove Press, 1993.

Belton, John. *Widescreen Cinema*. Cambridge: Harvard University Press, 1992.

Birchard, Robert S. *King Cowboy: Tom Mix and the Movies*. Burbank: Riverwood Press, 1993.

Curtis, James. *Between Flops: A Biography of Preston Sturges*. New York: Harcourt, Brace & Jovanovich, 1982.

Custen, George F. *Twentieth Century's Fox: Darryl F. Zanuck and the Culture of Hollywood*. New York: Basic Books, 1997.

Dunne, John Gregory. *The Studio*. New York: Farrar, Straus & Giroux, 1968.

Eyman, Scott, *Ernst Lubitsch: Laughter in Paradise*. New York: Simon & Schuster, 1993.

Fuller, Samuel. *A Third Face*. New York: Knopf, 2002.

Gussow, Mel. *Darryl F. Zanuck: Don't Say Yes Until I Finish Talking*. New York: Doubleday, 1971.

Harris, Marlys J. *The Zanuck's of Hollywood*. New York: Crown, 1989.

Jewell, Richard B. *RKO Radio Pictures: A Titan is Born*. Berkeley: University of California Press, 2012.

Kobal, John. *People Will Talk*. New York: Alfred A. Knopf, 1985.

Krefft, Vanda. *The Man Who Made the Movies: The Meteoric Rise and Tragic Fall of William Fox*. New York: Harper, 2017.

Mann, Denise. *Hollywood Independents*. Minneapolis: University of Minnesota, 2008.

McGilligan, Patrick and Paul Buhle. *Tender Comrades: A Backstory of the Hollywood Backlist*. New York: St. Martin's, 1997.

Merigeau, Pascal. *Jean Renoir: A Biography*. Philadelphia: Running Press, 2016.

Mordden, Ethan. *The Hollywood Studios*. New York: Knopf, 1988.

Mosley, Leonard. *Zanuck: The Rise and Fall of Hollywood's Last Tycoon*. Boston: Little, Brown, 1984.

Semenov, Lillian Wurtzel, and Carla Winter. *William Fox, Sol M. Wurtzel and the Early Fox Film Corporation, 1917-1923*. Jefferson: McFarland, 2001.

Silverman, Stephen. *The Fox That Got Away*. Secaucus: Lyle Stuart, 1988.

Solomon, Aubrey. *The Fox Film Corporation 1915–1935*. Jefferson: McFarland, 2011.

Stern, Sydney Ladensohn. *The Brothers Mankiewicz: Hope, Heartbreak and Hollywood Classics*. Jackson: University Press of Mississippi, 2019.

≡ Notes ≡

INTRODUCTION

1   "It's a basic call": Neil Brand to SE.

2   "like a Swiss watch": Robert Wagner to SE.

2   Fox was born Wilhelm Fuchs: Vanda Krefft, *The Man Who Made The Movies,* p. 16.

3   "I decided to become": Marlys J. Harris, *The Zanuck's of Hollywood,* p. 14.

5   "We're talking major": Ethan Mordden, *The Hollywood Studios,* p. 241.

5   "Zanuck was a first-rate": Mordden, p. 272.

CHAPTER ONE: SUNRISE

10   Carrie, Arthur, and David: Vanda Krefft, *The Man Who Made The Movies,* p. 488.

10   Fox planned to pay off: Krefft, p. 5.

11   "Now I've got": Glendon Allvine, *The Greatest Fox of Them All,* p. 24.

12   "You must have known": Allvine, p. 129.

12   In October 1929: Allvine, p. 9.

12   "When a man reaches fifty": Allvine, p. 9.

13   As for Fox's Tri-Ergon: Allvine, p. 25.

14   "All I remember": Krefft, p. 19.

14   In the summer he would earn: Aubrey Solomon, *The Fox Film Corporation,* p. 9.

15   "I do not remember anything": Allvine, p. 172.

15   "It would have been so easy": Allvine, p. 39.

15   It was a big wedding: Krefft, p. 40.

16   The mills would ship: Solomon, *The Fox Film Corp.,* p. 10.

16　"invited enemies": *Los Angeles Times*, 5-21-78, p. 116; Angela Fox Dunn, 116.

16　"All of it": Allvine, p. 100.

17　"this little bit of a theater": Allvine, p. 102.

17　"Every time we got": Allvine, p. 104.

18　When he got enough money: Solomon, p. 11.

18　His patron at Tammany: Krefft, p. 69.

18　"The motion picture did not": Solomon, p. 15.

19　Based on a play by Edward Sheldon: Solomon, p. 15.

20　Within fourteen years: Solomon, p. 19.

21　"Among the early pioneers": Allvine, p. 171.

21　He didn't wear a watch: Angela Fox Dunn, *Los Angeles Times*, 5-21-78, p. 116.

22　In reality she had never been to Europe: Krefft, p. 137.

23　Bara propelled Fox Film: Krefft, p. 137.

23　In 1919, Bara was making: Allvine, p. 57.

24　Similarly, Tom Mix made: Robert S. Birchard, *King Cowboy,* p. 133.

24　William Fox hired Mix: Birchard, p. 115.

25　"He had a photographic memory": Birchard, p. 131.

26　"Mix was himself": Birchard, p. 122.

26　"Tom was temperamental": Birchard, p. 120.

27　*Riders of the Purple Sage* cost $141,000: Solomon, p. 75.

27　"Reviewed Buck Jones picture": Lillian Wurtzel Semenov and Carla Winter, *William Fox, Sol M. Wurtzel and the Early Fox Film Corporation,* p. 106.

27　Buck Jones's Fox pictures: Birchard, p. 124.

28　by hiring him as his general manager: Allvine, p. 80.

29　"I have over-burdened you": Semenov and Winter, p. 73.

29　"I don't want to grant": Semenov and Winter, p. 30.

29　"By what authority": Semenov and Winter, p. 76.

30　"The only thing I can say": Semenov and Winter, p. 92.

30　In time, Wurtzel developed: Paul Wurtzel to SE.

31   "I want you to make every effort": Semenov and Winter, p. 50.

31   "there is behind": Krefft, p. 295.

33   "Mr. Wurtzel is a special character": *Fortune*, "Body and Soul Is (Here) Put Together," August 1931, p. 33.

33   "I never encountered": Allvine, p. 173.

33   "This mug of mine": Allvine, p. 174.

33   "I always bragged": Allvine, p. 174.

34   "I reviewed *The Big Punch*": Semenov and Winter, p. 150.

34   It had world rentals: Solomon, p. 65.

35   Mix's last picture for Fox: Solomon, p. 113.

CHAPTER TWO: WHAT PRICE GLORY?

39   On July 23, 1926: Vanda Krefft, *The Man Who Made The Movies,* p. 391.

39   "Fox with his Movietone": Glendon Allvine, *The Greatest Fox of Them All,* p. 73.

41   "I only met him": Krefft, p. 467.

42   "They never use hokum": Krefft, p. 357.

42   "Mr. Murnau will have": Bergstrom, p. 430.

42   "the genius of his age": Allvine, p. 98.

43   "smooth-talking Mick": Krefft, p. 342.

44   "pleasantly goblinesque": *Fortune*, "Body and Soul Is (Here) Put Together," August 1931, p. 32.

44   "kindness, generosity, and consideration": Allvine, p. 80.

44   Sheehan liked to play the nice guy: Robert S. Birchard, *King Cowboy,* p. 119.

45   "Borzage is entitled": Aubrey Solomon, *The Fox Film Corp.*, p. 114.

46   "The importance of *Sunrise*": Solomon, p.114.

46   When John Cohen: Allvine, p. 119.

47   The new contract, which began in August: Bergstrom, p. 455.

47   "He resented the cans": Allvine, p. 113.

47 "Tell that bastard": Allvine, p. 114.

48 "this summer I should like": Bergstrom, p. 430.

48 "After my talk with you": Bergstrom, p. 435.

48 "the estimated cost": Bergstrom, p. 437.

49 "We'd spend a whole evening": Bergstrom, p. 439.

49 "I found it difficult": Bergstrom, p. 459.

49 "a gigantic apparatus": Bergstrom, p. 438.

50 "People fell back": Janet Gaynor oral history, recorded in 1958, Columbia University.

50 "From this sawdust story": *New York Times Film Reviews*, p. 472.

51 "overnight and like a tidal wave": Bergstrom, p. 434.

51 "We took a whole apple orchard": Bergstrom, p. 443.

51 "If talk should be added": Bergstrom, p. 430.

52 "I would take it out here": Bergstrom, p. 449.

52 "*Sunrise* was the only": Bergstrom, p. 448.

53 "the final version": David Shepard to SE.

CHAPTER THREE: OVER THE HILL

57 "The public be damned": Glendon Allvine, *The Greatest Fox of Them All,* pp. 69–70.

57 "He did . . . embark": Bergstrom, p. 436.

58 "the dominating tenor of the book": Aubrey Solomon, *The Fox Film Corp.*, p. 177.

59 "He did not say anything": Solomon, p. 178.

59 "Like all . . . Fox arguments": Solomon, p. 178.

60 He listed his assets: Vanda Krefft, *The Man Who Made The Movies,* p. 719.

60 In January 1941, William Fox: Krefft, p. 728.

60 The paintings brought: Allvine, p. 159.

60   "I started with nothing": Allvine, p. 160.

61   "His daring and initiative": Allvine, p. 176.

63   In July 1931, more than a year: Solomon, p. 153.

63   In 1930, Fox theaters: Allvine, p. 141.

63   *Film Daily* carried a notice: Solomon, p. 158.

64   *Variety* summed up the sad state: Solomon, p. 156.

64   Between the theaters and the film operation: Richard R. Jewell, *A Titan Is Born*, p. 68.

64   By May of that year: Solomon, p. 165.

64   in 1932: Allvine, p. 152.

65   "Understood here that the whole motivation": *Hollywood Reporter*, Jan. 19, 1933, p. 1.

66   Creditors had little choice: Solomon, pp. 173, 180.

66   Fox profits for the first quarter: Solomon, p. 193.

67   *Film Daily*'s review: Solomon, p. 164.

69   "Early in 1932": Solomon, p. 166.

69   In August 1933: *New York Times*, August 3, 1933, p. 20.

69   Fox would finance: Solomon, p. 166.

70   "Battlefront reports": *Hollywood Reporter*, March 1, 1934, p. 1.

70   But movie attendance: Solomon, p. 202.

CHAPTER FOUR: THE MARK OF ZANUCK

75   "I saw an extraordinary scene": Leonard Mosley, *The Rise and Fall of Hollywood's Last Tycoon,* p. 111.

76   "Everyone in this movie": Mosley, p. 115.

76   "I want to talk to you": Patrick McGilligan and Paul Buhle, *Tender Comrades*, pp. 139–140.

77   "Hollywood is divided into two camps": George F. Custen, *Darryl F. Zanuck and the Culture of Hollywood,* p. 156.

77   "And then, his love turned to hate": Marlys J. Harris, *The Zanuck's of Hollywood,* p. 33.

78   "betterment and correctment": Harris, p. 42.

79   "On April 10, as Head of Production": Custen, p. 172.

80   Schenck wanted to know: Custen, p. 176.

80   Schenck and Goetz put up: Custen, p. 177.

80   Zanuck's salary: Custen, p. 177.

81   His body had to be strapped: *Hollywood Reporter,* May 15, 1933, p. 1.

82   "Zanuck had a Geiger counter": Mosley, p. 144.

83   "We must forget entirely": Custen, p. 192.

84   "The most significant development": *Motion Picture Herald,* August 3, 1935, p. 30.

86   "Fox had the best": Mel Gussow, *Don't Say Yes Until I Finish Talking,* p. 63.

87   "overpriced crap": Mosley, p. 155.

CHAPTER FIVE: HOW GREEN WAS MY VALLEY

90   "a great creative executive": Rudy Behlmer, *The Golden Years at 20th Century Fox,* p. xiv.

90   "To work with": Mel Gussow, *Don't Say Yes Until I Finish Talking,* p. 142.

91   *Lucky Baldwin* was Zanuck's: Marlys J. Harris, *The Zanuck's of Hollywood,* p. 48.

91   "the great scene": Ethan Mordden, *The Hollywood Studios,* p. 265.

92   "I saw him treat": Philip Dunne to SE.

92   "I'll read the script": Leonard Mosley, *The Rise and Fall of Hollywood's Last Tycoon,* p. 145.

92   "had absolutely no respect": Mosley, p. 175.

93   "If you made a great picture": Stephen Silverman, *The Fox That Got Away,* p. 71.

94   Darryl had a brother: George F. Custen, *Darryl F. Zanuck and the Culture of Hollywood,* p. 28.

94 "Anyone who puts down": Custen, p. 29.

95 "If I had a gun": Gussow, p. 10.

95 "We have two engines": Harris, p. 16.

96 "Darryl was the type": Harris, p. 17.

96 "one month in quarters": Custen, p. 34.

96 "It was like being a catcher": Mosley, p. 28.

98 "And when I say": Custen, p. 45.

98 "The four short stories": Custen, p. 63.

99 "Working for Sennett": Mosley, p. 46.

99 "Five of us would sit around": Gussow, p. 27.

99 "Sennett taught me two things": Mosley, p. 46.

100 "If I was hanging": Harris, p. 24.

101 "he was always on the phone": Gussow, p. 31.

101 "Our first year": Gussow, p. 32.

101 Barbara Stanwyck would be chased: Robert Wagner to SE.

102 "They hadn't invented": Mosley, p. 61.

104 "I practically lived": Mosley, p. 75.

105 Gregory Rogers was usually: Custen, p. 75.

106 "Harry, being president": Gussow, p. 39.

107 "Sydney Chaplin was the greatest": Gussow, p. 41.

108 "The feeling around town": *Hollywood Reporter*, Jan. 19, 1933, p. 1.

CHAPTER SIX: STAND UP AND CHEER

112 Temple's mother had signed: George F. Custen, *Darryl F. Zanuck and the Culture of Hollywood*, p. 207.

112 "I class myself with Rin-Tin-Tin": Jeanine Basinger, *The Movie Musical!*, p. 360.

113 "Will and I fell in love": Kobal, pp. 300–301.

114   his son Jim Rogers: Jim Rogers to SE.

114   Fox's profits for the year: Aubrey Solomon, *The Fox Film Corp.*, p. 222.

115   One historian estimated: Custen, p. 200.

115   "Shave his eyebrows": Mel Gussow, *Don't Say Yes Until I Finish Talking*, p. 72.

115   "Ty was my first lover": Evie Johnson to SE.

116   "disregard the formula": Rudy Behlmer, *The Golden Years at 20th Century Fox,* p. 6.

117   "If you don't like it": Gussow, p. xxx.

117   "I have finally come to the conclusion": Gussow, pp. 163–164.

118   "You loved [the people]": Custen, p. 181.

118   "With Zanuck, when you'd run": Custen, p. 17.

121   In 1939, the studio: Glendon Allvine, *The Greatest Fox of Them All*, p. 179.

121   "As long as people": *New York Times*, "That Beautiful Hunk of Man," Aljean Harmetz, 12-12-71. All Victor Mature quotes derive from this interview.

122   "Fox pictures were like Darryl": Stephen Silverman, *The Fox That Got Away,* p. 103.

123   "I was as fond": Custen, p. 67.

123   "I read the novel": Custen, p. 273.

124   "I think it would be a criminal": Pascal Merigeau, *Jean Renoir,* p. 430.

124   "I have come to the conclusion": Merigeau, p. 433.

125   "In the first place": Merigeau, p. 439.

126   "It's really a factory": Merigeau, p. 442.

126   "There's no pleasure": Merigeau, p. 443.

126   "Never would I have believed": Merigeau, p. 446.

127   "It was not the filmmaking system": Jean Renoir to SE.

128   The car was painted Zanuck green: Marlys J. Harris, *The Zanuck's of Hollywood,* p. 73.

128   "It was the same kind of setup": Harris, p. 47.

129 Patricia Morrison would advise: Silverman, p. 78.

129 "nearly paralyzed with fright": Silverman, p. 49.

129 "a sort of half-star": Loy, p. 60.

130 "Zanuck was a very complex man": Evie Johnson to SE.

130 "When I think of women": Fowler to Schenck, 7-9-47, Schenck to Fowler, 7-18-47, both letters in author's collection.

131 "I used to plow": Gussow, p. 51.

132 "If Aidan understands a script": Leonard Mosley, *The Rise and Fall of Hollywood's Last Tycoon,* p. 185.

133 "It was like a slaughterhouse": John Gregory Dunne, *The Studio,* p. 164

135 *"This is a roundelay, this is a song"*: Mosley, p. 6.

135 "I watched Zanuck play croquet": Mosley, p. 233.

136 "He always won": Gussow, p. 133.

136 "He was never there when I needed him": Selznick, "Growing Up in Hollywood," "M," vol. 8, issue 5, February 1991.

137 "we didn't really have": Gussow, p. 131.

137 "She loved being": Harris, p. 77.

137 One weekend Tyrone Power: Mosley, p. 72.

138 "She scared him a lot of the time": Selznick, "Growing Up in Hollywood," op cit.

138 "He was a very frightening person": Selznick, "Growing Up in Hollywood," op cit.

139 Richard remembered his father: Gussow, p. 132.

139 "What he did": Harris, p. 92.

140 Darryl would ask his son: Harris, p. 91.

140 "Darryl was *very* proud": David Brown to SE.

140 "That was my first experience": Gussow, p. 137.

141 "Darryl always thought of himself": Mosley, p. 137.

141 "the kind of thing": Behlmer, p. 172.

142 "That man could": Ethan Mordden, *The Hollywood Studios*, p. 272.

142   "a sneak preview": Behlmer, p. 155.

143   "We pay entirely too much": Behlmer, p. 39.

146   "We were confident": Gussow, p. 107, 111.

149   "She was a piece of work": Evie Johnson to SE.

151   "Nick Castle *presented* them": Bruce Goldstein to SE.

152   George Custen did the math: Custen, p. 403.

153   "We are going to eliminate": USC Cinematic Arts Library, Fox collection, *Gentleman Prefer Blondes* conference with Mr. Zanuck, on temporary script of 9-25-52, 9-27-52. Courtesy of Alan Rode.

155   "I dropped the key": *Films in Review*, "Alice Faye," by Michael Buckley, Nov. 1982, p. 517.

157   "This is a revolutionary type of story": Gussow, p. 94.

157   "Now is the time": Gussow, p. 94.

158   "When I think of what I got away with": Gussow, p. 95.

158   "Laura is a mess": Behlmer, p. 68.

159   The script had been written: Scott Eyman, *Laughter in Paradise*, p. 313.

161   "if he gets a hit": Custen, p. 333.

161   "If his death resulted": Custen, p. 335.

162   "I would like to see": Custen, p. 337.

162   "I realize you have no desire": Mosley, p. 228.

163   "a most extraordinary and ingenious": Gussow, p. 144.

163   "I recognize that there'll always be a market": Custen, p. 271.

164   "In every picture I have seen": Gussow, p. 120.

165   "I can tell you": Behlmer, p. 78.

166   The script was completed: Much of the background for the section derives from John Wiseman's "Darryl F. Zanuck and the Failure of One World," in *Historical Journal of Film, Radio and Television*, vol. 7, no. 3, 1987.

CHAPTER SEVEN: NO WAY OUT

172   "Even if only one superfluous": Rudy Behlmer, *The Golden Years at 20th Century Fox,* pp. 141–144.

173   *"The Treasure of the Sierra Madre"*: Mel Gussow, *Don't Say Yes Until I Finish Talking,* p. 82.

173   "fact and drama": Behlmer, p. 123.

173   "if we do not get Ben Hecht": Behlmer, p. 113.

174   "Darryl . . . was the best": Behlmer, p. xix.

174   "I sort of liked": Leonard Mosley, *The Rise and Fall of Hollywood's Last Tycoon,* p. 240.

175   "I would rather get it good": Mosley, p. 230.

176   On August 4: Much of the material about *Forever Amber* derives from Gary Smith's article "The First Amber" in *Films in Review,* February 1989.

178   "Coming to my house": Patrick McGilligan and Paul Buhle, *Tender Comrades,* p. 208.

178   "a mensch": Bruce Goldstein to SE.

179   "To my mind *Stagecoach*": Gussow, p. 160.

180   "If they wanted an ugly man": Behlmer, p. 190.

181   "completely impractical and impossible": Behlmer, p. 206.

182   "this is a tough business": George F. Custen, *Darryl F. Zanuck and the Culture of Hollywood,* p. 320.

183   "the process has many technical limitations": Stephen Huntley, "Sponable's CinemaScope," *Film History,* vol. 5, 1993.

184   "Directors hand-waved their way": Huntley, op cit. p. 305

185   "He is a pleasant old fellow": Huntley, op cit. p. 305

185   According to Zanuck: John Belton, *Widescreen Cinema,* pp. 120–122.

185   "AM ABSOLUTELY CONVINCED": Behlmer, p. 223.

186   the name had been copyrighted: Herbert Bragg, "The Development of CinemaScope," *Film History,* vol. 2, 1988, p. 370.

186   Because of Fox's determination: Belton, p. 140.

187   The great Technicolor cameraman Jack Cardiff: "Jack Cardiff," *The Perfect Vision*, May 1994, p. 64.

187   "We have no protection lenses": Huntley, op cit. p. 305.

188   Fox's investment: Herbert Bragg, "The Development of CinemaScope," *Film History*, vol. 2, 1988, p. 363.

188   "I was in Hollywood": "Freddie Young" *The Perfect Vision*, June 1994, p. 57.

188   "the superiority of CinemaScope": Behlmer, p. 232.

189   "this was the biggest": Glendon Allvine, *The Greatest Fox of Them All*, p. 182.

191   Fox announced: Allvine, p. 182.

192   "Was this the end of the close shot": David Bordwell, *Poetics of Cinema*, "CinemaScope," p. 292, Routledge, 2008.

192   "In some strange way": Behlmer, p. 246.

193   The last Fox picture: Belton, p. 155.

194   "he was the only mogul": Samuel Fuller, *A Third Face,* p. 265.

194   "With unknown actors": Fuller, p. 280.

195   "He was terribly chic": Swope to SE. All the quotes from Swope derive from this interview.

198   "She's got zip": Gussow, p. 181.

199   "Gambling was absolutely": Gussow, p. 189.

199   "I was really rocked": Selznick, "Growing Up in Hollywood."

200   The story that went around: Marlys J. Harris, *The Zanuck's of Hollywood*, p. 84.

200   "I was still infatuated": Gussow, p. 183.

200   "My separation": Gussow, p. 184.

201   "In a very short time": Custen, p. 355.

201   She was pointedly: Custen, p. 354.

202   Zanuck would get: Harris, p. 101.

202   "I just got . . . fed up": Behlmer, p. 259.

205   "I have had very little": Gussow, p. 237.

206   They returned worldwide rentals: Aubrey Solomon, *The Fox Film Corporation,* p. 144.

206   "Utterly idiotic": Stephen Silverman, *The Fox That Got Away,* p. 105.

206   "I would close down the studio": Mosley, p. 340.

208   Errol Flynn attributed: Harris, p. 103.

208   "An American businessman": Gussow, p. 208.

208   "He wasn't thinking as clearly": Custen, pp. 358–359.

209   "It was a one-sided": Silverman, p. 83.

209   "In some peculiar way": Harris, p. 110.

209   "When someone asked her": Silverman, p. 84.

210   Zanuck decided: Custen, p. 362.

211   "I suppose I had enough experience": Mosley, p. 338.

211   "This is a cinch": Custen, p. 363.

CHAPTER EIGHT: THE RAZOR'S EDGE

216   And then Elizabeth Taylor and Richard Burton: The chronology and most of the incidents described of the tortuous production of *Cleopatra* derive from Sydney Ladensohn Stern's *The Brothers Mankiewicz.*

217   "Preminger," Zanuck said: Leonard Mosley, *The Rise and Fall of Hollywood's Last Tycoon,* p. 341.

218   "There isn't anybody better": Marlys J. Harris, *The Zanuck's of Hollywood,* p. 112.

219   "When I last talked to you": Rudy Behlmer, *The Golden Years at 20th Century Fox,* p. 260.

CHAPTER NINE: WHAT A WAY TO GO!

222   people who had been canned: John Gregory Dunne, *The Studio,* p. 14.

222   "No self-respecting picture-maker": Mel Gussow, *Don't Say Yes Until I Finish Talking,* p. 252.

222 "Sweat or go crazy": Glendon Allvine, *The Greatest Fox of Them All*, p. 223.

223 "I can't pretend": Fred Hift, "Darryl F. Zanuck Remembered: Intense, Impetuous, Cruel," *Variety*, May 10–16, 1989.

227 Fox then hired: Dunne, p. 36.

227 "We've got $50 million": Dunne, pp. 242–245.

229 "I was proud of the movie": Gussow, p. 266.

230 "The last 15 years of his life": Daniel Selznick, "Growing Up in Hollywood."

231 "WE SHOULD HOLD OFF": Stephen Silverman, *The Fox That Got Away,* p. 255.

231 That same month: Silverman, p. 226.

232 Somehow, they anted up: Silverman, p. 242.

233 "Dick and Darryl": Silverman, p. 144.

233 "IN ADDITION TO PREVIOUS ECONOMIES": Silverman, pp. 197–198.

236 "He came to hate me": Silverman, p. 22.

236 "I like women": Russ Meyer to SE.

237 *The Only Game in Town* lost $7.5 million: Silverman, p. 259.

238 There was a large diamond: Marlys J. Harris, *The Zanuck's of Hollywood,* p. 142.

238 "I had a very large loathing": Silverman, p. 239.

238 "What happened fundamentally": Leonard Mosley, *The Rise and Fall of Hollywood's Last Tycoon*, p. 367.

239 *The Grasshopper* opened: "The Pitch," by Jerry Belson

242 "He was showing some very early": Silverman, p. 239.

243 To be specific: Silverman, p. 266.

243 "Idiots, this is a business": Silverman, p. 306.

243 "It was like an execution": George F. Custen, *Darryl F. Zanuck and the Culture of Hollywood,* p. 368.

244 "At any moment": Silverman, p. 277.

244 "I do not know": Silverman, p. 292.

245 Zanuck was concerned: Harris, p. 164.

245   "Shortly after that": Mosley, p. 388.

246   "DEAR GENEVIEVE": Harris, p. 167.

246   A November deposition: Harris, p. 167.

247   He was in bad shape: Harris, p. 206.

247   "It was a very sour period": Silverman, p. 297.

248   "I get up about 8:30": Silverman, p. 300.

248   He wasn't to be left alone: Harris, p. 251.

248   Another visitor: Harris, p. 269.

249   "In some ways": Custen, p. 371.

249   "If I did something really outrageous": *Variety*, Jan. 1, 1980.

250   She had been living: Harris, p. 278.

250   A 1971 will: Harris, p. 162.

250   A 1973 will: Harris, p. 293.

251   "I've always thought": Silverman, p. 306.

252   Richard Zanuck would say: I interviewed Richard Zanuck several times in the 1980s and '90s.

252   "For a little guy": Custen, p. 128.

CHAPTER TEN: THE TURNING POINT

254   Fox paid no dividends: Stephen Silverman, *The Fox That Got Away,* p. 286.

255   "The industry got too much": Silverman, p. 172.

259   In 1981, Marvin Davis: Silverman, p. 288.

260   He sold 50 percent of the company: Silverman, p. 289.

264   In December 2017: *USA Today*, Mike Snider, "Disney to buy key 21st Century Fox assets for $52.4 Billion," 12-14-17.

265   The deal finally closed: *Wall Street Journal*, Keach Hagey and Erich Schwartzel, "21st Century Fox Agrees to Higher Offer from Disney," 6-20-18.

265   "a race for scale": *Wall Street Journal*, Erich Schwartzel and Joe Flint, "Disney Closes $71.4 Billion Deal for 21st Century Fox Assets," 3-20-19.

Index

CHECK OUT OTHER TITLES IN THE LIBRARY

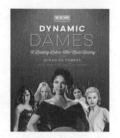

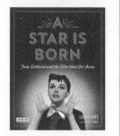

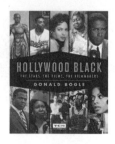

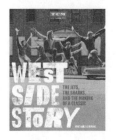

RUNNING
PRESS